*Five Tales for the Theatre*

Portrait of Carlo Gozzi, reproduced from *Opere del Cónte Carlo Gozzi*, vol. 1 (Venice, 1772.) Courtesy of The University of Chicago Libraries

# *Carlo Gozzi*

# FIVE TALES
## FOR THE
# THEATRE

Edited and translated by
## Albert Bermel and Ted Emery

Notes by Ted Emery

The University of Chicago Press
Chicago and London

ALBERT BERMEL is professor of theatre at Lehman College and the Graduate Center of the City University of New York. TED EMERY is assistant professor of Italian at New York University.

The University of Chicago Press, Chicago 60637
The University of Chicago Press, Ltd., London
© 1989 by Albert Bermel and Ted Emery
All rights reserved. Published 1989
Printed in the United States of America
98 97 96 95 94 93 92 91 90 89   54321

Library of Congress Cataloging-in-Publication Data

Gozzi, Carlo, 1720–1806.
    Five tales for the theatre / Carlo Gozzi ; edited and translated
by Albert Bermel and Ted Emery.
        p.   cm.
    Contents: The raven — The king stag — Turandot — The serpent
woman — The green bird.
    I. Bermel, Albert.   II. Emery, Ted.   III. Title.   IV. Title: 5
tales for the theatre.
    PQ4703.A6   1989
    852'.914—dc19                                          89-30641
    ISBN 0-226-30579-1 (cloth)                               CIP
    ISBN 0-226-30580-5 (paper)

♾ The paper used in this publication meets the minimum requirements of the American National Standard for Information Sciences—Permanence of Paper for Printed Materials, ANSI Z39.48-1984.

# Contents

## Introduction

# Carlo Gozzi in Context

### Ted Emery

In the insular tradition of the Italian theatre, Carlo Gozzi (1720–1806) is something of a rarity. While playwrights of the stature of Bibbiena and Alfieri are little known outside Italy, and others such as Ariosto, Machiavelli, and Verga are admired largely for their nontheatrical writings, the plays of Gozzi, like those of Pirandello, have long enjoyed international recognition. In his own time, Gozzi was highly regarded throughout Europe. Lessing admired him, Schiller adapted his *Turandot* for a production directed by Goethe, and Giuseppe Baretti, a member of Samuel Johnson's circle, compared him to Shakespeare. In the following years the German romantics came to view Gozzi as their spiritual and artistic predecessor, A. W. Schlegel finding in the Venetian his own concept of irony, Paul his view of humor, Tieck his own technique of mixing levels of reality, and Hoffmann a model for his fantasy.[1] In France, Madame de Staël lionized Gozzi as the ideal representative of Italy's national spirit for his defense of the "authentic and spontaneous" commedia dell'arte, while much later, in the Soviet Union, formalist writers and directors such as Meyerhold and Vakhtangov saw him as a model of pure theatricality to be opposed to the naturalism of Chekhov and Stanislavsky. Crossing the boundaries between genres as easily as those between nations, Gozzi's *Tales for the Theatre* have often been adapted as opera libretti: Puccini's *Turandot* and Prokofiev's *The Love of Three Oranges* are the most famous of many examples.

Paradoxically, Gozzi has long been less esteemed in his own country than abroad. This is in part due to the influence of traditional literary historiography, which tended to see him in a negative light as the rival of Carlo Goldoni, by any standard one of Italy's greatest playrights. A second influence is surely the style of Gozzi's *Tales,* which in the original contain long sections of literary verse rarely appreciated by modern audiences, and generally recast in prose by translators. (Indeed, even Goldoni's popularity is based on his prose comedies, for of his verse plays only *Il campiello* is regularly produced.) Outside Italy, these objections have carried much less weight. Since the early nineteenth century, Gozzi has been more popular with non-Italian audiences than with his countrymen, and until quite recently was more frequently performed in translation than in the original.[2]

The extent and variety of Gozzi's foreign reception might seem to suggest that his plays are somehow universal, that the innovation and sheer theatrical exuberance for which they have often been praised raise them above the limited historical and cultural context in which and for which they are written. Yet few playwrights have closer links to their times and their surroundings than Gozzi, for his *Tales* were in large part literary satires or cultural diatribes whose targets are now often recognizable only to specialists. This is the fundamental paradox of Gozzi's posthumous success: the ideological messages his plays were intended to transmit are rarely understood (especially in translation) by modern audiences, yet the *Tales* continue to be revived and enjoyed both in Italy and abroad. Can it be that the ideological elements of these plays have atrophied over time and are now of merely historical interest? Are the *Tales for the Theatre* universal because they can easily be appreciated out of context as examples of pure theatre? I think not. Paradoxically, Gozzi is a universal writer not despite his ideology, but largely because of it: his view of his world, deeply embedded in the fabric of his fairy-tale plots, still speaks to a modern, international audience.

Gozzi was born into a family of Venice's minor aristocracy, a class of noblemen, often fallen on hard times, who were rigorously excluded from the city's ruling class because they traced their origins not to the great families whose names were inscribed in the Golden Book, but to the less privileged and less prestigious nobility of Venice's mainland provinces.[3] His parents' continual financial difficulties had serious consequences for him, the sixth of eleven children: while his elder brother Gasparo was sent to a good Jesuit school, the family's poverty prevented Carlo from receiving a rigorous classical education. As a young man, Gozzi briefly sought his fortune in a military career and served in Venice's Dalmatian provinces from 1741 to 1744. On his return to the city, he found that his family's economic woes had been exacerbated by his father's illness and subsequent paralysis, by Gasparo's preoccupation with literature and his incompetence as head of the household, and above all by the meddling of Gasparo's wife, the poet Luisa Bergalli. In 1747, he broke off relations with his family, left their "poetic madhouse," and began litigation to save what remained of his inheritance. As a distraction from these troubles he helped found a literary academy, the Accademia dei Granelleschi, which elaborated a doctrine of literary and linguistic purism, and bitterly attacked two playwrights whose artistic rivalry had become the talk of Venice: Carlo Goldoni and Pietro Chiari.

Gozzi's literary career begins with his contribution to this polemic. In 1757, he accused Goldoni and Chiari of vulgarity and bad style, in the verse almanac *The Tartan of Invisible Influences for the Leap Year 1756*. Next, he satirized Goldoni's theatrical reform, in the prose dialogue *The Comic The-*

*atre at the Pilgrim Inn* (1758). Stung, Goldoni replied that the popular success of his plays was proof of their worth. Gozzi could not resist the challenge: "I thought to myself that if I could attract a large audience to a play that had a puerile title and the most frivolous, the most unrealistic of plots, then I could demonstrate to Signor Goldoni that the popularity of his comedies did not mean that they were good."[4] With that polemical intention he wrote *The Love of Three Oranges* (1761), the first of the ten *Tales for the Theatre* in which he championed the traditional improvised theatre of the commedia dell'arte against the "realistic" plays of its would-be reformers.[5]

The commedia dell'arte was Italy's first form of professional theatre (*arte* meant trade or profession) and had flourished since the middle of the sixteenth century. The skill of the commedia actors made possible a shift away from the literary comedy of the Renaissance, written texts usually performed by amateurs, toward a more popular theatre of improvisation. Commedia actors assumed one character for their entire careers, and those roles were invariably stereotyped: the wily servant Brighella; the foolish servant Arlecchino (also called Truffaldino); Pantalone, a Venetian merchant and senile skirt chaser; the soubrette Colombina (or Smeraldina); the *innamorati*, or lovers; and others. Some commedia characters, like Brighella, Arlecchino, and Pantalone, wore masks, further emphasizing their stereotypical personalities. All spoke in the characteristic language of their place of origin: Pantalone in Venetian, the two servants in Venetian colored by expressions from the dialect of Bergamo, and the *innamorati* in literary Tuscan, drawing heavily on the style of Petrarch. Each actor kept a notebook, or *zibaldone*, of monologues, dialogues, and tag lines appropriate to his character in a given dramatic situation—a love scene between *innamorati*, for instance, or a quarrel between master and servant—and these set pieces became the basis of their improvised lines. In addition, the *zibaldoni* of comic characters listed sight gags or verbal quips called *lazzi*, many of them extremely vulgar. The order of events in a commedia dell'arte play was established by a plot outline called a *canovaccio*, which listed necessary directions such as the entrances and exits of each character, their actions while on stage, and a summary of what they might say, without providing any dialogue. Improvising from this *canovaccio* and from their *zibaldoni*, the actors could vary a given play from performance to performance or from moment to moment, and this exciting unpredictability was responsible for much of the commedia dell'arte's liveliness and apparent spontaneity.

By the eighteenth century, however, the once-spontaneous commedia dell'arte had gone stale, its plots and routines familiar from long use. Increasingly middle-class audiences began to be dissatisfied with its slapstick and often vulgar comedy, preferring plays that would be morally instructive as well as entertaining. This is the position taken up by Goldoni in the preface to the Bettinelli edition of his works (1750), in which he describes his project of theatrical reform:

> The comic theatre in Italy had for more than a century been so corrupt that it had become an abominable object of scorn for the rest of Europe. Nothing appeared on public stages except filthy harlequinades, dirty and scandalous love scenes and jokes, poorly invented and poorly developed plots, with no morals and no order, and which, far from correcting vice—the original and most noble purpose of comedy—fomented it instead. It made the ignorant lower classes, dissolute young men, and mannerless boors laugh, but it bored and angered people of culture and good morals.[6]

Goldoni proposed his plays as a moral and refined antidote to the improvised theatre. He purged the obscene and unrealistic elements of the commedia dell'arte, substituted a written text for the *canovaccio* in order to limit the actors' improvisation, gradually eliminated the stereotypical characters and replaced them with others drawn from life, and so created a kind of theatre capable of satisfying the taste of a public in which the middle class had acquired an important place.

A bitter opponent of this reform for reasons I shall examine below, Gozzi countered Goldoni by asserting the superiority of the traditional improvised theatre. He makes this point in *The Love of Three Oranges* by way of a simple, satirical allegory. In the *Tale*'s first act, Prince Tartaglia (the Venetian public) is dying of an attack of melancholy brought on by undigested Martellian verses—a form much used by Goldoni and Chiari. Despite the machinations of Morgan Le Fay (Chiari) and the magician Celio (Goldoni), Truffaldino (the commedia dell'arte) succeeds in making Tartaglia laugh, and cures him. In plain words, the older comedy is funny, while the plays of the reformers are not, a conclusion Gozzi later repeats in the *Ingenuous Disquisition and Sincere History of My Ten Tales for the Theatre* (1772). In the hands of good actors, he tells us, the commedia dell'arte "will never fail to have a sure effect on the people, who will always have the right to enjoy what they like and to laugh at what they find funny, without paying any attention to the masked Catos [i.e., the reformers] who want to prevent them from liking it" (*Opere*, 1036). Where Goldoni views the commedia dell'arte as an object of international scorn, Gozzi defends it on nationalistic grounds: "No other nation can carry it off. The Italians are the only brave wits who for so many centuries have been able to manage this genre of improvised theatre. . . . I see in the commedia dell'arte one of the glories of Italy" (*Opere*, 1037).

However, while Gozzi is a staunch defender of the popular tradition, his *Tales* are not themselves commedia dell'arte plays, as is sometimes assumed. Though he originally wrote *The Love of Three Oranges* as a *canovac-*

*cio,* Gozzi published it as a "reflexive analysis," adding to the plot outline extended critical glosses on its satirical content and numerous indications of the words to be spoken, including complete dialogue for one scene. The *Tales* that followed were written out more fully. They progressively limit the improvisational element, restricting it almost entirely to the comic characters Truffaldino, Brighella, and more rarely Pantalone and Tartaglia. Moreover, even when these characters are allowed to improvise, Gozzi's directions to them are far more detailed than the ordinary *canovaccio,* often providing nearly complete dialogues in indirect discourse. Like the commedia dell'arte, the *Tales* are plurilingual, Venetian characters using their own dialect and non-Venetians speaking Tuscan—yet in Gozzi the serious characters generally declaim formal, literary verse, a step away from the deliberately nonacademic commedia dell'arte. Many of the characters of the older comedy are found in Gozzi, but often they do not accurately reproduce the traditional stereotypes. For example, Smeraldina is no longer the lusty wench of the commedia, perennially attracted to Truffaldino, and Pantalone evolves from a farcical dirty old man into an emblem of Venetian popular virtue. What is more, the tone of the *Tales* tends to be melodramatic and their plots are dominated by the serious characters, found in greater number and in greater textual prominence than in the commedia dell'arte. This serious material derives not from the tradition of improvised theatre, but from Italian and oriental fairy tales and their theatrical adaptations in the French Théâtre de la Foire.[7] While exoticism and magic were not unknown to the commedia dell'arte, the emphasis Gozzi gives to fairytale material, and the fusion of that material with elements of literary theatre and with a literary-cultural polemic, suggest that the *Tales* differ substantially from the tradition that had preceded them. There is more to Gozzi's plays than a simple restoration of the commedia dell'arte.

Gozzi's hostility to Goldoni was not grounded solely in an aesthetic disagreement over the improvised theatre. True, he sometimes criticizes Goldoni's realism on what seems to be purely artistic grounds, complaining that his rival merely copies the world around him rather than imaginatively reexpressing it: "He portrayed on stage all the truths he saw before him, exactly transcribed in the most trivial way, and not imitated from nature with the elegance necessary to a writer" (*Opere,* 1075). But the objection is not really so much to the manner of that theatrical transcription as to its content. Gozzi repeatedly describes Goldoni's plays as "low" or "plebeian," asserting that "many of his comedies are no more than a collection of scenes which may contain truths, but truths so low, so vulgar, so common, that . . . I could never understand how an author could bring himself to transcribe them from the swamps of the lower classes and raise them to the dignity of a theatre" (*Opere,* 1076). Why Gozzi objects to this sort of realism is evident from a closer look at the ideological ramifications of Goldoni's reform.

The son of a doctor and himself formerly a lawyer, Goldoni was a member of the Venetian middle class whose theatrical tastes he wished to satisfy and whose reality he wished to reflect on stage. In his hands the senile skirt chaser Pantalone becomes a productive merchant, worthy of respect for his economic contribution to society and whose highly moral conduct is characterized by hard work, professional honesty, and love of family. This new theatrical dignity that Goldoni gives to the middle class is in deliberate contrast to his view of the impoverished minor nobility, seen as arrogant social parasites, whose morals are usually licentious and who rarely have any sense of family responsibility. Goldoni satirizes Gozzi's class and allows the bourgeoisie to take the stage in plays that, within the eighteenth-century limits of the term, "realistically" reflect middle-class concerns and legitimize a middle-class world view. In his mature masterpieces, such as *The Chioggian Brawls*, Goldoni did much the same for the lower classes, drawing a sympathetic portrait entirely new in the Italian theatre.

The aristocratic Gozzi saw in such bourgeois realism a pernicious threat to the social order of his city. Indeed, this is one reason for his support of the commedia dell'arte, which privileged pure, slapstick entertainment and excluded any ideologically charged idealization of reality. In his autobiography, the *Useless Memoirs,* he claims, "I maintained and I proved that in his theatrical productions [Goldoni] had frequently portrayed his noble characters as frauds, cardsharps, and fools, while giving the serious actions of heroism and generosity to his plebeian characters, to attract the good will of the restless, noisy lower classes, who always resent the superior orders. [His comedies were] a bad public example against the indispensable order of subordination."[8] That phrase, "the indispensable order of subordination," is a refrain that returns repeatedly in Gozzi's autobiography and in the *Ingenuous Disquisition.* The concept is fundamental to Gozzi's world view: a simple, conservative ideology that idealizes the principle of order and hierarchy. As a political creed, this is perhaps most clearly expressed in the last of the *Tales, Zeim, King of the Genies,* where the slave girl Dugmè explains the lessons a mysterious old man taught her as a child:

> DUGMÈ. He always told me that sacred, inscrutable Providence had planned everything, and that the position of great men was a wonder of God. He said it was a heavenly sight to see all the people, rank by rank down to the most humble peasants, subordinated to their betters. "Oh," he said, "don't be led astray by those malicious sophists who claim that there is liberty outside this beautiful order which Heaven has given us. They only sow confusion and disturb the peace, and often they are murderers, thieves, and heathens who end up on the gallows. Daughter, respect the great ones, love them, and however heavy your state may be to you, do not be envious of them. In the eyes of Heaven, the good works of the great are no better than those of their lowest ser-

vants, and the way to immortality is open to a commoner as much as to a king." (act 2, scene 4)

Gozzi's words, in the mouth of his character, describe an ideal world in which the throne and the altar support each other, obliterating any distinction between social and moral misconduct. The hope of future spiritual salvation is enlisted to justify present social inequality, political submission becomes a religious virtue, disobedience to the "great ones" is presented as an abomination in the eyes of God, and intellectual dissenters are equated with common criminals.[9] Goldoni and Chiari are not the only "malicious sophists" that Gozzi has in mind in this passage, for he views the two playwrights as Venetian reflections of a broader danger: the corrupting intellectual influence of the European Enlightenment. While in *The Love of Three Oranges* Gozzi had limited himself to literary satire, later *Tales* such as *The Blue Monster, The Green Bird,* and *Zeim, King of the Genies* direct their diatribes at the egalitarian rationalism—for Gozzi, revolutionary atheism—of the *philosophes* and their Italian adherents. *The Green Bird* is liberally peppered with derogatory references to the Enlightenment. Truffaldino is described as "a sex fiend, a cuckold, and a bankrupt—a genuine modern philosopher" (2.3), while he sums up his credo this way: "Figuring out the world and getting what you want by hook or by crook—*that's* the real modern philosophy" (4.9). In a more serious vein, the moralist Calmon hints that the *philosophes* are "heathens who seek to excuse their faults by mocking the exquisite workmanship of our eternal Maker" (1.10). Renzo and Barbarina are disciples of modern philosophy who, apparently in imitation of Helvétius's *De l'esprit,* see self-love as the root of all human actions and feelings, even those that seem to arise from purely generous motives. In condemning self-love, Renzo proposes a vague notion of secular stoicism, to which Calmon replies by insisting that self-love and human reason must guide men to the love of God—an implicit rejection of the anthropocentric rationalism of so much Enlightenment thinking. Made rich by magic, the twins quickly fall victim to unbridled passions and vices, demonstrating that a philosophy that rejects submission to God cannot lead men to virtue and self-control.[10] After the usual magical transformations, Renzo and Barbarina admit that Calmon is right, and the play ends with a final anti-Enlightenment quip: "So mend your ways, everyone, and take your philosophy with a grain of salt. As for us [the actors] up here, if our fairy tale can turn a profit, we'll conclude that such foolishness is the best philosophy of all."

How seriously are we to take Gozzi's literary and cultural polemics? In his own comments on the *Tales,* the playwright often privileges their didactic aspect. The preface to *The Raven* makes reference to Gozzi's intended "moral lesson" and "criticism of mores and manners," while his autobiography later insists that

there is no one who does not know that the masks of the commedia dell'arte, an expedient I used in many (but not all) of my
plays in order to give wholesome entertainment to those in my
audience who rightly loved them, in fact played a small role [in
the *Tales*]. It was their basis of a sound moral lesson, and the vigorous passions expressed by the serious characters that were the
real cause of their continuing success. (*Memorie* 1 : 250)

Despite such claims, readers may have difficulty seeing the *Tales* as pri-
marily moral or ideological statements. For one thing, their polemical content is far from uniform: after *The Love of Three Oranges*, extended literary
satire is rare, while prior to *The Green Bird* attacks against "philosophy"
are isolated outbursts only tenuously connected to the plot (see, for example, Gozzi's mockery of modern science—a sacred cow of the Enlightenment—in the final lines of *The King Stag*). What is more, the *Tales*
often seem to be motivated less by a common ideological intention than
by a purely theatrical one: they consistently mix melodrama and commedia
dell'arte farce with exotic spectacle or special effects in a style that deliberately draws attention to its own theatricality.

This elaboration of an insistently *theatrical* theatre was an important innovation, and one that has made the eighteenth-century Venetian seem
surprisingly relevant to later audiences. While Gozzi looks to the past for
the main elements of his *Tales* (the masks and improvisation of the commedia dell'arte, the fairy-tale exoticism of the Théâtre de la Foire, and the
machines and special effects of baroque opera), his use of that material
often foreshadows modern approaches to the theatre. Both the romantics
and the formalists were fascinated by the jarring anomaly of these plots in
which serious and comic elements are present at the same time, and in
which exotic oriental characters are indiscriminately mixed with the typi-
cally Italian and Venetian masks of the commedia dell'arte. This juxtaposition of contradictory elements, the guiding stylistic principle of the *Tales*,
is the source of Gozzi's apparent modernity, for the playwright's emphatic
heterogeneity allows him not merely to avoid his adversaries' realism, but
to *subvert* it.

For an implacable foe of realism, Gozzi is often oddly concerned to
stress that his theatrical fantasies are meant to seem convincingly real. In
his preface to *Turandot*, for example, he emphasizes his ability to hold an
audience's attention by creating a completely *believable* theatrical illusion
even in the objectively unbelievable moments of magical transformation.

The transformations I used in my tales for the theatre were for the
most part painful afflictions, and consisted of nothing more than
the final outcome of dramatic circumstances prepared and developed long before the physical changes occurred. *They always had
the power of holding the audience's attention for as long as I wished,*

*and of maintaining a convincing and varied illusion, even during the transformation itself.* [italics mine]

Gozzi's illusions are not only visually convincing (in a sense realistic); they are also closely connected to the psychological development of the serious characters, in plots that stress their romantic woes and desperate perils— that is, the tragic part of what Gozzi generally labels "tragicomic tales for the theatre." However exaggerated by modern standards, such unabashed melodrama was a form of emotional realism common in some varieties of eighteenth-century theatre, where human passions were indulged on stage in order to engage the sentiments of the audience. This is the pattern of the French *comédies larmoyantes* and *drames bourgeois*—those forerunners of modern soap operas which had become popular in translation in the Venice of the 1760s and 1770s and which Gozzi attacked not so much for their artistic vulgarity as for the bad social and moral lesson he felt they transmitted (*Opere,* 1051–73).[11] Indeed, he claims that his *Tales* are just as emotionally effective as these tearjerkers, while at the same time more morally sound: "if the effect of these [tearful dramas] is to make the people laugh and cry, and to hold an audience's attention, then no one can deny that I produced the same effect, while maintaining good morals, in my *Raven,* my *Serpent Woman,* my *Blue Monster,* my *Donna Elvira,* and others" (*Opere,* 41–42).

On one hand, then, Gozzi wants to create a believable theatrical illusion out of the unbelievable events of the fairy tale, encouraging the same kind of emotional empathy that characterizes the style of his realistic adversaries. At the same time, however, the illusion and the empathy of the melodramatic plots are continually broken by a serious of devices that Albert Bermel, in his afterword to this volume, has perceptively characterized as forerunners of the Brechtian *Verfremdungseffekt.* Serious characters are found side by side with comic ones, melodrama is brought up short by slapstick humor, realistic illusion is overturned by deliberate dramatic alienation, and exotic fairy-tale settings improbably harbor references to the real world of eighteenth-century Venice (as in the last of Turandot's riddles). The empathic relationship between serious characters and spectators, constructed by the "vigorous passions" of the melodramatic plots, is continually *deconstructed* by the abrupt juxtaposition of such contradictory elements. This is an extraordinarily modern approach to the stage—an approach that seems to find its raison d'être less in the author's ostensibly polemical intentions than in pure, unadulterated theatrical *play.*

The striking theatricality of the *Tales* is more immediately evident to today's audiences (and perhaps to those of Gozzi's time) than any intended moral or social comment. Indeed, it would not be difficult to see the Venetian as an ideologue whose native talent for the theatre causes him, in the end, to prefer his medium to his message. If this is so, then can we conclude—Gozzi's own statements notwithstanding—that his plays are more important for their form than their content? Is the author's ideology only a minor element in his *Tales for the Theatre,* unnecessary for their enjoyment and unrelated to their enduring success?

I think not. Such a conclusion, by no means uncommon, is possible only if we limit what we see as ideological in the *Tales* to the element of overt satire. But Gozzi's ideology, his obsessive idealization of order and subordination, is also expressed at a more fundamental level of the plays, as reflected in their formal structures, in their characterization, and in the development of their plots. In the final analysis, the radical Gozzi, the forward-looking man of the theatre, cannot be separated from the conservative social ideologue, nostalgic for the past and opposed to modern "corruption."

It must be emphasized that Gozzi's stress on fantasy and theatrical play is itself ideologically motivated. His rival Goldoni, like many eighteenth-century theorists of the theatre, frequently speaks of the stage as a "mirror" of society in which the audience may recognize both its own virtues and its own vices. Spectators are expected to draw a lesson from a comedy, modelling themselves on the theatrical fiction and reproducing its idealized world in their own daily lives. Such a view of the theatre has clear ideological implications, for the plays of Goldoni's reform often portray aristocratic vices and middle-class virtues, implicitly encouraging audiences to subscribe to a bourgeois way of life. Gozzi rejects this conception of the theatre as a social mirror, undermines the empathy between characters and audience, and substitutes a theatre of entertainment and fantasy. In thus challenging the realistic form of Goldoni's theatre, Gozzi also strikes at the world view that that form transmits. By privileging the theatre's power to create entertaining fantasies, Gozzi prevents it from constituting a model of what, for him, is an undesirable reality.

Moreover, as Giuseppe Petronio has noted in his introduction to Gozzi's *Opere* (p. 33), the playwright's hierarchical view of society is reflected in the formal organization of his plays. Divisions between classes of characters are marked, in the original, by linguistic and stylistic distinctions: nobles speak in Italian verses, and their lines are fully written out, rarely if ever improvised; "middle-class" characters speak in prose, Pantalone in Venetian and Tartaglia in Italian, improvising only occasionally; and the lower-class Truffaldino and Brighella generally improvise in Venetian slang on the basis of the author's *canovaccio.* There are a few exceptions to these rules—for example, when the commedia mask Tartaglia is cast as a king in *The Green Bird,* the tone of his lines is less literary—but for the most part the stylistic hierarchy is quite stable. Furthermore, Gozzi's characterizations involve a rigid barrier between the serious and comic characters. Serious characters are aristocrats, whose noble passions of love and despair are featured in the often melodramatic plots of the *Tales*. Comic characters are middle or lower class and provide a foil for the melodrama of their social betters. With the sole exception of Tartaglia and Tartagliona in *The Green Bird*, aristocrats are never comic characters nor comic characters aristocrats—again, a stable hierarchy.[12] Also, the distinction "middle class" is only a term of convenience when referring to Gozzi's *Tales*, for none of his characters or settings is recognizably bourgeois. While Goldoni had portrayed Pantalone as an independent merchant, Gozzi's version of the character is always found in a client relationship to a king or a prince, raised by aristocratic favor (and always "beyond his merit") from poverty to the status of a minister, admiral, or secretary. The middle class as a productive economic force, and one that might in some circumstances challenge Gozzi's own class, is naturally banished from the fairy-tale world of his plays.

In their plots, too, the *Tales for the Theatre* may subtly reflect their author's world view even when they do not incorporate explicit anti-Enlightenment attacks or easily decoded allegories. In the *Useless Memoirs* and the *Ingenuous Disquisition*, Gozzi's most substantial ideological statements, the author's constant idealization of order is invariably accompanied by the perception of a threatening disorder: good art is menaced by the stylistic vulgarities of the reformers, an orderly class structure is undermined by the bad example found in Goldoni's plays, traditional morality is imperilled by "enlightened" sexual promiscuity, and revealed religion is endangered by philosophical freethinking. This same opposition of order/disorder is basic to the plots of the *Tales for the Theatre*. In all of these plays, the happiness and stability of a fictional kingdom are endangered by a threat to its order. That threat may take many forms: a mysterious curse (*The Raven*), a traitorous minister (*The King Stag, The Fortunate Beggars*), even an evil ruler (*Zobeide*).[13] The conflict between order and disorder usually culminates in a physical transformation which can be reversed only by a heroic act or, more often, by the intervention of an outside force such as a powerful magician. In *The King Stag*, for example, the serenity of the realm of Serendippo is threatened by the ambition and lust of the evil minister Tartaglia, who envies Deramo's position and desires his bride. He first attempts to kill his master, then steals his body by means of a magic spell, leaving Deramo in the form of a stag. Tartaglia's political and sexual usurpation can be countered only by the wizard Durandarte, who punishes the minister and restores order.

On the surface, there may not seem to be much of a link between this simple plot structure and Gozzi's view of the world—after all, conflicts between order and disorder are structurally necessary to carry forward the plot of any play and are found in comedy from the very beginnings of the genre. It is in Gozzi's manner of elaborating this conflict that we may find a link between his theatrical expression and his social outlook. A closer examination of the concept of transformation will help us see the relevance of this simple fictional pattern to Gozzi's world view.

Physical transformations are found in the great majority of the *Tales for the Theatre:* men are changed into beasts or statues, women into men or beasts, and so on. These transformations have generally been taken as an audience-pleasing exercise in special effects: that is, as pure theatricality. However, there is more to these scenes than meets the eye. A suggestive passage of Gozzi's *Memoirs* describes the cultural corruption caused by the Enlightenment as a series of *transformations* observed and condemned by the narrator throughout his life.

> I watched women become men, men become women, women and men become monkeys, as they all immersed themselves in new discoveries, especially the inventions and the innumerable follies of fashion. They all tried to seduce each other like hounds in heat, ruining themselves and their families by vying with each other in lust and luxury . . . changing indecency into decency and calling anyone who disagreed a hypocrite. (*Memorie* 2 : 154–55)

In the autobiographer's view, philosophical corruption has broken down society's traditional sexual roles and moral constrictions. This blurring of crucial distinctions—between male and female behavior, between decency and indecency—is then expressed metaphorically as a *physical* transformation. Something very similar occurs in Gozzi's *Tales*. Though some of the transformations found in the plays are merely punishments meted out to bad characters in the final scene, most occur at the culminating moment of the conflict between order and disorder: when Tartaglia tries to kill his king, when King Millo sentences his brother to death, or when Farruscad curses his wife. The play's disorder is concretized in a transformation that blurs normal physical distinctions (between a man and a statue, for instance) in the same way that cultural corruption, in the real world, subverts the normal categories of social behavior. The "pure" theatrical spectacle of transformation thus allows Gozzi to displace his perception of a threatening disorder from the realm of reality to that of fantasy, where its danger may be more easily defused.

While in the *Memoirs* the autobiographer can do no more than observe and deplore the metaphorical transformation of society, in the *Tales* the physical transformation can be reversed by the figure of the magician (Durandarte, Geonca, Calmon, etc.). For the most part, these mighty wizards are psychologically flat characters, peripheral to the plays' plots; they exist to intervene with advice or magic at crucial moments, and thus represent a convenient means of *authorial* intervention in the *Tales*.[14] In the real world, Gozzi may condemn social corruption but can do nothing to stem the tide of the Enlightenment. In his plays, however, disorder may be allowed free play, indulged for several acts before it is safely and predictably repressed at the play's end. In short, the *Tales for the Theatre* are a ritual of wish fulfillment in which Gozzi magically accomplishes what he is unable to do in real life: impose order on the threat of disorder and heal the fairy-tale society.

In *The Raven* and *The King Stag*, this resolution of disorder, while reflecting a preoccupation basic to Gozzi's ideological *Weltanschauung*, does not take us much beyond theatrical play for its own sake, and it is fair to say that aside from the occasional polemical outburst we are in these plays more often aware of the playwright as artist than as ideologue. In other *Tales*, however, the development of the order/disorder opposition reveals the presence of an important ideological substratum in what seem, initially, no more than playful fantasies. This is clearest where the threat to order is represented by a female character. In the *Useless Memoirs*, Gozzi repeatedly insists on the connection between women and social disorder.[15] It is women who are most easily corrupted by false philosophy and who cause chaos by ignoring their responsibilities and their proper position in society.

> [The philosophers] called it an old-fashioned and barbarous prejudice to restrict women to the home, so that they might watch over sons and daughters, servants, the work of the household, and the family budget. And women quickly emerged from their houses, as wild as the ancient Bacchae, and shouting "Liberty! Liberty!" they filled all the streets, forgetting about sons, daughters, servants, housework, and budgets. With nothing but silliness in their heads, abandoned to their own whims and instigated by their philosophical counselors, they concerned themselves solely with fashions, with frivolous inventions and imitations, with making a lavish appearance, with partying, gambling, flirting, and lovemaking. Husbands no longer had the courage to oppose this destruction of their honor, of their fortunes, of their families, this bad example to their children, for fear of being tainted by the word "prejudice." (*Memorie* 1:197)

Whether for their weakness, ambition, vanity, or greed, women are the vulnerable link in society's defense against moral corruption. If weak men allow them to become insubordinate, to escape from their proper restricted place in society, women may constitute a serious threat to social order.

In the *Tales for the Theatre*, this view of women as a threat to order is displaced to the level of the plot. It is most obvious in the bad women who, like the bad ministers, are deliberately subversive. In *The Blue Monster*, Gulindì, a former slave, has seduced and married the aged ruler of Nanking. Having virtually seized control of the government, she derides traditional morality as the "foolish philosophy of ancient times" and boasts of the power her sex gives her over men: "What a pleasure it is to be a woman, and to have such beauty and such winning ways that a joke or a laugh will make men tremble" (2.2). Because of her licentiousness and pride the city is under a curse, ravaged by magical monsters—an obvious fairy-tale representation of social disorder. In *The Green Bird,* too, we find a similar subversive woman: the queen mother Tartagliona, whose sexual morals are nearly as suspect as Gulindì's and who in her son's absence has accused her daughter-in-law of adultery, imprisoned her to starve in the royal sewers, and ordered that her two children be killed. The social threat these women represent is at least partly due to the weakness of the men of the plays, one of whom is senile, while the other has been absent from his kingdom for eighteen years and, on his return, behaves as capriciously as a small child. Predictably, both women are punished through divine (i.e., authorial) intervention: it is Gulindì's destiny to die when the monsters threatening Nanking are slain, while the green bird transforms Tartagliona into a turtle and condemns her to life in a swamp.

Gozzi's portrayals of women are not limited to such caricatures. There are many positive heroines in the *Tales,* examples of constancy in love such as Dardanè in *The Blue Monster* and Cherestanì in *The Serpent Woman,* or more ambiguous but by no means wholly negative women such as Turandot. Often, though, even Gozzi's positive heroines embody an involuntary threat to order, displaced in ways that may not be immediately apparent. For example, *Turandot* and *The Serpent Woman* are among the least overtly ideological of Gozzi's *Tales.* In the first, Gozzi concentrates on melodrama and exotic, oriental spectacle, while the second combines melodrama with impressive transformations and special effects. The figure of the evil minister is barely present (Badur in *The Serpent Woman* has a mere two scenes), and there are no obvious female equivalents to Gulindì and Tartagliona. Yet each of the two heroines is in her own way a threat to order, and each must be dealt with in the same theatrical ritual of reordering that we saw above.

An ultra-feminist who swears that "the very word 'wife' is enough to kill [her]" (2.5), the Chinese princess Turandot is the ultimate castrating female. She has tricked her father into vowing that she may ask her suitors to solve three riddles: if the prospective husband succeeds, she must marry him; if he does not, he will be beheaded. The execution of the many failed candidates has embroiled the empire in wars with its neighbors and has alienated the emperor's own subjects, who abhor his daughter's cruelty. Gozzi's point is clear: a weak man has allowed female insubordination to cause social disorder.

Turandot's threat to order is also played out at a more fundamentally menacing level. She is unimaginably intelligent and beautiful, "as wise as a sage, and so lovely that no painter can do her justice" (1.1). Neither images nor words can adequately describe her: "No painter has captured all her beauty. . . . But neither could the highest eloquence of the finest speaker succeed in describing her pride, her ambition, the rancor and perversity in her heart" (1.3). Despite its inadequacy as a signifier for her superhuman signified, Turandot's portrait—"a few signs daubed by a painter"—has an irresistible force, "such power of fascination that young men who glimpse it rush blindly to their death" (1.1). In other words, Gozzi's heroine cannot be reduced to the terms of language, the primary structure of order upon which all other symbolic systems—culture, custom, law, and so forth—inevitably depend. She is the emblem of an ultimate power and plenitude, beyond our ken and threatening precisely because it may not be described, quantified, *ordered* within the constraints of the symbolic systems by which our consciousness is limited.

To nullify this menace, Turandot must be incorporated into proper structures of linguistic and social order. The two types of structure are in fact linked in the plot, for the princess can avoid accepting her social role as wife only by an adroit manipulation of language. In her riddles, she charges communication with ambiguity, accentuating the distance between words and meaning, between signifier and signified. Turandot subverts language's power to signify, hoping to escape social domination in the linguistic interstices she has opened. But in answering the riddles, Calaf remorselessly reorders their linguistic disorder, reestablishing the link between word and meaning. In so doing, he fixes Turandot in the realm not only of language, but of law and society as well, as she is "sentenced to marriage" (2.5).

If the *Tale* ended with its climax in the riddle scene, Turandot would be little different from the bad women Gulindì and Tartagliona, save that her subversion of order is played out at a more fundamental and therefore more threatening level. Unlike those caricatures of female evil, however, Turandot is a strikingly ambiguous figure. In order to create a dramatically convincing character, Gozzi must allow Turandot to speak her mind, sympathetically underscoring the essential unfairness of her position as an object of matrimonial barter. This presents the playwright with a problem: the "bad" princess, caught in a conflict between a passionate attachment to liberty and a burgeoning passion for the nameless prince, is far more interesting than the "good" but colorless Calaf. The playwright instinctively sympathizes with the character of greatest dramatic interest, while the ideologue still finds it necessary to brand her as a danger to patriarchal order. Suggestively, it is the ideologue who prevails. In the end, Gozzi tries to erase the ambiguity of his attitude toward Turandot by turning her into a positive character. This is possible only because her solitary plenitude is revealed to be less than fully satisfying. Turandot experiences new and disquieting feelings at her first sight of the prince, and is plagued by them throughout the play (see 2.5, 3.2, and 4.3). Not truly powerful, not whole and sufficient unto herself, Turandot feels *desire*—the sign of a lack which may be filled only when she voluntarily accepts her place in the social order by agreeing to marry Calaf. Her story is thus not merely the taming of a shrew. Rather, it is a ritualistic idealization of a concept of order in which the menace of woman as Other is defused by male intelligence and love, and voluntarily renounced in an act of female complicity. It must have been a comforting conclusion for Gozzi and the men of his audience when the ice princess stepped forward in the final scene, repented, and begged their forgiveness.

Like Turandot, Cherestanì is a figure of power: she is a half-fairy, the immortal queen of a hidden realm, capable of superhuman feats of magic. This apparent power is in direct contrast to the passivity of her husband Farruscad, a kept man of sorts who lives for eight years in his wife's magical palace without being allowed to ask her name and country. Here, husband is subordinated to wife, she magically potent, he passive and subject to her law (the prohibition against asking her name) in a clear reversal of the sexual roles considered proper in Gozzi's idealized patriarchal order. It is no accident that at one point Farruscad is referred to as a "timid waverer . . . *more like a weak woman than a man*" (3.3; italics mine).

This perversion of proper sexual order has disastrous social consequences: in Farruscad's long, irresponsible absence, his father has died and his kingdom is on the point of destruction, unable to defend itself against invaders without the prince's leadership. But though Cherestanì has in a sense caused this disorder, having kept Farruscad from his responsibilities, she is not a deliberately evil figure; indeed, the ambivalence we noted in Gozzi's treatment of Turandot is evident here as well. Cherestanì's greatest desire is to give up her immortality and her powers to become a normal woman living a normal life as Farruscad's wife. In order to do so, she must subject her husband to cruel treatment, seeming to burn his children alive and destroying the provisions that will save his kingdom from starvation. If he bears all this without complaint, firm in his love, the king of the fairies will allow Cherestanì to shed her immortality and magical powers, but if Farruscad curses her, she will be transformed into a serpent. This stipulation introduces another element of disorder into the world of *The Serpent Woman:* again, the problem of meaning and ambiguity. Like Turandot, Cherestanì does not say what she means, for she is forbidden to tell the secret of Farruscad's trial. Her lack of a true name and country, her mysterious oracular pronouncements—intelligible to the audience but not to the other characters, who continually misinterpret her—create tension and confusion until, after Farruscad's curse, she can finally reveal the true significance of her words and actions. However involuntarily, Cherestanì, like Turandot, is a distorter of meaning.

Cherestanì's transformation into a serpent is a fictional concretization of the reversal of roles that characterizes her relationship with her husband. The shape she assumes is not only an obvious phallic symbol, but also an emblem of power—she is by far the most fierce and threatening of the creatures Farruscad must overcome at the play's end. The first two of these monsters are vanquished by a sort of castration: the magical bull disappears when Farruscad cuts off his horn, while the giant is disposed of when the prince severs his head and an ear. The serpent cannot be defeated in this way, for Farruscad must kiss it (without, of course, knowing that it is his wife). Urged on by the paternal guidance of the magician Geonca, timid Farruscad, "more like a weak woman than a man," accomplishes his most forceful act of the play by embracing this phallic emblem of masculine power—an embrace that is both literal and metaphorical, signifying Farruscad's acceptance of male potency and of man's proper role in society. With his embrace, the disorder of the play is at once resolved: Cherestanì regains human form, becomes mortal, and offers Farruscad her kingdom; Canzade marries the vizier Togrul, who will rule her realm; Smeraldina weds Truffaldino, and Brighella is promised a bride at a later date. Again, the ritual of reordering is complete, as the woman who had constituted an involuntary menace to patriarchal order triumphantly sloughs off her threatening, unwanted potency and surrenders it, her kingdom, and herself to the proper authority of her husband.

Beyond their occasional anti-Goldoni or anti-Enlightenment polemics, and beyond their more consistent emphasis on entertainment and supposedly pure theatricality, Gozzi's *Tales* thus have an important element in common: the existence, at the root of their plots, of a fundamental conflict between order and disorder, ritualistically resolved in the course of the play.[16] Perhaps the *Tales* may best be understood as a reaction to a disquieting (for some) sense of cultural instability, a sense that the traditional categories of meaning and behavior were being called into question. If so, the historical situation of the *Tales* is strikingly similar to Fredric Jameson's characterization of romance:

> Romance as a form . . . expresses a transitional moment, yet one of a very special type: its contemporaries must feel their society torn between past and future in such a way that the alternatives are grasped as hostile but somehow unrelated worlds. . . . the archaic character of the categories of romance (magic, good and evil, otherness) suggests that the genre expresses a nostalgia for a social order in the process of being undermined by nascent capitalism, yet still for the moment coexisting side by side with the latter.[17]

Such a sense of cultural anxiety, the feeling that the rules of the game were somehow in question, is of course by no means specific to the eighteenth century. I do not think it an exaggeration to assert that this ideological angst is in fact a constant of modern society: certainly it was present in Germany during the early nineteenth century and in the Soviet

Union immediately after the revolution—both hospitable to major Gozzi revivals. If this is true (and I think it is), then it should be clear that Gozzi's seeming fantasies offer to modern audiences what they offered his contemporaries: escape into a world where plurality and disorder can be dominated, and a comforting (if imaginary) stability restored. Gozzi's universal appeal is thus due to more than the impressive formal innovations which so often seem to foreshadow the modern theatre. Beyond the sheer technical bravura of the *Tales,* beyond their play of seemingly escapist fairy-tale fantasy, an important part of Gozzi's art is this embedding of ideology— that is, of a coherent system of social values—in the very fabric of his plots. Even if we consciously reject Gozzi's view of the world, we cannot help but feel the pull of his plays, for the fundamental issues they confront through theatrical displacement—authority and subordination, male and female roles, the security of stability and the threat of change—are still pertinent to our lives today. And that, perhaps, is the secret of the continuing success of the *Tales for the Theatre* nearly two centuries after their author's death: in a very real sense, Carlo Gozzi's context is still our own.

## Notes

1. Kurt Ringger, "Carlo Gozzi's *Fiabe teatrali:* Wirklichkeit und romantischer Mythos," *Germanisch-romanisch Monatsschrift,* neue Folge 18 (1968): 15.

2. Goldoni's comedies have also been widely translated, but are more often read than performed abroad, particularly in the English-speaking world. Certainly, they have had less influence on non-Italian playwrights and directors than Gozzi's *Tales.*

3. Paradoxically, these minor nobles (called *barnaboti*) were fiercely protective of Venice's aristocratic system, though excluded from any real share of the state's political and financial power. Gozzi's ideology often reflects the positions typical of his class, and conflicts with the views of some members of the greater aristocracy who were cautiously open to social and economic reforms. Suggestively, the latter were often supporters of Goldoni.

4. Carlo Gozzi, *Opere: Teatro e polemiche teatrali,* edited and introduced by Giuseppe Petronio (Milan: Rizzoli, 1962), 1085. Further references to the *Opere* will be in the text.

5. Written within the brief space of five years, Gozzi's *Tales* include *The Love of Three Oranges* and *The Raven* (both 1761); *The King Stag, Turandot,* and *The Serpent Woman* (1762); *Zobeide* (1763); *The Fortunate Beggars* and *The Blue Monster* (1764); *The Green Bird* and *Zeim, King of the Genies* (1765).

6. From the "Prefazione dell'autore alla prima raccolta delle commedie," in Carlo Goldoni, *Tutte le opere di Carlo Goldoni,* edited by Giuseppe Ortolani, 14 vols. (Milano: Mondadori, 1935–56), 1:765. The translation is my own.

7. Gozzi's primary folkloric sources are Giambattista Basile's *Pentamerone* or *Lo cunto de li cunti,* Pompeo Sarnelli's *La Posilecheata,* the *Thousand and One Nights,* and the various collections of oriental or pseudo-oriental folktales in *Le Cabinet des fées,* published in 1716. The Parisian Théâtre de la Foire, or "fairground theatre,"

was a forerunner of the Opéra Comique; Gozzi was familiar with the work of at least one of the principal authors connected with it: Alain-René Lesage (1668–1747).

8. Carlo Gozzi, *Memorie inutili,* edited by Giuseppe Prezzolini, 2 vols. (Bari: Laterza, 1910), 1:214. Further references to *Memorie* are in the text.

9. Petronio, in Gozzi's *Opere,* 12.

10. Norbert Jonard, "Les Structures idéologiques de *L'augellino belverde* de C. Gozzi," *Romanistische Zeitschrift für Literaturgeschichte* 2 (1978): 10–20.

11. Some of Goldoni's plays were also influenced by this style of theatre: see for example *La buona moglie, Pamela,* and the "Ircana" trilogy.

12. The anomalies of *The Green Bird* may perhaps be explained by the fact that its plot and characters continue Gozzi's first *Tale, The Love of Three Oranges,* written as a *canovaccio* before the playwright had a clear plan for the literary project to come.

13. The fact that Gozzi criticizes a ruler in *Zobeide* and *The Green Bird* does not contradict his idealization of authority, since these characters have failed to live up to their responsibilities as monarchs. Individual sovereigns may be portrayed negatively, but the value of an aristocratic *order* is never questioned.

14. Norando in the *Raven* is perhaps an exception, since his role is that of an adversary rather than a helper of the hero. Still, at the play's end his enmity is revealed as having all along been no more than a pose required by the conditions of the curse, and it is he who expresses Gozzi's explicit mockery of theatrical realism in the final scene.

15. Ted Emery, "Autobiographer as Critic: The Structure and 'Utility' of Gozzi's *Useless Memoirs,*" *Italian Quarterly* 94 (Fall, 1983): 43–49.

16. It is of course possible that much of the deep structure of Gozzi's plots was already present in his sources, perhaps a primary reason for his choice of the genre of "fairy drama" in the first place. Gozzi's use of fairy-tale material has never been studied from an ideological perspective. I suspect, nonetheless, that in modifying his folkloric sources, he consistently stressed their inherent order/disorder dichotomy so as to facilitate the ideological displacement I have described. In any case, the playwright's frequent denigration of his fairy-tale sources as peurile or silly should be taken with a grain of salt.

17. Fredric Jameson, "Magical Narratives: Romance as Genre," *New Literary History* 7 (1975): 158.

# The Raven

## A Tragicomic Tale for the Theatre in Five Acts

### Preface

The popularity of the *Tale* of the three oranges caused controversy and debate throughout Venice.[1]

The critics, whose opinions—when they are intelligent—are for the most part based on the size of the audience, praised this fairy tale in their newspapers.

In addition to the parodies I had intended my *Tale* to express, they discovered profound allegories I had never dreamed were in it.[2]

The two playwrights and their supporters criticized me so bitterly that they offended everyone who had praised me. Rather than saddening me, that reflection made me laugh. I saw my literary enemies themselves opening up the way for my plan, and contributing to their own disaster.

The huge claque opposed to the *Oranges* maintained that the *Tale*'s success was due only to its popular and plebeian style of comedy, to the wit and skill of the commedia dell'arte actors who performed it, and to the striking theatrical effects of its transformations. Signor Goldoni became very angry and had the actress Bresciani, prima donna of the San Salvatore Theatre for which he wrote his comedies, make malicious and satirical remarks about my *Tale* in the sonnet that is always recited on stage at the close of the spring season.[3]

Without becoming at all angry, I proposed that a silly, unrealistic, puerile plot, if developed with skill, artistry, and elegance, could have an effect on the emotions of an audience, commanding their attention, and even moving them to tears.

I wrote *The Raven* in order to prove the truth of my proposition.

This fairy tale is commonly told to children, and I took its plot from a Neapolitan book entitled *Lo cunto de li cunti.*[4]

I could hardly have found a better source to carry out my threat—but whoever reads the tale of the raven in that book and tries to compare it to my play, will find that it is impossible to do so.

I warn my readers that this is true not only for *The Raven,* but for all of the *Tales* which I subsequently wrote, and in which I retained only the titles and some of the dramatic circumstances of my sources.

I did not ban the commedia dell'arte characters from this *Tale*, since I had sworn to support them, but I brought them on stage sparingly, as you will see, in creating a seriocomic play based on a highly unrealistic, infantile plot.

The Sacchi troupe performed it for the first time on the stage of the Royal Theatre of Milan. Contrary to their habit, the Milanese audience insisted that it be repeated for many performances.

It made its Venetian premier at the San Samuele Theatre, played by the same company, on the twenty-fourth of October 1761, causing a notable stir.

I brought the audience from laughter to tears with the greatest of ease, fulfilling my intention and proving my ability.

To make people cry in the midst of an openly silly plot requires an emotionally charged situation. In *The Raven*, that situation is based on circumstances that are in themselves unrealistic and laughable, lacking in the dramatic preparation, rhetorical embellishments, and fine eloquence which can create an illusion by imitating nature. Let my rivals try to draw tears in such circumstances—those honorable journalists, honorable literary hacks, honorable bestial novelists, who love to pass sentence without having the power to carry out their judgments, and who can convince no one to enforce their decisions.[5]

I was inspired to undertake this challenge by those three immortal geniuses Boiardo, Ariosto, and Tasso, who gave poetic truth to impossible, marvelous events, and whose work has such power over the human heart.

In Norando, the necromancer of this *Tale*, my reader may see the noble character I wanted to give my wizards, which are unlike the silly magicians of the commedia dell'arte.

*The Raven* was repeated for sixteen performances in that autumn and the following spring season, and despite the torrential rains that plagued it, it always had full houses.[6]

It was poorly plagiarized by some rival theatrical companies, and it is still successful when they revive it. Sacchi's troupe produces it every year, with good results.

You will find that it is written partly in verse and partly in prose, and that it has some small scenes that give only an outline of the plot.[7]

Anyone who wants to help Sacchi's company and support the masks of the commedia dell'arte will do the same, or he will botch it.

Signor Chiari insisted on having his masked characters speak in verses. He filled their mouths with gross stupidities—and in mocking his characters, he mocked himself. The seventh scene of the third act of *The Raven* is a little parody along these lines.

No one will ever be able to write the part of Truffaldino in prose, let alone verse, and Sacchi is one of those Truffaldinos who can improvise from the outline of a scene so well that he surpasses any playwright who could try to write it.[8]

However, all of the scenes in *The Raven*, whether in prose, verse, or outline, are necessary to the development of the plot and suited to the genre of the theatrical fairy tale. If those hypochondriacal pamphleteers who criticize me had ever read the collections of French theatre published by Grand, Girardi, and others, they would never have let their literary vapors go to their heads, and would not have called my *Tales* a jumble of formless scenes, badly planned and barely written out.[9]

I am having them printed just as they were performed.[10] In subjecting them even in their printed form to the verdict of the public, I choose for them a judge far different from a malicious, arrogant, stupid, or starving publisher.

In choosing whether to write in verse or prose, I was not moved by a whim, but by the necessities of art. In situations involving strong passion I wrote in verse, knowing that the harmony of a well-written verse dialogue gave nobility to the circumstances of the serious characters and rhetorical force to their speeches.[11] I do not presume, however, that I succeeded in my intention.

I would have little difficulty in rewriting my plays entirely in prose or entirely in verse—but I promised to publish them exactly as they had been performed, and when I make a promise I do not lie.

Since I do not believe my *Tales* are worthy of passing mountains and oceans, to be read by foreigners who do not know the Venetian dialect— necessary to my Pantalone and my Brighella—I will not waste my time adding footnotes to those characters' parts so as to explain, for example, that *osello* means "bird" or that *aseo* means "vinegar," as Signor Goldoni was good enough to do in his published works, to the considerable enlightenment of his foreign readers.[12]

You may see from this that I am a humble man. I don't claim that my fairy tales are worthy of being entirely understood abroad, though it is indispensable for foreigners to appreciate all of the beauties and dignities of *The Chioggian Brawls*, with its important arguments about roast squash.[13] It will be enough for me if the Italians understand the criticism of mores and manners, and the moral lesson I tried to embody in these two characters.

Since I have followed the above pattern regarding the use of prose, verse, and scene outlines in all of the comedies that I wrote to support Sacchi and his company, I inform my dear readers that they may expect the same not only in *The Raven*, but in most of my other plays.[14]

I proposed to entertain and to move audiences with a new theatrical genre, but I always intended to be humble in my art, and to conserve something of the infantile silliness of fairy tales—if only to satisfy my own poetic whim, and to have the freedom to invent without the limitations of literary rules and stodginess. This new genre is free, daring, and immoderately filled with artifice and invention. If anyone reads these *Tales* with the intention of comparing them to the Marquis Maffei's *Merope*—itself not exempt from criticism—or similar works, he'll find it easy to play the critic, but will do so without foundation or merit.[15]

# The Raven

MILLO (MEE-loh), king of Frattombrosa
JENNARO (jenn-AH-roh), a prince, his brother
LEANDRO (lay-AN-droh), a minister
TARTAGLIA (tarr-TAHL-yah), another minister
ARMILLA (arr-MEE-lah), princess of Damascus
SMERALDINA (SMAY-rahl-DEE-nah), her lady in waiting
NORANDO (noh-RAHN-doh), a magician
TRUFFALDINO (troof-ahl-DEE-noh), king's huntsman
BRIGHELLA (bree-GHEL-ah), another of the king's huntsmen
PANTALONE (PANT-ah-LOH-nay), admiral
TWO DOVES, who can speak
SAILORS, including galley crew
SOLDIERS
SLAVES
A DRAGON

The scene is the imaginary city of Frattombrosa and nearby.

## Act One

*A seashore with some trees. Behind it, the sea. Squalls, rain clouds, thunder, and lightning*

SCENE I

PANTALONE, *on the bridge of a galley caught in the storm, blows his mariner's whistle and yells orders, but the sounds are lost in the storm. The storm eases up and the galley approaches the shore.*

PANTALONE    (*Lashing the* SAILORS *with a rope as he shouts*). Let go of the helm. Scum! Slacken that sheet. Take it in, you jellyfish!

CREW.   Land, land!

PANTALONE.    Land, land? You'd be dead, you deadbeats, if you didn't have me here to look out for you. (*A piercing whistle*) Now, rats: down with the anchor!

CREW.   Anchor down, sir.

(*They pull the galley ashore and lower a ladder.*)

PANTALONE.    Bark your thanks to heaven, you dogs.

(*He blows three times on the whistle. Each time the* CREW *responds with a howl of gratitude.* PANTALONE *descends the ladder, together with Prince* JENNARO, *who is dressed as an oriental merchant.*)

## Scene 2

JENNARO.   What a storm, Pantalone—I thought I was done for.

PANTALONE.   What? when you know where I come from?

JENNARO.   All right, from Venice. You've told me a thousand times.

PANTALONE.   Damn right. A Venetian from the island of Giudecca.[16]
With a Giudecca Venetian on board no ship's ever in danger. I got my
education the hard way. Why, for years I sailed the trade route to Turkey and back—wore out half a dozen boats at it, too. You call this a
storm? Well, it gave me a shiver now and then, not for myself—I'm
used to these capers—but for Your Highness. God almighty! I saw you
born. I carried you around in these arms when you were only this big.
My wife Pandora, bless her soul, you grew up on her milk. I used to
bounce you on my knees. I smothered you in kisses. And you'd push my
face away with your tiny fingers and say, "Pantalone, your beard is
scratching me." What I mean is you're like my own flesh and blood, and
I was more afraid for you than for myself. Besides, I owe everything to
your family—my living, my happiness. I've enjoyed I don't know how
many kindnesses from them over these past thirty years, all the way back
to when your dear father was king. And if that isn't enough, I have the
loyal heart of a Venetian.

JENNARO.   That's the truth. I have plenty of evidence of your stout
heart and your skill as a navigator. To bring us safe into port through a
storm like that one is enough to make your name as an admiral live forever. How far are we from our kingdom of Frattombrosa? How does
the weather look?

PANTALONE.   This port is called Sportella. We're only ten miles from
Frattombrosa. The weather's getting better; the wind is dying down.
It'll be sunny again in two or three hours, and after a quick hour and a
half at most, we'll be home again. Your brother Millo will be relieved.
His ears must have been burning all this time. You never stopped talking about him. He'll be worried to death at not having had any news
about you. What a wonder for brothers to be so devoted! Can I tell her
yet that you're the brother of a king?

JENNARO.   Yes, now you can. (*He looks back at the galley.* ARMILLA
*and* SMERALDINA, *in tears, are leaving it, followed by two* SLAVES.)
Ah, the princess is coming. She looks so unhappy. Leave us together.

Set up two tents on the beach here. We can rest after the storm. Send a messenger by land ahead of us to let my brother know we're coming.

PANTALONE.   I won't waste one second. I'm so excited, so delighted! What a wedding we'll put on in Frattombrosa! Maybe you'll say I'm crazy to look forward to a wedding when I'm seventy-five years old. But when I hear the word "wedding," I think back to all those fairy tales they used to tell when I was a little boy, with the prince and the princess who got married and the wedding feast of turnip brew, skinned rats, and flayed cats.[17] I think of that and . . . I'm a kid again. (*To the princess, who is still weeping*) There, there, little one. When you find out who we are, you won't cry any more, let me tell you. (*Exit.*)

SCENE 3

*The* SLAVES *escorting* ARMILLA *and* SMERALDINA *retire. The princess and her maid are also dressed in "oriental" fashion.* ARMILLA *has very dark hair and eyebrows, artificially darkened.*

JENNARO.   Armilla, your tears are like accusations. But you have far less reason to weep than you think.

ARMILLA.   You heartless pirate!

SMERALDINA.   Kidnaper! Traitor!

JENNARO.   It's true: I am cruel, wicked, and a traitor. But, princess, let me explain—

SMERALDINA.   What is there to explain, robber?

JENNARO.   I want to tell her—

SMERALDINA.   Murderer, what *can* you tell her? That you lured a princess aboard your boat by prayers and lies to show her laces and fabrics and jewels and ribbons and ornaments, the most beautiful ones in the world, you said, for her to choose whatever suited her best? That you took advantage of her woman's vanity? And will you dare remember that while this innocent girl wavered between these hundreds of attractions, you raised the anchor and set sail out into the open sea with us? Is that how you snatch two young women from their families? Thief! Scum! You deserve to be hung, drawn, quartered, and beheaded.

JENNARO. Slaves! Remove this impudent babbler.

ARMILLA (*As the* SLAVES *approach*). Bully! Do you want me alone with you? I know what you mean to do. But I'll die before—

JENNARO. No, princess. I only want to defend myself. But I will not listen to affronts from an angry woman who won't give me a chance to explain. I make no excuses, but if you listen I may be able to put a better face on my actions and calm you. (*To the* SLAVES) Take her.

SMERALDINA. Oh, punish this wicked man, you heavens! (*Aside.*) Will my premonitions come true? (*Exit, escorted by* SLAVES.)

SCENE 4

ARMILLA. Barbarian, what do you have to tell me? Keep away from me, you vicious buccaneer. And if you fear nothing else, at least respect the daughter of Norando, the prince of Damascus. Tremble at the thought of his power and expect a ferocious revenge.

JENNARO. Let it come! But first, let me tell you this: I am no evil man, no pirate, but Prince Jennaro, the younger brother of Millo, king of Frattombrosa.

ARMILLA. You are King Millo's brother? And yet you dress as a merchant, entice an innocent princess onto your boat, and carry her away?

JENNARO. Armilla, it was my affection for my brother, your father's stony heart, and the unkindness of fate that forced me to kidnap you.

ARMILLA. What fate could drive a king's brother to behave with such baseness?

JENNARO. Judge for yourself, Armilla. My brother adored hunting; he talked of nothing else. Three years ago he went into a forest in pursuit of some quail and hares. He noticed a raven in an oak tree, aimed his bow and sent an arrow into it. Directly beneath the oak there stood a white marble tomb. The dead raven fell onto the tomb, staining the marble with its blood. The forest suddenly shook to a clap of thunder. From a grotto nearby an ogre appeared, the raven's owner. My God, what a terrifying creature: a giant with flaming eyes, a furious face, the tusks of a wild boar protruding from his cave of a mouth, and blood foaming on his lips. "King Millo, my curse be on you!" he shouted, and uttered this fearsome incantation, which still rings in my brain:

30

"You must seek a woman whose skin
Is as white as this marble tomb,
Whose lips are scarlet, akin
To my raven's blood, and whom
The gods have given black hair,
As black as his every plume.
If you find her not, I swear
By Pluto to seal your doom!"

He vanished and (marvel of marvels!) my brother stared in fascination at the dead raven, the blood, and the marble. He was tormented by apprehension and rage. He would not move from there. I had to drag him out of the forest and back to the palace. Since that time he will not listen to either quiet reason or desperate entreaties. Sighs, tears, and unshakable sadness are consuming my poor brother. Like a maniac he runs through the palace crying, "Who will bring me a woman with hair as black as the raven's wing, lips as scarlet as his blood, and skin as white as the marble on which he lies dead?"

ARMILLA  (*Aside*). Truly an extraordinary tale! I've heard of nothing like it.

JENNARO.   In my anxiety, I sent envoys and spies to every country in search of such a woman. All in vain. They could not find anyone with the whiteness of marble, the red of blood, and the black of the raven's feathers. Meanwhile, I watched my dear brother dying. In desperation, I fitted out a ship and sailed from India to Arabia, searching for her in every port. I saw a thousand cities and numberless women, even the rare beauties of Venice, young and fair, slim and voluptuous, shy and majestic. But I could not discover one with the whiteness of marble, the blackness of the raven's down, and the scarlet of his blood. Three days ago I arrived in Damascus. An old man, taking pity on my plight, told me about you and how I might kidnap you and escape your father's wrath. I observed you at your window . . . and recognized in you the qualities I was seeking. I tricked you into coming aboard my ship. The rest you know.

ARMILLA.   Why did you hide this from me during our two days at sea?

JENNARO.   I felt ashamed. You were in tears and in horror of me. It seemed wiser to leave you alone until you calmed down and I could tell you the truth. Love for my brother, sheer necessity, and a horrible fate compelled me to do this. And if your heart is as sweet and generous as your looks, Armilla, I beg you: forgive me. (*He kneels.*)

ARMILLA.   Jennaro: rise. Since you mean to make me the bride of a king, I can confess that I hated being cruelly locked up by my father, no better than a prisoner. I do forgive you, and I admire you for setting so unusual an example of brotherly devotion.

JENNARO   (*Rising*). Princess, you're as wise and kind as you are beautiful.

ARMILLA.   But what use is my forgiveness? I pity you, Jennaro. You are the most unlucky of men.

JENNARO.   What misfortune could make me unhappy? My brother's live is saved. You have forgiven me. What could spoil . . . ?

ARMILLA.   My father Norando is an implacable ruler, and so powerful a magician that he can stop the sun in its course, overturn mountains, change men into plants—he can bring about whatever he desires. He will never forgive you for kidnaping me. I feel sorry for King Millo and you and everybody else responsible for bringing me here. That storm today was surely his doing. I tremble to think of the catastrophes to come.

JENNARO.   Let the gods decide. I feel so joyful that I can't think about anything sad. (*He points to a tent that has been put up.*) Rest there, princess. (*Pointing to another tent that has been erected during the scene*) I'll do the same here. In a few hours the storm will calm down and a short trip will take us to my brother.

ARMILLA.   I'll rest now, but before long we shall be weeping, not sleeping. (*Exit.*)


SCENE 5

PANTALONE   (*Entering*). What about this? Good things come in bunches, like cherries. Highness, my boy, I have some news, not exactly spectacular maybe, but nothing to sneer at, either, seeing as how you love your brother as much as he loves hunting and horses.

JENNARO.   What news, my dear old Pantalone?

PANTALONE.   While you were chatting with the princess, I kept out of your way, as I should, by taking a stroll along the beach. All at once, a huntsman appeared on a horse. And what a horse! Me, I was born and raised in Venice, and my specialty is boats, but I've seen plenty of horses in my time. This one's as handsome as a painting. A strapping piebald with a mighty chest and cruppers, small head, large eyes, an ear only that big. He cantered, he jumped, he danced all sorts of steps, and so daintily that if he'd been a mare I'd swear he was the prima ballerina of our century and that her soul had passed into that horsey body by what Pythagoras and the lunatics used to call transmigration.

JENNARO.   We must buy this marvel for my brother.

PANTALONE.   Slow down, boy! Listen and wonder. The huntsman kept a magnificent falcon on his wrist while he rode the great black horse. This shoreline must be full of game. As he galloped, six partridges flew away in front of him, plus three or four quails, I couldn't tell you how many water hens, and two ptarmigans. The huntsman released his falcon. And then I saw the impossible. The falcon seized a partridge in one claw and in the other a quail. He clamped his beak on a water hen—all this, mind you, in one flying movement—and with his tail—no, you won't believe what comes next—but with his tail—you know I'd never lie to you, Your Highness—he scooped up a ptarmigan.

JENNARO   (*Laughing*). Is this the kind of story they tell in Venice?

PANTALONE.   Let the sky drop on my head if I'm telling a fib. With a partridge in one claw, a quail in the other, and a water hen in his beak, the damn bird grabbed a ptarmigan with his tail.

JENNARO.   We must buy the horse *and* the falcon. By adding these prodigies to the princess, I'll make my brother the happiest man in the world.

PANTALONE.   Don't bother.

JENNARO.   What?

PANTALONE.   I've already bought them.

JENNARO.   For how much?

PANTALONE.   Next to nothing. As much as I wanted to give. A couple of coins. Six million in gold pieces. Look, Your Highness, after all the benefits I've received from you, don't I have the right to show some gratitude? I give you the horse and the falcon and I don't want you to say another word about it. Now you're grown up, I'd like you to give in to me sometimes the way you did when you were a child. So go and get some rest. The weather's cleared up and it'll be fine for the last leg of our voyage. Where's the princess, by the way? Did she calm down?

JENNARO.   Yes, and she knows everything. About the gifts: I insist on repaying you. No? Very well, we'll talk about it later.

PANTALONE.   To hell with that, my little pisser. Get into your bed and stop pestering me. (*Aside*) I spent no less than two hundred ducats, and if I had to, I'd have given one of my eyes. Why? First of all, because I love this young prince the way I love my guts, and then to show that a Venetian like me, even when he's not rich, can be as generous as a king. (*Exit.*)

JENNARO   (*Alone*). You old golden heart, a model for mankind! Now I should feel cheerful, but Armilla's warning about her father's powers has troubled me. Must get some sleep. I need it.

(*He lies down on a sofa in the tent which his men have put up under a tree in full view of the audience.*)

## SCENE 6

*Two* DOVES *alight on the branch of the tree over the tent of* JENNARO, *who is resting.*

FIRST DOVE.   Poor Jennaro! Unlucky prince!

SECOND DOVE.   What is wrong, my dearest? Why is he unlucky?

JENNARO   (*Sitting up*). A miracle. Doves that speak! About me! I'd better listen.

FIRST DOVE.   That falcon he now owns . . . as soon as he presents it to his brother, the falcon will pluck out the king's eyes. But if he doesn't give it, if he conceals the fact that he has it, or if he mentions this curse to anybody, or even hints at it, Jennaro himself will turn into a marble statue.

JENNARO   (*Aside*). Horrible! Can this be true?

FIRST DOVE.   Poor Jennaro! Unlucky prince!

SECOND DOVE.   Is that the worst danger that threatens him?

FIRST DOVE.  As soon as his brother gets on the horse, it will kill him. But if Jennaro doesn't give him the horse, if he conceals the fact that he has it, or if he mentions this curse to anybody, or even hints at it, or makes any attempt to avoid it, Jennaro will turn into a marble statue.

JENNARO  (*Aside*). Am I awake or dreaming? What an unmerciful punishment!

FIRST DOVE.  Poor Jennaro! Unlucky prince!

SECOND DOVE.  And is that the worst danger that threatens him?

FIRST DOVE.  If the king marries Armilla, on his wedding night he will be devoured by a monster. But if Jennaro doesn't give Armilla to his brother, if he conceals the fact that he abducted her, or if he mentions this curse to anybody, or even hints at it, or makes any attempt to avoid it, Jennaro will turn into a marble statue.

JENNARO.  Evil birds! Are they doves—or crows? If only I had my bow . . . I'll go back for it to the boat. (*He stands up. The* DOVES *fly off.*) Thank heaven they've gone.

### SCENE 7

NORANDO, *old, venerable, and terrifying in appearance, and dressed in "oriental" garb, emerges from the waves, seated on a sea dragon. He dismounts and points a majestic arm at* JENNARO.

NORANDO.  Do not move, you thief, foolhardy ravisher! I am Norando. Those doves were my messengers. They spoke the truth. I sent you the falcon and the horse. Take my beautiful daughter Armilla to your brother. You will both pay for having insulted me. Norando, prince of Damascus, does not tolerate such affronts. If the tempest I raised has not convinced you of my power, you will soon see the prediction of the doves come true.

JENNARO.  Please hear me, Norando—

NORANDO.  I will not. Couldn't I take Armilla from you by force, if I wished to? Revenge is what I want, revenge on you and your family. I will slaughter you all and punish Armilla for disobeying me. Present Armilla, the horse, and the falcon to your brother or you will turn to marble. One word of what I have said to anyone else and you will be cold stone. I leave you to the contemplation of your rewards. (*He disappears into the waves.*)

JENNARO.   Good God, what should I do? If I tell Millo about the curse, I'll turn to stone, but if I carry out Norando's sentence, my brother will be blinded by the falcon or killed by the horse or swallowed up by a monster. Oh, my dear brother, are these the gifts I brought to cure your long sufferings and terrors and tears?

## SCENE 8

PANTALONE *enters with two* SLAVES, *one of them leading a richly decked-out courser, the other with a large, splendid falcon on his wrist.*

PANTALONE.   What's this? You're not asleep?

JENNARO.   No, Pantalone, I'm not.

PANTALONE.   Here, just take a look at these two beauties. (*To the* SLAVES) Hey, boys, bring the horse and falcon forward and let the prince feast his eyes on 'em. (*As the horse passes in front of* JENNARO, *it goes up on points like a dancer.*) Gorgeous creature! If I wasn't so old, I'd leap on his back and put him through his paces for you, take him through four somersaults.

JENNARO   (*Sighing*). Ah, my friend . . .

PANTALONE.   It can't be! You're not weeping?

JENNARO.   With pleasure. (*Aside*) Perhaps I've already said too much. I'm beginning to feel as cold inside as marble.

PANTALONE.   Yes, magnificent, aren't they? You never saw anything like 'em before. Good, the sky's clear at last. I'll take 'em aboard. I was keeping the princess company. She couldn't sleep, either. Too nervous and upset. You poor kids—if it's not one of you crying, it's the other. The sound breaks my heart! This is no time for sadness. (JENNARO *bursts into tears.*) Well, for the love of . . . You *are* crying. What's the matter with you?

JENNARO   (*Aside*). I mustn't tell him. (*Aloud*) Only a dream, old friend, a frightening dream . . . hallucinations. Where is the princess?

PANTALONE.   Only a dream? Come on now, you ought to be ashamed of yourself. Dreams, phantoms—nothing but silliness. Let's cheer up. The princess is coming and I must get us ready for the trip. (*To the* SLAVES) Let's go. Take it easy there with that animal. Don't let him hurt himself. (*To the* CREW) Ho there, you lazy pigs, you scullions and skivvies, drag her offshore. Up with the sails! Out with the oars . . . (*He boards the boat.*)

JENNARO   (*Aside*). What do I do? Leave the horse and falcon here on the beach? Take Armilla back to her father? No, I must give them all to my brother or I'll turn to marble. But my brother will die! Can I be his executioner? I can't think which way to move. And if I give away so much as a hint of the secret . . . O God, help me, advise me! Yes, God is kind. He will assist me. I think I feel His light on me, directing me. Courage, Jennaro!

## SCENE 9

*On the beach before the boat.* JENNARO, ARMILLA, *and* SMERALDINA

JENNARO.   We're ready, Armilla. Time to leave. (*He offers her his arm.*)

SMERALDINA.   Prince, forgive my harsh words. I took you for a pirate, not the brother of a king.

JENNARO.   I do forgive you. (*Aside*) Heaven help me now.

PANTALONE   (*From the deck*). Come on, you beggars. A cheer for the prince and princess!

(*He whistles three times. Each time the* CREW *responds with a loud "Hurrah!" When everybody is aboard, the sails are unfurled, the oars dip in the water, and the galley disappears from sight.*)

## Act Two

*A room in the palace of Frattombrosa*

## SCENE 1

KING MILLO, *at rear, is asleep on some cushions. Enter* TRUFFALDINO *in hunting outfit.*

TRUFFALDINO.  Quiet, mustn't wake the king.
What?
I said *QUIET!*
I heard you.
Poor king. What he only looks like since he shot that rotten raven. He's
  slimmed down a lot.
Slimmed down! He's practically transparent. He used to have a decent-
  sized belly. Now look at him.
Not only his belly. He's also lost his wits. Once that ogre put the hex on
  him, he started having fits instead of wits. He walked around talking
  nonsense.
That's not nonsense: it's poetry.
How can you tell?
It rhymes.

> "O raven, o raven, I must find a spouse
> With white skin and scarlet lips and black hair and brows . . ."

I've heard those words so often they're printed on my brain, even though
  it's a tiny brain as brains go.
Poor king. I'm sorry for him.
I'm sorry for myself. If we lose our king, how can I still be master of the
  royal hunt?
He's not crazy. Not all the time. But once he goes into that "O raven, o
  raven" act, watch out.
He asked me to wake him at nine so he can go hunting. That's his only
  enjoyment. If I wake him before—or after—nine o'clock and he's in
  one of his fits, he'll hunt *me*.
I don't know the time.
(*A clock begins to chime the hour.*)
There it is!
(*When the clock reaches the fourth chime,* TRUFFALDINO *begins to count,*
  *"One, two . . ." As the clock chimes nine,* TRUFFALDINO *has reached*
  *six.*)
Oh my God, I'm three hours early! Rush away quietly.
What?
I said *QUIETLY!*

SCENE 2

*As he hurries out on tiptoe with tiny steps, enter* BRIGHELLA *noisily.*
*TRUFFALDINO makes threatening gestures to warn him not to disturb*
*the* KING.

BRIGHELLA.  But it's nine o'clock.

TRUFFALDINO   (*Whispering*). No. Six. I counted.

BRIGHELLA   (*Shouting*). Nine! I heard the chimes.

TRUFFALDINO   (*Whispering*). Shush! If you rouse him, I'll kill you.

BRIGHELLA   (*Shouting*). If you let him sleep late, I'll kill you.

(*Improvisation: They circle each other with threatening movements, ready to square off. They hurl themselves at each other and miss. Other business. The* KING *sits up, shakes his head.*)

KING.   What's that? Who's making that infernal noise? I'll kill him. (*He paces the stage in a fury crying out, "O raven, o raven!"* TRUFFALDINO *and* BRIGHELLA *run off to either side.*) . . . I must find a spouse with white skin and scarlet lips . . .
Where am I? Where was I? That wretched day when I fired the arrow has wrecked my entire life. My subjects are anxious, the palace has become a chamber of mourning, and my dear brother has been snatched away. God only knows what has become of him while he's roaming the oceans. He must have died.

## SCENE 3

*Enter* TARTAGLIA, *holding a handkerchief to his face.*

TARTAGLIA.   Your Majesty, Your Majesty! Important news!

KING.   News, Tartaglia? Now what? More misfortune?

TARTAGLIA.   One moment, please. The news is so important that I'm all choked up. A messenger has just announced that your brother—(*He blows his nose and wipes his eyes.*)

KING.   You're crying. My dear brother—he's dead.

TARTAGLIA.   No, no. I'm crying because I'm happy. They've sighted his ship. He'll be here shortly. He's brought you a princess stolen from her father, Prince Norando of Damascus. She has cheeks as red as the goddam blood, skin as white as the goddam marble, and hair and eyebrows as black as the goddam feathers on that double-damned crow.

KING.   My dear Tartaglia!

TARTAGLIA.   There's no doubt about it. The prince sent a messenger from Sportella, where they put in during the storm. The weather's better. They should be here any minute.

KING.   My cherished brother: how much I owe him! Tartaglia, assemble my courtiers and send someone to the port to see whether the lookouts have caught sight of them coming in to land. We'll all hurry there to welcome him. (*Exit.*)

TARTAGLIA.   What a rush he's in! Let's take a look at this inimitable beauty, this star who has held an entire kingdom under her spell for three years, and why? Because she looks like a crow.

SCENE 4

*At the port of Frattombrosa: a tower with cannons mounted on its roof.* TRUFFALDINO, BRIGHELLA, *and a* SENTRY *are on the tower.* TRUFFALDINO *has a telescope, but instead of looking out to sea, he looks the other way, at the audience. He improvises some jokes about what he sees in the house, with moderation and discretion.*

TRUFFALDINO.   I don't see any galley.

BRIGHELLA   (*Snatching the telescope and looking out to sea*). I do. Just a speck on the water. You need keen eyes to make it out.

TRUFFALDINO   (*Snatching the telescope back and pointing it at the audience, especially the boxes*). That's not a galley. It's a flight of pigeons, a flock of sitting ducks.

BRIGHELLA.   A galley!

TRUFFALDINO   (*Using his hand as an eyeshade*). A donkey, an elephant, an anthill!

(*They continue to squabble and wrestle for the telescope.*)

SENTRY.   Galley ahoy! North by nor'east. (*He rings the tower bell.*)

TRUFFALDINO.   What did I tell you? I'll warn the king.

BRIGHELLA.   You stay here. I'll warn him.

(*More buffoonery between them as each tries to reach the exit first. Three cannon shots are heard from the galley, which is still not in sight. The cannons from the tower fire three shots in reply and are answered by three more from the galley, as is the proper naval practice. Pantalone's whistle and the shouts of his* CREW *are heard.*)

PANTALONE'S VOICE.   They've seen us. Row, row harder, you vermin!

## SCENE 5

*The galley appears, covered with flags and pennants, to the sound of trumpets and kettledrums. On the lookout tower, a gong is struck.* PANTALONE *orders his men to lower the gangplank, and* JENNARO, ARMILLA, *and* SMERALDINA *leave the galley.*

JENNARO.   This, Armilla, is the capital of Frattombrosa, and you will soon be its queen.

SMERALDINA.   Pretty town. Charming. Cheerful.

ARMILLA.   So it is. This peaceful sea, the vivid green hills on the out-skirts, and the fragrant air . . . we are finally safe. (*Ironically*) But Prince Jennaro seems worried, though he's trying to hide it from us. Perhaps my future here is less bright than he promised.

JENNARO   (*Coming out of his reverie*). Possibly you haven't quite for-given me. You find yourself far from home among a strange people, and in spite of your better feelings, you are suspicious. (*Aside*) If only I could tell her what is at stake . . . (*Aloud*) But look, princess, my brother's coming to greet you. Let's dispel all misgivings. Please don't make him bitter. He has suffered enough. (*Hastening toward the* KING) Millo! At last!

## SCENE 6

*Enter the* KING, TARTAGLIA, LEANDRO, *and* SOLDIERS.

KING.   My dearest Jennaro! How I've waited for this moment! (*He em-braces him, holds him away and studies him.*)

LEANDRO   (*To* TARTAGLIA). Loving brothers—a splendid example to us all.

TARTAGLIA.   Not like my brother Pancrazio, boy! That stinker robbed me blind and now he's suing me for all I've got.[18]

KING.   And this is the princess?

JENNARO.   Yes, Armilla of Damascus. I put her in your charge.

KING.   What wondrous beauty! (*Aside*) There at last is the perfect complexion and the jet-black hair I've longed for. I feel full of joy. My melancholy has gone. (*He embraces* JENNARO *again.*)

SMERALDINA   (*To* ARMILLA). How do you like the king?

ARMILLA.   I do like him.

KING.   Tartaglia, go back to the palace. Make sure everything is ready for the feast. Leandro, go straight to the temple and tell the priest to prepare the altar for our marriage.

TARTAGLIA   (*Aside, rubbing his hands*). He's certainly eager! This means he's cured at last! (*Aloud*) I will carry out Your Majesty's wishes without delay.

LEANDRO.   Immediately, Your Highness.

JENNARO   (*In agitation*). No, wait, Leandro. (*To the* KING) We've hardly arrived, Millo. This is so hasty.

KING.   Why should we wait? Princess, you've turned the sorrow that overwhelmed me into joy. My brother must have told you our story. My only regret is that I am responsible for having taken you from your home. But I beg your forgiveness and, in compensation, I offer you a royal husband. You may perhaps resent me now, but my only desire is to please you and be the husband you desire. If you'll allow me to try, let us be married at once. I've waited fervently for this moment. My life hangs on your lips. Or my death. I will not coerce you. If necessary, I know how to die.

SMERALDINA   (*Softly, to* ARMILLA). He's good-looking, tender, considerate. He's the king. He adores you and you don't dislike him. What are you waiting for?

ARMILLA.   Your Majesty, I accept.

KING. Generous and gracious princess! Leandro, conduct the queen to her suite in the palace where she can rest. Then take my orders to the temple.

SMERALDINA *(Softly, to* ARMILLA). You don't look very cheerful.

ARMILLA *(Softly, to* SMERALDINA). Oh, Smeraldina, I want to, but I can't. *(After a worried look at* JENNARO, *who seems dejected, she follows* LEANDRO *out.)*

SMERALDINA *(Aside).* I feel sorry for her. If she knew the awful prediction . . . But maybe it's nonsense. We mustn't spoil the wedding. *(Exit.)*

### SCENE 7

KING. Why did you try to delay my marriage, Jennaro?

JENNARO. I thought that, after such a long voyage . . . It doesn't matter. *(Aside)* I know what Norando will do if I speak. *(Aloud, noticing the arrival of* PANTALONE *with the two* SLAVES *who bring on the horse and falcon)* The gifts are here. *(Aside)* This is the dangerous moment. Help me, God! Save my brother and show me how to avoid the terrible consequences.

KING *(Aside).* What's wrong with my brother? I hardly know him.

PANTALONE. Will you allow this poor and useless servant to kiss your hand?

KING. Useless? You? I consider you the most useful of all my courtiers. I know that it was your bravery that saved the lives of my brother and my precious queen during the storm.

PANTALONE. Heaven supported my meager skills. Give thanks to heaven first, and then to the courage and love of your brother Jennaro, who, if I may say so, has done more for you than you can ever repay.

KING. Yes, I admit that. *(Looking at the horse and falcon)* But pardon my curiosity, Pantalone. You know how much I love hunting, and I've never seen finer animals than these. Whom do they belong to?

PANTALONE. You. They're presents from your younger brother. He never loses an opportunity to do you some kindness.

KING.   I'm very grateful to him.

JENNARO   (*Deeply moved, aside*). We've come to the decision. Be bold.
(*Aloud*) Yes, Millo, allow me to present you with this miraculous falcon. (*He takes the falcon from the servant's wrist and approaches the* KING.)

KING.   A treasure. Thank you.

JENNARO   (*Aside*). This is the only way to save my brother's eyes . . .
(*He takes a dagger from his belt, cuts off the falcon's head, and flings the
dead bird far away, then remains standing as if stunned.*)

KING.   Jennaro, what do you mean by this extravagance?

PANTALONE.   Why the devil did he do that? To a falcon that picks up
ptarmigans with its tail! I'm stupefied. I don't understand a thing!

KING.   It was yours to begin with, Jennaro. If you wanted it yourself,
why not simply keep it? I may be your brother, but you'd better remember I am also your monarch.

JENNARO.   I'm sorry, Majesty . . . hallucinations . . . an attack of madness . . . (*Aside, in despair*) I dare not tell him. (*Aloud*) This wonderful
stallion will console you for the loss of the falcon. You'll forget my lapse
as soon as you climb on his back and experience how sensitive and re-
sponsive he is, more so than any horse you rode before.

KING   (*Aside*). I'm dreaming. I don't understand . . . (*Aloud*) I accept
your gift. I'll put him through his paces on the way back to the palace.
You can return with the admiral in my coach.

(*The* SLAVES *bring the horse forward. The* KING *takes the reins.*)

JENNARO   (*Aside*). God, lend me strength. Let me save my brother.

PANTALONE.   One moment, Your Majesty. I want the honor of holding your stirrup.

(*He holds the stirrup. The* KING *puts his foot in the other stirrup and is about
to swing up into the saddle when* JENNARO *takes out his sword and cuts
the horse's hamstrings. As the animal falls, it lands on* PANTALONE.)

Help! I knew it! A fortune teller warned me to stay aboard ships and away from horses. (SLAVES *pull the horse off him; he gets up and limps out.*)

KING   (*To* JENNARO) At last I see what you're up to. Delaying my marriage, and now these two murderous insults. You're in love with Armilla and you hate me. But don't abuse my brotherly affection. One more such error and I'll be forced to punish you. (*Aside*) A suspicion! The thought makes me mad with jealousy. Armilla is so lovely. He's my brother, it's true, but love has no regard for family ties and won't stop at insolence or displays of hatred. My God, I don't know what to think.

(*He strides out followed by his* GUARDS.)

JENNARO.   Millo! He despises me, and I can't defend myself. How could he guess that I kept him from death—twice? What if I had told him the fatal secret and been frozen into marble? And now, if he marries Armilla, how can I save him from the monster? I must exert all my ingenuity and protect him from Norando's power, even if I die in the attempt.

## Act Three

*A room in the palace*

### SCENE 1

*The* KING *and* ARMILLA

KING.   Armilla, my dearest one, my heart's ambition . . . (*Hotly*) My torment and my ruin! I can't stand this.

ARMILLA.   Torment? What do you mean?

KING.   Jennaro loves you. You're aware of his passion, yet you say nothing to me about it. Don't be cruel: knowing for sure will destroy me, but not knowing will destroy me even more painfully.

ARMILLA.   This is madness, Millo.

KING.   I am anything but mad, you ungrateful woman. His offensive behavior toward me proves it. And since then my ministers have seen him prowling gloomily through the palace as if he had lost touch with himself. He sighs, he weeps, and tries to hide from us. Have pity on me. Relieve me once and for all of this torture.

ARMILLA.   I won't deny that these sighs and tears and erratic actions you speak of do arouse my suspicions. But you are the one I love, Millo, and if I am lying may heaven strike me down! I am eager to become your wife. I can't give you a more sincere sign of my love. You may think it strange that I conceived such a warm affection for you so quickly, as if this were all some improbable, romantic story. But it is mostly your brother's doing. During the voyage he spoke of you all the time and so favorably as he praised your graciousness, your thoughtful manner, and your serene temperament that I could not help loving you before I had seen you. I can say no more, if Jennaro is to be condemned for his generosity.

KING.   But why those insults? And the sighing? And the objection he raised to our marriage? Armilla, I tell you he has been overtaken by a sudden infatuation. And seeing himself deprived of you, its object, he trembles for fear of revealing it to you or to me. Here he comes. My dear one, for the sake of our love, our peace of mind, and in the name of the sacred tie that will shortly bind us until death, allow me to hide and overhear what he says to you. Pardon this jealousy, which consumes me. All I long for is to be able to call you mine and mine entirely.

ARMILLA.   Your longing shall be satisfied. It doesn't offend me in the least.

## SCENE 2

*The* KING *hides.* JENNARO *enters. He is preoccupied and does not see* ARMILLA.

JENNARO   (*Aside*). So far, I've forestalled my brother's death. But the wedding will shortly take place, and I can't find any way to save him from the dragon Norando swore would devour him. I'm so terrified I can't think—and all because I dare not reveal the terrible cause of my anguish. (*Noticing* ARMILLA) She is here! What if she heard me? This terror dries me up so that I can hardly speak, and chills me: I feel as if I were already turning to stone.

ARMILLA.   Jennaro, is this the joy you said awaited me in the palace? You sigh, you weep and act strangely, you start quarrels with your brother. Is this any way to celebrate my wedding, which you strove so hard to bring about? The truth now, Jennaro: is it the fear of my father that has made you become so unlike yourself?

JENNARO   (*Aside*) She did hear. (*Aloud*) How can you think that, Armilla? We are absolutely safe here.

ARMILLA.   Then why do you upset your brother and me by opposing our marriage? Tell me candidly. Perhaps . . . could it be that you're smitten with me? Is that it? No, Jennaro. Impossible. You could never deceive your brother, could you? If he knew, he would die. What's this? Jennaro! You're weeping.

JENNARO.   You are wrong, Armilla. I love my brother more than myself. And I should and do love you, but as my brother's bride. I mustn't, I can't, say any more. If you love the king and if you feel any pity for me, call off this marriage. (*He kneels to her.*)

KING   (*Emerging*). You traitor—you are no brother to me. I knew it. Armilla, the altar is ready for us. Never fear. I know how to deal with the schemes and insults of a rival. If he persists with this importunity he'll pay for it. Come, it's growing late and my patience is at an end.

ARMILLA   (*Aside*). This will be a joyless wedding. (*The* KING *gives her his arm. They leave.*)

JENNARO.   I curse the day when my brother struck down the raven with his arrow. I am now loathsome in the eyes of Armilla, the king, the court, and the people. What good is it if I'm innocent, yet have no proof?

## SCENE 3

*One of the drapes rises and* NORANDO *steps forward, accompanied by "magical" special effects.*

NORANDO.   Try to prove your innocence and see what happens to you.

JENNARO.   Norando! How did you get into the palace?

NORANDO.   I go wherever I wish. Your murders of my falcon and my courser have enraged me more than before. You succeeded in putting off my punishment, but this night the dragon devours your brother. Say one word about this to anybody and you know what awaits you. I'll have my revenge if the whole world has to pay for it.

JENNARO.  Let me speak, Norando, my lord—

NORANDO.  I don't want to hear. You're beginning to learn the consequences of your felony. (*He steps behind the drape, which falls again.*)

JENNARO.  Implacable and hellish creature, you follow me like my shadow. You squirm and twist in my mind like a nest of vipers.

## SCENE 4

JENNARO *and* PANTALONE, *who has his arm in a sling and his head bandaged*

JENNARO.  My dear and faithful old friend! What are you doing here. I heard you had been seriously hurt. How can I apologize? I was the cause of your injury.

PANTALONE.  No apologies necessary, my lord. Since you were in your cradle, I've wanted nothing better than to serve you. In Venice we say a loyal heart never wavers. The surgeon has put me to rights. My hand did get a bit buckled under the horse and I cracked my skull and I couldn't move. But words, my dear boy, words heal faster than any medical treatment. While I lay there, I heard people around me saying, "The king's angry, the prince has offended him, the king threatened the prince, and if we don't watch out, we could walk right into a tragedy." And that's what made me forget the agonizing pain and gave new strength to this poor old body, which is mostly Venetian heart. So here I am to hear from your own mouth what all this trouble's about, give you my sincere advice, and if there's no other way to defend you, to sacrifice what's left of an old man's life.

JENNARO.  Everything you say is true, Pantalone, but don't worry about it. Let me bear the distress alone.

PANTALONE.  My dear son, excuse me if I speak to you as a father, and not as your subject or servant. Tell me what the hell is wrong. Why these sudden excesses, these provocations? I know how fond you are of your brother. If you have some complaint, if somebody has insulted you, let me know. If you're justified, I'll be the first, old as I am, to advise you to take revenge. A noble and suitable revenge, of course. But slitting a falcon's throat and chopping a horse's legs when someone's in the middle of mounting it, that's what we Venetians call a butcher's revenge. It's unworthy of a prince like you. For friendship's sake, for the love of God, spit it out, take me into your confidence. Don't leave me thinking the worst. That's like sticking a hundred daggers into this Venetian heart.

JENNARO.   Pantalone, you're the most faithful of servants. And your courage does honor to the city you come from. But when you try to ease my distress, you only torture me further. (*Aside*) Have I said too much? I feel as cold as ice.

PANTALONE.   Dear boy, enough of this oracle talk! Tell me everything. Come with me to the temple and, in front of all the people at the wedding ceremony, act cheerful, embrace your brother, and put a stop to the envious, malicious tongues of those who'd like nothing better than to see a rift between the two of you.

JENNARO   (*Agitated*).   So my brother is already in the temple for the ceremony?

PANTALONE.   Wait a minute . . . you're not upset about this marriage, are you? Have you fallen for . . . ? Well, why not? You're young. It's natural. We can't always help what we do. You should have told me while we were still aboard the galley. I would have turned the ship right around and sailed you off to—I don't know, maybe Venice.

JENNARO   (*Aside*).   Every word I speak terrifies me. I keep imagining that I see Norando, that I'm turning into stone. I must concentrate on Millo. If there is still time to rescue him, then the danger be damned. (*Aloud*) Pantalone, I know that everybody but you is against me, and I need your loyalty still. I swear, and God is my witness, that I love my brother as I do myself, that I cherish Armilla, but as his wife, and that everything I've done today I had to do. I can't tell you more than that. My honor and my innocence are in your hands. I must go. (*Aside*) May heaven inspire me. I must save Millo's life, even if I lose my own.

PANTALONE.   No, I want to come with you. Don't leave me. Listen—

JENNARO.   Stay here. I order you to. Good-by. (*Exit.*)

PANTALONE.   So I'll stay. I'm a servant. I mustn't disobey. But what the devil did he mean by that strange talk: "Everything I've done I had to do?" I don't get it. And yet I'll bet every drop of blood in my veins that he wasn't lying. I know that youngster. From his earliest days he's been the soul of sincerity. Couldn't tell a fib if he wanted to. When he broke a cup or filched an apple or peed in his pants he never did what my late wife, bless her memory, advised him: blame the cat, blame a servant. It was always: "My fault. I'm sorry. I won't do it again." Ever since he learned to speak! And at twenty he still hasn't told a single lie. I know how he felt when he had to trick the princess into coming aboard the ship. He went along with it only because his brother's life was at stake. He felt he had to. God almighty, how can I prove he's innocent? I'm the only one who still believes in him.

### SCENE 5

LEANDRO *enters rapidly.*

LEANDRO.   Admiral, have you seen Prince Jennaro?

PANTALONE.   Why do you ask?

LEANDRO.   Because the king sent me for him.

PANTALONE   (*Aside*). I don't like this. (*Aloud*) What instructions did he give you, my dear Leandro?

LEANDRO.   Have you seen him, yes or no?

PANTALONE.   Yes. But do me a favor: what are your orders?

LEANDRO.   Where is he? I must find him immediately.

PANTALONE.   When I know your instructions, I'll tell you.

LEANDRO.   I am not at liberty to reveal the king's commands. I'll find him without you. (*Swift exit.*)

PANTALONE.   You dogs! I can guess what those orders are. And they want me to help. They want to take him away from me!

### SCENE 6

TARTAGLIA *enters rapidly.*

TARTAGLIA.   Admiral, have you seen Leandro?

PANTALONE.   Yes. Why do you want him? (*Ironically*) You look as jolly as a jester. You must have good news for him.

TARTAGLIA.   Where is he? Don't hedge. I'm obeying the king's orders.

PANTALONE.   You too? My dear Tartaglia, what are those orders? Tell your best friend.

TARTAGLIA.   Nothing complicated. You may as well know. Leandro has to put the prince under house arrest. My orders go further. The king decided that house arrest was not enough. He's worried about Jennaro. Wants him taken right away to the Isle of Tears and locked up there.

PANTALONE.   Not on the Isle of Tears! How can the king do such a cruel thing to his own blood? My poor innocent prince!

TARTAGLIA.   Innocent! He slew the horse and the falcon. You can't have forgotten. Because of it you have your arm in a sling and a busted head.

PANTALONE.   Makes no difference. Nobody but me knows why it happened. Or rather, I know but I don't know. Still, I do know he's innocent.

TARTAGLIA.   Besides, after all that impertinence, the king found him on his knees in front of the princess. He kissed her hands, fondled her, and implored her with tears in his eyes, "My darling, my life, don't marry my brother unless you want me to die." That's what you call innocent.

PANTALONE   (*Aside*). Good God! This is serious. (*Aloud*) That's nothing. How can you know what he really meant?

TARTAGLIA.   Isn't it obvious? The king's suspicions grew when Jennaro didn't attend the ceremony in the temple. It's only common sense to put away a brother who might dream up more dangerous plots, and possibly, out of jealousy, slay the king and queen just when they're settled cozily in their bedchamber. The prince has scandalized and irritated the court and enraged the public. We must nip this thing in the bud. Look at your head. You must have dislodged your brain. You're talking like a lunatic.

PANTALONE.   And you like a man with no heart, faithless; one of those people who proverbially kick a man when he's down. You inflame the king's anger for your own ambition and profit. You stoke the fire instead of throwing water on it. You don't give a damn for the scandal and catastrophe that have overtaken these brothers—no, you find joy in their misfortune, when you should be weeping at it. Yes, weeping, as this poor old man is weeping, because I'll never find peace again. I may die this very evening because of all the heartache. (*Weeps bitterly*).

TARTAGLIA.   You're not the only one who's weeping, my dear admiral. And I'm doing it despite all the insulting things you said. I'm aware of your devotion to the prince. But he's responsible for what he did. I'm not. I'm only carrying out his majesty's commands.

PANTALONE.   It's true: the king is the ruler. If I'd been there, I, this humble lad from Venice, would have tried to calm him. And if he insisted on persecuting his brother, I'd have been honorable enough to resign, lose my place in the court, be chained up in the dungeons, rather than bring the news of such disgrace and mortification to a boy like Jennaro.

TARTAGLIA.   In Naples, my lord Pantalone, we don't have the fancy manners of you Venetians. When the king commands, we obey instantly and without any show of heroism.

PANTALONE.   Go ahead. Carry out the commands. But maybe a Venetian like me can teach you how to give up comfort and security to spend your last days in exile in the company of a poor youngster who's been abandoned by everybody else. Me, I still love him like my own tripes.

SCENE 7

TRUFFALDINO *whirls in.*

TRUFFALDINO.   Heard the big news?

PANTALONE.   Don't say the prince has made it up with the king?

TARTAGLIA.   Don't say Jennaro has done something else idiotic?

TRUFFALDINO   (*Striking a tragedian's pose*). While our attentive and expectant people . . . (*Relaxing his pose*) One moment. I'd better explain something. Be patient, will you? A poet told me what happened. I'm supposed to recite it in verse. I hope I don't fluff it or forget any lines. (*He resumes his tragic pose, illustrating his narrative with pompous gestures.*)

> While our attentive and expectant people
> Congregate for the wedding in the temple
> The priest adorns the altar, as the king
> Escorts his bride, and mellow trumpets sing

In harmony with lute and drum and lyre,
Followed by murmurous chanting of a choir.
They'll tie the knot—that sacred knot—but what
Is wrong? The temple air grows thick and hot.
It's crowded with the whirring flight of owls
And other night fowls. Evil omen! Howls
From hundreds of invading hounds now sound
Throughout the darkened precincts. Every hound
Takes up a spot. Abruptly, from the wall,
We see a mirror break away and fall,
Crashing into a thousand shards. A vase
Of salt placed on the altar tips—now sprays
Its contents. Next, a bird of prey descends
Upon King Millo's head. Another rends
The hairdo of the princess, that creation
Of jet-black strands . . .

I've lost my inspiration.[19] (*He wipes his forehead.*)

PANTALONE.   Then what? Don't leave us dangling.

TRUFFALDINO.   Verse is too terse. It doesn't suit my character. In-dulge me, please. I will conclude in the purest prose. Those nasty omens frighten the king and the people. Leandro comes back to announce that he cannot locate Prince Jennaro anywhere. The king says he fears his brother may start and lead a rebellion. He orders his soldiers to go armed and his courtiers to remain on guard throughout the night. Then he retires with the princess to their nuptial chamber.

PANTALONE.   Where has Jennaro gone? Could he have tried to drown himself? Oh, God, my poor boy! Shall I ever see you again? (*Exit, wailing.*)

TARTAGLIA.   Well, if I'm going to be on guard all night, I might as well get a pouchful of tobacco to keep me awake. (*Exit on the opposite side.*)

TRUFFALDINO.   I'll release my hunting dogs. If Jennaro tries any more of his crazy tricks during the night, they'll bite some sense into him. (*Exit down the middle.*)


## Act Four

*An antechamber in the royal apartments. Offstage, behind a large door, cen-ter, is the king's bedchamber. Night. A flagstone in the floor rises, and*

JENNARO *scrambles through it. He carries a lighted torch in one hand and in the other a sword.*

## SCENE 1

JENNARO.   The twists and turns in these underground vaults slowed me down. But I kept going. My brother's life counts for me above all else, even though he now persecutes me. This is the only passage by which the monster can reach the king's bedroom. And here I must die. My words can't argue my innocence, but my death will. (*Flashes of lightning offstage*) Explosions of flame, heat. And a sickening stench! I can hardly breathe. This is the monster's breath. He must be approaching. Yes, I see him now. A gigantic dragon! O heaven, guard me, strengthen my arm, lighten my sword, and prepare me to submit to your will. (*He puts the torch in a socket on the wall. A* DRAGON *covered in scales and vomiting fire, appears out of the darkness.* JENNARO *goes at him with the sword.*) Foul creature, I'll be your first victim. No use! His scales are as hard as porphyry or diamond. (*He attacks furiously.*) Millo, Millo, I can't protect you! (*The* DRAGON *pushes* JENNARO *aside and makes for the door to the royal apartment.*) One last try, before it's too late. (*Swings his sword in both hands. He strikes the door. The* DRAGON *has vanished. He stands there stupefied before the open door.*)

## SCENE 2

*The* KING *appears in the doorway, also holding a lighted torch and a sword. He sees* JENNARO *and takes a step back.*

KING.   Traitor! So you turn up at night in my palace, with a sword in your hand, breaking open this door to your brother's room.

JENNARO   (*Flabbergasted*). The dragon—has it gone?

KING.   And you hoped to kill me while I slept. Here I am. We shall see who gets killed. (*He raises his sword en garde.*)

JENNARO.   Millo, you don't understand. How could you? I came here to— (*Aside*) No! I almost told him.

KING.   Guards! Here, quickly!

## SCENE 3

*Enter* TARTAGLIA, LEANDRO, *and* SOLDIERS.

TARTAGLIA. Your Majesty, at your service. (*Noticing* JENNARO) What in hell—Jennaro, here?

LEANDRO. How did he get in?

KING. Is this how you protect your monarch's life? By letting traitors into his bedroom? Disarm this fratricide. I want to know who admitted him against my orders.

TARTAGLIA. I don't understand . . .

LEANDRO. Your Majesty, we have no idea.

JENNARO. These men are not responsible. I came in through a secret passageway underground, driven by my concern for you . . . Yes, I'm holding a sword. And I broke down the door—out of love for you.

KING. Love! Listen to that outrageous excuse.

JENNARO. Don't ask me to explain. I swear I did it out of love.

KING. For love, perhaps, but not love of me. These stupid lies are proof of your guilty conscience. Disarm him and then imprison him! Assemble the royal council to pronounce on his fate. (*Exit.*)

JENNARO (*Throwing down his sword*). You ungrateful fool! Here's my sword. Take my life and free me from this nightmare! The day will come when my brother sheds tears on my tombstone and calls me innocent and tries to call me back. (*Aside*). Are you satisfied, Norando? Drain my blood, so long as you let my brother enjoy happiness from now on with Armilla!

LEANDRO. Prince Jennaro, how could you bring yourself to commit such a crime?

TARTAGLIA. I can still hardly believe it. Out of love, did he say?

JENNARO. Enough! I spurn your reproaches. Aren't you the king's ministers? Then follow his orders. Take me away.

LEANDRO. We will, we will.

TARTAGLIA. We certainly will.

(JENNARO *goes out proudly, escorted by* SOLDIERS. TARTAGLIA *follows.* LEANDRO *goes after the* KING.)

## SCENE 4

ARMILLA, *in sleeping attire, enters from the door of the royal bedchamber, center.* SMERALDINA *enters from one side.*

SMERALDINA.   Princess, what's all the din? Torches burning in the middle of the night. Soldiers. Shouting. What happened?

ARMILLA.   Leave me, Smeraldina. Oh . . . Jennaro slipped into this room, broke open the door of our bedchamber, and tried to kill the king. My husband. His own brother! They've thrown him in prison. Instead of joyful celebrations, all I expect now is death and destruction.

SMERALDINA.   Unbelievable! Where is the king?

ARMILLA.   He looked at me with tears in his eyes. He sighed, then went and locked himself in his private chamber. I pleaded, but he refused to let me in. I could hear him in there, sobbing.

SMERALDINA.   Armilla, princess, my child—we must run away from here, to the mountains. It's time to tell you about a prediction I've kept hidden.

ARMILLA.   Hidden from me? What is it?

SMERALDINA.   When you were born your father consulted his wise men about your future. They said that, because of the killing of a certain raven belonging to an ogre, you would be abducted. Misfortunes, even massacres, would follow. And Norando himself, under the influence of a fateful star, would become your persecutor. That's why he always kept you guarded in isolation. But mere human precautions couldn't prevail against fate. The oracle has come true. That's why we must run away, save ourselves while we still can, before the massacre.

ARMILLA.   I will never run away. What, from a husband I love? Never! Perhaps if I stay here I can do something about these calamities. I'm not afraid of death; at worst, it could put an end to my griefs. (*Exit.*)

SMERALDINA   (*Hurrying after her*). My poor little one . . .

## SCENE 5

*A prison cell.* JENNARO *is in chains.*

JENNARO.  Damp walls, dark prison: will you alone know that I died in the effort to save my brother's life? I can tell you all about it, but if I breathe a word to any living person, I will turn to stone. Norando, you're lurking there close by, invisible, I'm sure of it. Tell me at least whether my brother's misfortunes will end when I die.

## SCENE 6

NORANDO *steps magically through the wall into the cell.*

NORANDO  (*Fiercely*). Die now, kidnaper, die while everyone thinks you are a traitor. Or if you wish, proclaim your innocence. And turn into a statue. You will never know your brother's fate, or the fate of Armilla . . . my dear daughter . . . (*He catches himself.*) That is your destiny. And my will.

JENNARO.  Cruel man, you must listen—

NORANDO.  I will not listen. You did not listen when you stole a princess. Now endure the penalty. (*He disappears.*)

JENNARO.  God, You who see all and are just, now help me. I have no other recourse. I am lost.

## SCENE 7

*Enter* PANTALONE.

PANTALONE.  Jennaro, my son, my dear boy, I won't ask you why you committed those crimes. I won't scold you; there isn't time. The king's council is in session. The only question being discussed is how they're going to execute you. When I hear the word death applied to you, my guts turn cold. I've bribed the guards with everything I have. A fast ship's waiting to take us away. Let's hope for better luck elsewhere. I don't need money. I'll feel rich if I can save your life. Hurry now: this way!

JENNARO.  Escape? My dear and only friend, I thank you. But I mustn't sneak away or I'll seem guilty. Innocent I am and innocent I must die.

PANTALONE. It's past the time for talk of innocence. Say you were crazy, say anything you like, but—

JENNARO. So you do believe I'm guilty?

PANTALONE. You're innocent, of course, whatever you say. But does it make any difference? If you escape, you play for time, let things cool down. Some day you'll come back, justify everything you did, and make it up with your brother. To be condemned as a traitor, as a rebel, as the murderer of your nearest blood relative, all this means death for sure, a shameful death, in public, on a gallows, at the hands of the executioner—that's what makes you guilty in the minds of others, and there's no remedy for it, and it will leave a stain on your reputation. Take my hand, my own boy, and be brave.

JENNARO. It's only too true, everything you say. Death makes me appear guilty, but flight is dishonorable. So if I must not die and not run away . . . (*Reflecting*) There's one other possibility.

PANTALONE. Then tell me fast—what could be better than escaping?

JENNARO. The only way to establish my innocence. For me it will be worse than dying. The mere prospect makes me shudder, but it's my destiny. At least, I will not leave a shameful memory behind me.

PANTALONE. My dear lad, don't abandon yourself to hollow dreams. If you really do know of a way out, take it fast! Death is hanging over you. I think I hear—

JENNARO. Go to my brother. Tell him that before I die, I must speak to him. If I've ever done anything he can remember with affection, he won't refuse me this last concession. If you do what I say, I will not have to scuttle away with you and I will not die in disgrace.

PANTALONE (*Ecstatically*). Are you sure?

JENNARO. Absolutely. If he comes, he'll be satisfied with what he hears.

PANTALONE. You've put new life into me. Here! (*He hugs him.*) I'll run all the way. I'll beg, I'll weep, I'll go down on these creaking knees. I feel so light and young. One more hug and I'm gone. (*He hugs him again and goes.*)

JENNARO.   Poor old fellow, you certainly will weep. So will my brother, and the court, and the whole kingdom. But I'll be more miserable than all of you.

## SCENE 8

*Enter* TARTAGLIA, *holding a scroll and accompanied by* SOLDIERS.

TARTAGLIA.   Heaven alone knows, Highness, how sad I am, how broken-hearted to present myself before you here. My voice f-f-falters. I don't know how to begin.[20] But as minister—

JENNARO.   It's all right, Tartaglia. I understand. I'm condemned to die, isn't that it?

TARTAGLIA   (*Nodding*). At your service. I have this warrant. I'm not sure I can bear to read it aloud. But you'll definitely get the gist of it. (*As he reads, he interrupts himself with frequent sobs and attacks of stuttering.*) The royal council, having examined the deeds of Jennaro, especially his armed assault at night in the palace, and finding the attempt on the life of his brother the monarch to be a clear and indefensible outrage . . . (*Breaking down*) . . . condemns Jennaro to be publicly decapitated.

JENNARO.   And the king signed it?

TARTAGLIA.   As you see. At your service. (*Displays the scroll*) Millo, King of Frattombrosa.

JENNARO.   A brother? A beast!

TARTAGLIA   (*Mopping his eyes*). Forgive me and have pity on me for what I am compelled to do. Guards, I consign His Highness to you. Make sure the sentence is carried out within the hour. I must leave because I sense that I am about to break down. Your Highness, good day. (*Exit.*)

## SCENE 9

*The* KING *enters with* SOLDIERS.

KING.   I am here in answer to your plea, and because the admiral swore you could establish that you're innocent. I know you are lying to delay your execution. I feel sympathy for you. I want you to prove your innocence. But I cannot believe in it. Your offenses were too blatant. Enough of that . . . I don't wish to be cruel. I came to listen to you, and I will. (*To the* SOLDIERS) Unchain him. (*To* JENNARO) Be seated.

(*The* SOLDIERS *release* JENNARO *from his chains and bring cushions for him and the* KING *to sit on, placing them near where the transformation will occur.*)

JENNARO.   I didn't guess you were so cruel. Would to God I'd never seen your signature on that death warrant.

KING   (*Emotionally*). The royal council . . . your crimes . . . the law . . . reasons of state . . . But I did not come here to listen to rebukes. All I hope for is to find that you really are innocent. No, I am not cruel.

JENNARO   (*Aside*). This is the moment of terror. I want to speak, but I'm trembling. (*Aloud*) Don't you remember when we were children, our affection, how we could not bear to be parted? We never had the slightest quarrel. Remember all those gifts we exchanged? We shared every toy we owned. And we always played together. You can't have forgotten how I took the blame for your faults, as you did for mine. If one of us ran a fever, the other cried, and took his hands to rub them, and stayed beside the bed, and wiped his forehead, and chased away the flies, and tasted the bitter medicines first, encouraging his brother to take them bravely. Now I ask you to tell me if you remember a single act I ever performed that was not done out of love for you. Since you killed the raven, haven't I shown the pain I felt for you? Didn't I repeatedly risk my life on that voyage? Didn't I bring back the princess? That fatal abduction saved your life. And now you think me guilty of planning to murder you! Not cruel? When you're the one who condemned me to die like a felon!

KING.   Your deeds condemn you. I'm not here to listen to pretty speeches. Prove your innocence, or I'll leave.

JENNARO   (*Aside*). Can I dare to say any more? (*Aloud*) Millo, I swear I am innocent and that you have condemned me unjustly. Don't force me to go further . . . (*He weeps.*)

KING   (*Rising*). Your tears do not prove your innocence. I leave you to your remorse. And your fate.

JENNARO   (*Also rising, in despair*). Wait, barbarian! I will give you the proofs of my innocence. But be ready to weep for me when it will be too late to mourn and to know I've been wronged. Norando, let your revenge come! Yes, I killed the horse and the falcon I gave you and I did oppose your marriage with Armilla. Why? While I rested on the beach at Sportello, two magic doves perched on a branch above me and revealed a terrifying secret. Suddenly Norando, Armilla's father, appeared and confirmed what the doves had said. (*Aside*) God save me, I'm approaching the metamorphosis . . . (*Aloud*) Listen to what the doves and Norando said:

> As soon as he presents the falcon to his brother, the bird will pluck out the king's eyes. But if he doesn't give it, if he conceals the fact that he has it, or if he mentions this curse to anybody, or even hints at it, Jennaro himself will turn into a marble statue.

I had to give you the falcon, you see, and then kill it, to preserve your sight, and then keep silent to preserve my life. (*A clap of thunder*) It's done. It's happening!

(*From his feet up to his knees* JENNARO *becomes white marble. The* KING, *frightened by the thunder, wants to flee, but Jennaro's words hold him back.*)

Don't run away. Listen to what else the doves said:

> As soon as the king gets on the horse, it will kill him. But if Jennaro doesn't give it, if he conceals the fact that he has it, or if he mentions this curse to anybody, or even hints at it, or makes any attempt to avoid it, Jennaro will turn into a marble statue.

I had to give you the horse, then kill it to preserve your life, and then keep silent to preserve mine.

(*Another thunder clap. Jennaro's body and arms become white marble up to his head.*)

KING (*Terrified by what he sees*). Jennaro, stop! I believe you. You're innocent. Don't say another word.

JENNARO. Listen, inhuman being, and suffer! You wanted my proofs and you shall pay for them. Now hear the final one.

KING. No, please, Jennaro, have mercy . . .

JENNARO (*With a last burst of resolve*). Here it is. The doves also said,

> If the king marries Armilla, on that very wedding night he will be devoured by a monster. But if Jennaro doesn't give Armilla to his brother, if he conceals the fact that he abducted her, or if he men-

tions this curse to anybody, or even hints at it, or makes any attempt to avoid it, Jennaro will turn into a marble statue.

(*His voice growing feebler*) I fought the dragon and struck your door open. That blow saved your life. And that is why I now . . . why I cannot . . . Rescue yourself from Norando. I cannot speak. Farewell . . .

(*Another thunder clap. Jennaro's head is now white marble, like the rest of his body. He stands motionless. Enter all the characters from the earlier scenes.*)

KING.   Heaven strike me down! I have killed my own brother. Soldiers, servants, ministers, my brother was innocent. I am the traitor. He warned me and I refused to believe him. Take this statue to the palace. I will die of grief at his feet.

(*He falls to the ground in front of Jennaro's statue.*)

## Act Five

*A room in the palace*

### SCENE I

TRUFFALDINO *and* BRIGHELLA *meet, carrying all their personal effects in sacks and knotted kerchiefs.*

BRIGHELLA.   Ready to leave?

TRUFFALDINO.   Ready to leave. You have everything with you?

BRIGHELLA.   Everything except a couple of tables, a sideboard, half a dozen chairs, and of course, my bed. I'll come back for them.

TRUFFALDINO.   We're not coming back. Give them away.

BRIGHELLA.   I will not.

TRUFFALDINO.   You're a miser.

BRIGHELLA.   I'm thrifty. You're a parasite.

TRUFFALDINO.   I'm friendly.

BRIGHELLA.   I hate to leave all that furniture. It's in tiptop shape. I bought it for a song. But I can't stand the gloomy atmosphere here.

TRUFFALDINO.   Everybody's too thin.

BRIGHELLA.   No more hunting. No more handouts. A pheasant here, a brace of rabbits there.

TRUFFALDINO.   No decent meals. The cuisine has gone downhill. I'm famished for a heaping plate of meat.

BRIGHELLA.   I'm out of place. I'm a daisy trying to grow in midocean. I'm a whale trying to swim across a field.

TRUFFALDINO.   A shark.

BRIGHELLA.   A salmon.

TRUFFALDINO.   Don't mention salmon. You make my insides weep. I'm lost. I'm a glass of water served to a drunk.

BRIGHELLA.   We're two actors in a show with no audience.

TRUFFALDINO.   What did the king ever do for us?

BRIGHELLA.   Or the prince?

TRUFFALDINO.   They paid us, fed us, clothed us in gorgeous hunting outfits.

BRIGHELLA.   They spoiled us, ruined us.

TRUFFALDINO.   We're drying up.

BRIGHELLA.   Not appreciated. Out of commission.

TRUFFALDINO.   And commissions.

(*They each pick up the other's bag and start to move off.*)

BRIGHELLA.   That's mine. What were you trying—to steal my silver plate?

TRUFFALDINO.   You never had any silver plate.

BRIGHELLA.   I do now. Give it back.

TRUFFALDINO.   Not till you give back my gold coin collection.

BRIGHELLA.   Where did you get gold coins from?

TRUFFALDINO.   I found them.

(*They go out, squabbling.*)

## SCENE 2

*Another room, a larger one, with funereal drapes and tapestries. Near the center stands the statue of* JENNARO *in the same pose as at the end of the prison scene. There is a seat on either side of the statue. Enter* PANTALONE.

PANTALONE.   Where has my boy got to? Flesh of my flesh, blood of my innocent blood! Forever lost. (*He comes face to face with the statue and stops.*) O my son, image of innocence, example of all the virtues, I can still hear your last words to me: "I will not die in disgrace and you will be happy to know I am innocent." Happy! When I was the one who brought this about! I didn't mean to. How could I know the hideous secret you were hiding from me? And yet, I ask your forgiveness. (*He kneels and kisses the statue's feet.*) Let these tears speak for me. If I could open up my heart and show you its depths, you'd see that I'd give you my life to buy back yours. But would you want it? You'd be even more miserable than you are now, because there's nobody who relishes life less than this old sailor from Venice. (*He stands, studying the statue's face.*) That honest mouth will never speak again. How I loved it! I haven't the strength to remain here or the courage to look at you in this condition. My sight is going. I can hardly move my limbs. I'll make a last effort to drag myself to the darkest room in the palace, where I can weep myself to death. (*Exit.*)

## SCENE 3

*A funeral march sounds. Enter the* KING, *in mourning, preceded by* SOLDIERS.

KING.   Leave me, friends. This is where I want to die. (*The others go out. He sits next to the statue, clasping its knees.*) Jennaro, how can I make you understand now that I signed that death warrant only to force you to reveal the secret? I would never have let you die, I swear to heaven. But you can't hear me, and if you could, you wouldn't believe me. Even God will not forgive me. Only my death will avenge you. That is why I have come here to die at your feet. There I'll fall and there I'll be buried. Your statue shall stand over my head like a trophy of victory. And on my tomb an inscription shall proclaim your virtues, the wrongs I did you, and the unspeakable cruelties of Norando.

(*The wall opens and* NORANDO *steps through it.*)

## SCENE 4

NORANDO.   Fate is relentless. I am no more than its agent.

KING.   You are . . . ?

NORANDO.   Norando of Damascus. I bring you no comfort, only further distress. Jennaro deserved to be turned to stone, and you deserve the pain you now feel in your heart. The raven's death and the ogre's curse were written in the book of fate. So were the abduction of Armilla and the prophecy that she will prove fatal to your house and to mine.

KING   (*Kneeling*). If you are Norando, you can do whatever you will. Take my life and restore my brother's.

NORANDO.   I cannot. It is useless for you to kneel. There is only one way to rescue Jennaro from this marble envelope. (*Aside*) How can I bear to say it? (*Aloud*) This dagger, let Armilla take it. (*He tosses a dagger at the statue's feet.*) She must be stabbed at the statue's feet, so that her blood collects on the marble. Perhaps it may revive Jennaro. Are you bold enough to employ this means? I have no other suggestion. If you do, I will suffer from it as much as you. (*He vanishes.*)

KING.   Stop, let me speak! . . . Monster, she is your own daughter! And my beloved wife. Oh, God, Armilla . . . !

## SCENE 5

*Enter* ARMILLA.

KING.   Escape, Armilla! You are in a worse plight than that of Oedipus. Escape from the tortures of hell!

ARMILLA.   Escape, dear husband? Yes, I have a plan for our escape, but together.

KING.   A plan?

ARMILLA.   Don't scorn it because it's a woman's idea. You and I must sail to Damascus and throw ourselves on the mercy of my father. I'll plead with him. I can move him. He'll restore your brother to life, pardon us, permit us to marry; and from then on we'll live in peace.

KING.  Your gentle words tear at me, my darling. We've lost our chance to live peacefully. All I have left now are despair, rage, tears, and death. Your father just appeared to me. I pleaded with him. He would not listen. He will do nothing for Jennaro or for me or for you. God, I said more than—

ARMILLA.  My father? In the palace? Oh, why couldn't I have been here? Did ask him whether your brother—?

KING.  I did ask him. I can't tell you what he replied.

ARMILLA.  I insist.

KING.  No. Don't try to find out.

ARMILLA  (*Taking his hand*). I must know. Tell me what he said.

KING.  My dearest wife, you have no idea what you're asking. My brother is lost to us forever.

ARMILLA.  What are you holding back?

KING.  Nothing. It would be useless. Impossible.

ARMILLA.  What?

KING.  He suggested—I can scarcely put it into words—that you must be stabbed with that dagger and fall at the statue's feet so that your blood stains the marble and, perhaps, restores Jennaro to life. Then he vanished, leaving me here in torment. Do you see it now, Armilla? There is no remedy at all. Only death can free me from this anguish. (*He rushes out, his head in his hands.*)

ARMILLA.  God, do I have the courage? I'm as cold within as marble, while my head feels on fire. This caps my misery: to have come into this world to be a prisoner and bring grief and terror to humanity! At last I understand my fate and my father's wishes. Father, you want me dead! You shall have your wish. (*She grasps the dagger and faces the statue.*) Jennaro, poor innocent victim, it's only right that my blood bathes you and frees you from this white stone. I am making a slight sacrifice. By dying I rise above this vale of tears and evil and give you back to a brother who loves you.

(*She kisses the statue, then stabs herself. The blood spurts on the marble, which recovers the colors of Jennaro's skin and clothing.* JENNARO *steps off the pedestal. At that same moment* SMERALDINA *enters. She screams as she sees* ARMILLA *stab herself.*)

## SCENE 6

JENNARO.   Who released me from that marble prison?

ARMILLA.   God, I am dying. (*She falls.*)

SMERALDINA.   Princess! Princess!

JENNARO.   Armilla! She's wounded. Who struck her? I'll avenge—

SMERALDINA.   No. (*Weeping*) She stabbed herself. I saw it.

ARMILLA   (*Lifting herself*). Jennaro, you cannot avenge me. My father wanted me to die, so that my blood could restore yours. I've given it. Live happily, you and Millo. If I deserve it, remember me kindly.

JENNARO.   You are too magnanimous to die! The wound may not be deadly. With the aid of doctors—

ARMILLA.   I no longer need them. I feel my soul on my lips. Say farewell for me to my husband . . . Tell my father I paid the debt. Let him remember . . . Say that I . . . no. No more . . . (*She dies.*)

(SMERALDINA *stands sobbing.*)

JENNARO (*Crying out at the top of his voice*).   Norando! Millo!

## SCENE 7

*The* KING *rushes in.*

KING.   Who cried out? (*Seeing* JENNARO, *who stands in front of* ARMILLA) Jennaro! You're alive! Oh, my dear brother. (*He goes to embrace* JENNARO, *who tries to fend him off and get him away.*) Armilla! Soaked in blood. Why did I tell her? I'm her murderer, Jennaro. I left her here. I was wrapped up in my own selfish thoughts. But I'll avenge her. (*He snatches up the dagger and is about to plunge it into himself.* JEN-NARO *prevents him.*)

JENNARO.   Millo, I forbid you. This is madness.

KING.   Let me alone. I abhor this life. Let it end.

(*The scene lightens and grows splendid. All the emblems of mourning are trans-formed and glow brightly. From the far end of the vast hall* NORANDO *appears.*)

### SCENE 8

NORANDO.   You have been punished enough. Only now am I per-mitted to cease my cruelty toward you. Fate willed that the raven's death would cause my daughter to be kidnaped—with those horrible consequences for all of us. My daughter's death has revived the dead raven. The ogre is pacified. The curse has run its course, like a mighty city burnt to ashes by a fire started with a single spark. Let no one seek to understand it.

KING.   Tyrant, who will revive my cherished wife?

NORANDO.   After so many complications, all arising from the death of a crow, after I have performed so many miracles, do you need to ask? Realism has no place in a fairy tale like this. But then, have you ever witnessed real realism in any play? (*He takes Armilla's hand.*) Rise, my child. Now that nothing threatens my rule, I can be kind again. Rise, Armilla, and let us all be comforted.

ARMILLA.   You woke me from a heavy sleep, father. Thank you. For the second time you have given me life.

(*The* KING *and* ARMILLA *embrace.* JENNARO *stands by, marveling.* SMERALDINA *plies Armilla's back and hair with kisses.*)

### SCENE 9

*Everybody floods onto the stage.*

LEANDRO.   The prince!

TARTAGLIA.   The statue!

PANTALONE.   My darling boy, let me kiss you. Let me hug you to bits.

BRIGHELLA.   Everything has changed.

TRUFFALDINO.   And nothing has changed.

BRIGHELLA.   His majesty's happy.

TRUFFALDINO.   We'll get a raise.

BRIGHELLA and TRUFFALDINO   (*Together*). But if we don't . . .

NORANDO.   Yes, everything has changed. I have renewed the life of this kingdom. You pair of fools! Would you walk out of paradise? (BRIGHELLA *and* TRUFFALDINO *vigorously shake their heads.*) Now let laughter banish sadness. We wanted to see if a false illusion could move an audience. Did we succeed? We shall soon know. (*He concludes with the following words, with which mothers and nurses end their fairy tales:*)

> You will live happily forever after
> With feasting in between your bouts of laughter.
> The wedding guests will dine on turnip stew,
> Flayed rats, and skinless cats—a savory stew!
> And if the grown-ups don't applaud on cue,
> Who cares, so long as all the children do?

The end of

# The Raven

# Notes

1. Gozzi is referring to his first play, *The Love of Three Oranges*, a *canovaccio* or plot outline for improvisation, published as a "reflexive analysis" (see Introduction, pp. 4–5, and the plot summary in note 5 to *The Green Bird*). Since the text cannot be performed without extensive adaptation, we have chosen not to include it here. The preface to *The Raven*, like the others in this volume, is taken from the first edition of Gozzi's collected works: *Opere del Co: Carlo Gozzi*, 7. vols. (Venice: Colombani, 1772).

2. A reference to Gasparo Gozzi's allegorical reading of *The Love of Three Oranges* in *La Gazzetta Veneta*, 28 January 1761.

3. Goldoni did indeed react bitterly in the *addio* to the spring 1761 season, saying that "Ghe vol altro che Fiabe a farse onor / E maghi e strighe e satire e schiamazzi, / Le vol esser Commedie e no strapazzi" (It takes more to excel [as a writer] than fairy tales / And wizards and witches and satires and noisemaking, / It takes comedies, and not personal attacks). The San Salvatore Theatre was situated near the border between the parishes of San Salvador and San Luca. During the first half of the eighteenth century (circa) it took its name from the former parish, while afterwards it was called the San Luca Theatre. Goldoni was connected with this theatre from 1753 until his departure from Venice in 1762.

4. *Lo cunto de li cunti* (1634–36), also called *Il pentamerone*, was a collection of fairy tales in Neapolitan dialect by Giambattista Basile (1575–1632). The literary source of *The Love of Three Oranges* may have been Basile's story "Le tre cetra" (the ninth story of the fifth day). However, recent scholarship suggests that the play has more in common with an oral version of the fairy tale. See Angelo Fabrizi, "Carlo Gozzi e la tradizione popolare. (A proposito de 'L'amore delle tre melarance')," *Italianistica* 7 (1978): 336–45.

5. Probably a reference to Pietro Chiari, who in addition to being a playwright was active as a journalist and novelist.

6. The Venetian theatrical year was divided into two parts: an autumn season from September 1 to November 30, and a spring season from Saint Stephen's Day (December 26) through the end of the pre-Lenten holiday of carnival (*carnevale*). In addition, operatic theatres had a short summer season for the Feast of the Ascension, beginning forty days after Easter and continuing until June 15.

7. In the original *Tales*, the scenes involving the commedia dell'arte characters are sometimes found in the form of a *canovaccio* (see Introduction, p. 5). In these translations, we have provided dialogue.

8. In the role of Truffaldino, Antonio Sacchi (or, rarely, Sacco) was in fact among the most celebrated comic actors of the eighteenth century, widely hailed by his Italian contemporaries and by numerous foreign visitors who witnessed his performances.

9. "Grand" is Marc-Antoine Legrand (1673–1728), actor at the Comédie Française and author of many comedies and farces performed at the Théâtre Italien. The reference is to his *Théâtre* in four volumes (Paris, 1731). "Girardi" is Evaristo Gherardi (1663–1700), a leading Arlecchino of the Théâtre Italien and compiler of a popular anthology of the plays performed there: *Le Théâtre Italien; ou, Le Recueil de toutes les scènes françaises qui ont été jouées sur le Théâtre Italien de l'Hotel de Bourgogne* (Paris, 1694).

10. Gozzi is less than candid here. Recent studies of the original manuscripts have shown that some of the *Tales* were substantially reelaborated, in all likelihood after the original performances. See Paolo Bosisio, "Gli autografi di 'Re cervo.' Una fiaba scenica di Carlo Gozzi dal palcoscenico alla stampa con le varianti dedotte dagli autografi marciani," *Acme* 34, no. 1 (1983): 61–146.

11. Gozzi suggests that his choice of verse or prose was based on a distinction between serious and comic characters, each of which had different expressive needs. While this is true, it should be noted that most of the serious characters are nobles, while the comic characters are plebeians. It is likely that the "necessities of art" are not alone in determining Gozzi's choice. See Introduction, pp. 10–11.

12. The Pasquali edition of Goldoni's works—published for the most part when the playwright was residing in France and could thus logically expect a certain number of foreign readers—has footnotes that translate some dialect words into Italian. Oddly, though, the words Goldoni chooses to gloss are often close to their Italian counterparts, as Gozzi suggests in these satirical examples: Venetian *osello* and *aseo* as compared to Italian *uccello* and *aceto*.

13. Another ironic swipe at Goldoni. Gozzi felt that comedies such as *The Chioggian Brawls*—today regarded as one of the masterpieces of the Italian theatre—were "low" and undignified for their attention to lower-class life. See Introduction, p. 5.

14. In addition to his *Tales,* Gozzi wrote many comedies based on the Spanish theatre of the Golden Age, also included in the Colombani edition of his works, from which this preface is taken. In the "Spanish" plays too, he mixes verse, prose, and improvisation, and juxtaposes serious characters with the comic masks of the commedia dell'arte.

15. Gozzi stresses the theatrically innovative character of his *Tales,* suggesting that they should not be expected to conform to the same rules or be judged by the same standards as the literary tragedies of the first part of the eighteenth century. *Merope* (1713), by the Marquis Scipione Maffei of Verona, was the most popular and most critically esteemed Italian tragedy prior to Alfieri.

16. Giudecca is one of the islands comprising the city of Venice. In the eighteenth century, it was home to many lower- and middle-class families. Gozzi is appealing to his audience's local patriotism, as well as deliberately underscoring an element that clashes with his fantastic setting.

17. These unlikely ingredients were always part of the wedding feast in the formulaic endings (similar to "and they lived happily ever after") found at the end of many Italian fairy tales of the period. See also *The King Stag,* 3.11.

18. An oblique allusion to the sometimes tense relations between Carlo and Gasparo Gozzi. The two brothers had been involved in numerous lawsuits over their inheritance, sometimes as allies and sometimes as adversaries. What is more, Gasparo had slyly satirized his younger brother in his *Esopo in città,* a free translation of a French comedy. Here, Carlo repays him in kind.

19. This passage is a parody of the bloated poetic style of Gozzi's rival Pietro Chiari. Gozzi particularly objected to Chiari's practice of having his commedia dell'arte characters declaim heroic verse.

20. Here, Gozzi is playing on a characteristic of the commedia dell'arte mask Tartaglia, traditionally a stuttering lawyer from Naples.

# The King Stag

## A Tragicomic Tale for the Theatre in Three Acts

### Preface

*The Love of Three Oranges* and *The Raven* made such a stir in the theatre that Signor Goldoni, who is not devoid of intelligence, said that he was beginning to think I might be worth something as a writer, since I had invented a new theatrical genre that had found favor with audiences.[1] With his usual prudence, the *abbé* Chiari harangued the public, calling it ignorant and attacking its bad taste. The journalists praised my *Tales* in their papers, and found in them all sorts of beautiful things I had not seen.[2]

Intelligent people whose interest had been aroused took a balanced look at my *Tales* and praised them in the sincere and impartial manner of honest, enlightened men—men, that is, who do not live by imposture, and who can distinguish trivialities used for an artistic purpose from those which issue from the pen of an untalented clod.

With such a different genre, and such infantile titles, it was difficult to win over the large audiences who were used to sleeping through the supposedly reformed and learned productions of Signors Goldoni and Chiari, falsely convinced that they were indeed "learned."

A great many people had seen my first two *Tales* and had been impressed by their intrinsic theatrical force, but were ashamed to praise comedies that had fairy-tale titles. They were afraid that their high culture and sublime intelligence would be lowered too far if they confessed that my plays had any merit.

To overcome such fears, I thought it necessary to be even more daring and to allow my imagination even freer reign in my new genre. And truly, readers of *The King Stag* will soon note the boldness of a whimsical mind.

The vigorous, tragic circumstances it contains drew tears from my audiences. The broad comedy of the masks, which I had sworn to continue in my plays, was intertwined with the serious material. It took nothing away from the fantastic solemnity of the impossible events, or from the *Tale's* allegorical moral lesson—despite the fact that at that time the Sacchi company had been relying on comedy, having few actors capable of carrying off serious roles with the necessary dignity, feeling, and skill. Indeed, in an unrealistic play the serious actors need twice the skill required to perform a realistic role, for they must illustrate truths that the roles themselves do not contain.

As you will see, the *Tale* of *The King Stag* began with a very comical prologue, spoken by a character named Cigolotti. This Cigolotti was a grotesque old man well known in Venice, who could often be found at the center of a group of listeners in Saint Mark's Square. There he told stories of paladins and magicians, in a tone of exaggerated solemnity and in a language he thought was purest Tuscan, but which he spoke with innumerable mistakes.

Antonio Zanagi, the very able Brighella of the Sacchi company, imitated this old man to perfection—his manner of dressing, his voice, and all his gestures—and was roundly applauded.

Even trivialities are worthy of applause when they are developed correctly and put in their proper light, and when an audience can see that an author has used them with a purpose in mind. The success of my *King Stag,* and indeed of all my *Tales,* in which I allowed myself a freedom unbounded by artistic scruples, justifies my opinion and condemns that of the few critics who called them fatuous and nauseating trivialities.

To hold the attention of eight or nine hundred people, cultured and uncultured, for three hours, and to thus render oneself useful to a commedia dell'arte troupe, one has to appeal to all kinds of tastes. The little writers who condemn everything in my *Tales,* such as they are, must have very poor stomachs, incapable of digesting any kind of food.

I don't say that *The King Stag,* written according to my methods, will be a hit in the theatre. I don't need to predict the future; it was a tremendous success. Produced by Sacchi and company at the San Samuele Theatre in Venice on 5 January 1762, it was performed sixteen times to full houses, and it is still revived every year.

If in its printed version my courteous readers find it worthless, I will accept their verdict with stoic humility.

# The King Stag

CIGOLOTTI (CHEE-goh-LOTT-ee), historian of the public square, a character from real life, prologue for the production
DERAMO (day-RAH-moh), king of Serendippo, who loves
ANGELA, daughter of
PANTALONE, second minister of Deramo
TARTAGLIA, prime minister and confidential secretary of Deramo, in love with Angela
CLARICE (clah-REE-chay), daughter of Tartaglia, in love with
LEANDRO, gentleman at court, son of Pantalone
BRIGHELLA, the king's valet
SMERALDINA, his sister
TRUFFALDINO, a bird catcher, in love with Smeraldina
DURANDARTE (DOO-rahn-DAHR-tay), magician
GUARDS, HUNTSMEN, PEASANTS
A STATUE
A PARROT
AN OLD MAN
A BEAR, STAGS

*The scene is Serendippo and the countryside nearby. All the characters, except Cigolotti, wear "oriental" costume.*

## Act One

*The stage represents a small square. The character of* CIGOLOTTI, *played with the costume, conversational style, and gestures of one who narrates fables and romances in the great square of Venice, doffs his cap, bows to the audience, puts on his cap again, and speaks.*[3]

CIGOLOTTI.   Most revered masters, I am here to unfold a wondrous tale . . . Five years ago there came to this city of Serendippo an astronomer, a magician who could command white magic, black magic, red, green, and, I believe, even blue. He was called the great Durandarte, and I was his loyal servant. As soon as Deramo, the king of this city, heard that my master had arrived at the Inn of the Ape, he summoned his trusted minister and said, "Tartaglia [for this was the heroic minister's name], go to the Inn of the Ape and bring back Durandarte the magician." The obedient Tartaglia conducted Durandarte to his monarch. I haven't the time to describe the rich treatment my master received, but I must tell you that when he left, he gave His Majesty two magic secrets, two marvels, two spells that were as follows . . .

But I'm not allowed to say because I'd dry up your curiosity and steal the pleasure that, heaven willing, lies in store for you. All I can tell you is that I had the honor of serving the necromancer Durandarte for forty years, and I never managed to learn anything of his great art. However, one day he said to me, "Cigolotti, woe to you if you reveal to anyone, before the year 1762, the two secrets I conferred upon the king of Serendippo. You must now put on a cassock of black, worn cloth, a woolen cap, and broken-down shoes. Shave off your beard every two months, and eke out a living by telling stories in the great square of Venice. In 1762, on January fifth, these two secrets will be the cause of great wonders.[4] At that time you will take me, in the shape of a parrot, to the Forest of Roncislappe. There you will leave me. The more potent of the two secrets that I gave the king of Serendippo will lead to a treacherous act; but through my intervention the treachery will be punished."

When he had delivered these instructions, he cried, "Good Cigolotti, my sentence is now being imposed. Demogorgon, the king of the fairies, ordains that for five years I live as a parrot. Note the date, January fifth, 1762, when you must let me loose in the Forest of Roncislappe where, after being captured by a bird catcher, I will work great spells and my punishment will end. That evening at six you shall have twenty pennies as a reward for your faithful service." With this he cast off his human form and to my great astonishment, became a magnificent parrot.

Hark then, revered ladies and gentlemen, to the extraordinary events for this day, January fifth, 1762. I will take Durandarte, the magic parrot, to the Forest of Roncislappe, and then, collecting the twenty lovely gold coins, I will proceed to the Inn of the Ape and drink a toast to the revered nobility, wishing you what you deserve—peace, wealth, and good cheer. (*He tips his hat, bows. Exit.*)

## SCENE 2

*A large room.* TARTAGLIA *and* CLARICE.

TARTAGLIA.   Daughter, we have certainly been lucky in this kingdom of Serendippo. You have become a lady of the court, I prime minister. Everyone fears me and the king favors me. But now, my darling Clarice, it is time for a great leap upward, for if you obey me, today will see you crowned queen.

CLARICE.   Queen? How?

TARTAGLIA.   Yes, queen, queen! You know that a few years ago King Deramo questioned two thousand, seven hundred and forty-eight damsels, princesses, and ladies in his private chamber, and—I have no idea why—turned them all down. For four years he's sworn he would never look for a wife again.

CLARICE.   I know. I can't believe he would want me for a consort after rejecting all those titled ladies.

TARTAGLIA (*Fiercely*). Girl, what I say is what will happen. Let me finish. I brought him around yesterday by sheer skill, reminding him that he has no heirs, and telling him the people feel unhappy, if not rebellious, over it; and I've at last persuaded him to take a wife. But he has this damn obsession about interviewing all the girls in the privacy of his study. And because we have no titled ladies left to question, he's announced that any young woman of any class may appear before him in his confounded study. He promises to select the one who pleases him most. Two hundred of them have been so informed and their names drawn from an urn to determine the order in which they see him. Yours came out first. Now you must prepare yourself for the interrogation. You're my daughter; you're not a monster; and if you present yourself to him properly, you'll be queen by the end of this day, and I'll be the most illustrious—the happiest—man on earth (*Softly*) Tell me, Daughter, you have no little . . . ah, affairs he might uncover, eh?

CLARICE.    Father dear, spare me this trial, I implore you!

TARTAGLIA.    What? Hey? Saucy girl! Get ready this instant. And make a good impression on the king, otherwise . . . You understand? You know me. Minx! Do you refuse to obey me? (*Softly*) So you do have some secret sin?

CLARICE.    No, none. But I'm nervous. I won't make that good impression at the interview—it's impossible—and he'll . . . reject me.

TARTAGLIA.    Nervous? Reject you? Out of the question. He has too much regard for me. Be brave. We must go. It's time. He's waiting for you in his study (*Takes her arm*).

CLARICE    (*Pulling away*). No, father, I can't. I won't.

TARTAGLIA.    I'll rip off your ears. I'll slit your nose. Come! And swear you'll behave properly at the interview, or else . . . (*Strikes her*).

CLARICE.    Father dear, I cannot. I may as well confess. I'm in love with Leandro. I won't have the strength, in front of the king, to disguise my feelings.

TARTAGLIA    (*Starting back, furious*). Leandro! The son of Pantalone, the second minister! A mere gentleman at court! You prefer Pantalone's boy to a king? My daughter? A wicked, unworthy daughter for Tartaglia the terrible! Now listen: if you mention this loathsome love of yours to the king . . . if you don't make him pick you . . . Listen . . . We're going to him right away. Don't make me say any more. (*He seizes her arm.*)

CLARICE.   Have pity. Let me go. How can I wrong my friend Angela by competing with her? She desperately loves the king.

TARTAGLIA   (*Starting back again*). In love with the king—Angela—Pantalone's daughter? (*Aside*) Angela, my heart! I meant to make her my wife this day, by love or by force. In love with the king! (*Aloud*) Listen, Clarice, and tremble. If you do not immediately appear before the king; if you do not behave perfectly when you're with him; if you mention that you love Leandro; if you don't *compel* the king to pick you; if you repeat one word of what I've said here . . . I have poison ready.

CLARICE   (*Terrified*). I'll obey, if you want to see me rejected, humiliated.

TARTAGLIA   (*Pulling at her violently*). No more delay! Do as I say, you sniveling, defiant brat, or look out for your life! (*Exeunt.*)

SCENE 3

PANTALONE *and* ANGELA

PANTALONE.   No one can say, dear daughter, no one can say. Two thousand, seven hundred and forty-eight princesses and ladies have already been turned down by the king. He leads them into his study, puts three or four questions to them, then politely sends them on their way. Does he dislike the voice, the personality? Do they show too sharp a wit or some half-hidden defect that doesn't suit him? Maybe he has a familiar spirit that ferrets out all their little secrets. No one can say. He's no madman. In all the time I've served him I've found him a wise and considerate ruler, with all the virtues a monarch could have; but there's something devilishly strange in this business.

ANGELA.   Father dear, why didn't you defend me from such humiliation? If he says no to me, as he did to the others, I'll die of shame.

PANTALONE.   He certainly will say no to you. But dear girl, I went down on my knees to him. I pleaded, beseeched, gave him reasons to let you off. I told him, true, we come from a good Venetian family; we're honest, if poor, folk—raised up in the world only through his bounty. I said we don't deserve such honor. You know what he answered? "I have declared this open to any and all women, and it would not be fair to allow your daughter the privilege of not taking part, like the others, in this great contest." I begged, I cajoled, I begged some more, but nothing doing. He just grew angry. He's already put your name in the urn, and you came out number three. What more can I do? We must go. Do you think I'll enjoy the gossip and mockery to come? My heart is breaking, Angela. My heart is breaking.

ANGELA.  I know I don't belong at that height. I shudder to think of the risk. And yet . . . if he is looking for sincerity, for love . . .

PANTALONE.  Well, I'll be . . . Are you in love, you silly lamb?

ANGELA.  Yes, Father. I confess, Father darling. I'm reckless enough to have fallen madly in love with my king . . . who will spurn me, Father. And then—I'll die. Not because a king has rejected me. A humble girl should not aim so high. But because I'll be turned away by the man who has my heart and is my life.

PANTALONE.  Poor me! What are you saying?

ANGELA.  But I'm most afraid of Tartaglia. He has ambitions for his daughter, but that is not the worst of it. He's been ogling me, sighing at me. This morning he suggested I pretend to be sick and not appear at the interview.

PANTALONE.  Astounding! So that big booby's in love again? May heaven guide you, my girl. I don't know what to say. But it's late. We must go. You're third on the list.

ANGELA.  Let love decide . . . (*Exeunt.*)

## SCENE 4

BRIGHELLA *and* SMERALDINA. *They are both in "oriental" garb.* SMERALDINA *has a huge fan with flowers and feathers painted on it.*

BRIGHELLA.  Come on! Keep your head up! Don't hold your arms so stiff, damn you! I've been coaching you for an hour, and you're worse than ever. You look like one of those screaming peddler women. (*Falsetto, as if crying his wares*) Chestnuts! Candy! Sugared rose petals!

SMERALDINA.  You tease, you! I know you think I'm dressed up enough to have a wild animal fall for me, never mind a king.

BRIGHELLA.   What dumb talk! Say something like that in front of the king and you'll kiss his fist. I'd like to see you got up in Venetian style, with a proper headdress and loose gown.

SMERALDINA.   Oh, you ninny! I'll bet that if I stood in Venice, dressed like this, everybody would worship my good taste. All the fashion designers there would steal the ideas and in three days they'd have every Venetian lady's purse empty.

BRIGHELLA.   Some hope! Nobody knows Venetian fashions here. If you'd only shown up dressed the way I'm telling you to, you'd have knocked the king's eyes out. This is the big time, remember. Win the king over and you become queen. Become queen, and I jump from valet to at least generalissimo.

SMERALDINA.   If that's all you want, leave it to me. He'll fall with a crash. For the past three days I've been studying Armida's love scenes from Tasso and the part of Corisca in *The Faithful Shepherd*. I practiced them with the most fetching moans and sighs you ever heard. Don't worry. I'll twist Deramo around my little finger. Go ahead: sing the famous lines from Ariosto: (*Singing*)

> "Love drove the man who had been wise and wary
> Into a state of hot, demented fury." [5]

BRIGHELLA.   That'll do. Pray God it'll happen as you say, but with that mug of yours and that figure . . . Enough, let's give it a try. (*They start to leave.*)

SCENE 5

TRUFFALDINO, SMERALDINA, *and* BRIGHELLA. TRUFFAL-DINO *is dressed in "oriental" style, in the green of a bird catcher, with many whistles [for bird calls] tied on his chest. The whistles are comically exaggerated in size.*

TRUFFALDINO.   Smeraldina and Brighella: my only friends! Smeraldina's looking bright and bouncy. Where are you off to?

BRIGHELLA.   To see the king in his study. To enter the queen contest.

TRUFFALDINO.   Say, Smeraldina—you're enough to make me double up.

SMERALDINA. Advise him that this is serious.

TRUFFALDINO. You don't mean it?

SMERALDINA. We absolutely do.

BRIGHELLA. No need to lower ourselves and waste time on this pathetic specimen. Here, Smeraldina, give me your arm. (*They start off, grossly aping formal, "noble" manners.*)

TRUFFALDINO. Wait, you can't do that! (*He tries to drag them back.*) She can't marry the king after she promised to marry me.

SMERALDINA. Royal commands supersede all private promises.

TRUFFALDINO. Tell his majesty there's been a mistake.

BRIGHELLA. That's a good one. Don't you understand? My sister aspires to a throne; she can't possibly wed a whistling bird catcher. Her status doesn't compare with yours any more, or with her own when she was born.

TRUFFALDINO. Any second now I'm going to cry.

SMERALDINA. Let us show compassion, and comfort him in his tragic plight. When we are queen, we will shed favors upon you. Bid good-by to Brighella.

TRUFFALDINO. My heart has collapsed.

### Scene 6

LEANDRO *and* TRUFFALDINO, *unaware of each other for the first seven lines.*

LEANDRO. I'm inconsolable.

TRUFFALDINO. I'm tormented.

LEANDRO. My lovely Clarice: the king wants her. Listen to this—

TRUFFALDINO. Listen to this: my lovely Smeraldina . . . I mocked her, drove her into the king's arms.

LEANDRO. How could she suddenly turn so faithless? It must have been her father who—

TRUFFALDINO. It must have been her brother who—

LEANDRO. Bear up, Truffaldino. The king will choose Clarice, I'm sad to say.

TRUFFALDINO. Cheer up, Leandro. The king will choose Smeraldina. I can't think why.

LEANDRO. I'm furious.

TRUFFALDINO. I'm worse than that.

LEANDRO. We're victims of the same affliction. What shall we do?

TRUFFALDINO. Wait and see what happens?

LEANDRO. The king's already rejected two thousand, seven hundred and forty-eight prospective queens. Perhaps Clarice will be number two thousand, seven hundred and forty-nine. (*Exit.*)

TRUFFALDINO. And Smeraldina number two thousand, seven hundred and fifty. But if the king doesn't take her, neither will I. I don't want anybody's rejects. (*Exit.*)

SCENE 7

DERAMO, *alone. The setting changes. It represents King Deramo's study, with a door to the outside. At the sides of the door are two niches and in them two busts, half-statues. The half-statue on the left will be played, from the waist up, by a live actor in white, so that the audience takes him for a stucco sculpture, like the one on the right. This "stucco" man takes part in the scenes that follow, as will be noted. The STATUE will prove to be one of the two great magic secrets given King* DERAMO *by* DURANDARTE *the necromancer, and signalled by* CIGOLOTTI *in the prologue. In the middle of the study are "oriental" cushions for seating.*

DERAMO. I must follow the sensible advice of my minister Tartaglia, and finally determine who will be my queen. (*He turns to the* STATUE.) I'm depending on you again, my precious gift, the first of my two secrets from Durandarte, the man of magic. When you laughed at lying women, you protected me from marriage and showed me their insincerity. Don't abandon me now. Reveal the truth with your laughter and show which ones are insincere today. I would rather leave my realm without an heir than be the victim of a lying woman who would betray my love and honor, a woman who'd hate me and whom I'd always suspect . . . It's time for the first one, Tartaglia's daughter. Let's find out whether she is sincere. After so long a search, I doubt whether any woman ever tells the truth. (*He sits.*)

## SCENE 8

CLARICE *and* DERAMO. GUARDS *lead* CLARICE *in through the door and stand to either side, in front of the statues. The king waves them out. They go, closing the door.*

DERAMO.   Be seated, Clarice. There's no need to feel awed because I am your king. Answer my questions frankly. Your father's services to me in war and peace have earned you the right to say what you think. Hold nothing back.

CLARICE   (*Sadly*). My lord, I thank you for your graciousness. I will sit in your presence, but only out of respect for your bidding (*Sits*).

DERAMO.   My task is to find a wife who's worthy of me. Tartaglia is my dearest friend. Doesn't his daughter deserve a crown? But first tell me: do you really desire this marriage?

CLARICE.   Wouldn't any woman welcome an illustrious match with a king who is so sympathetic and virtuous?

(DERAMO *glances at the stucco* STATUE, *which gives him no sign.*)

DERAMO.   No, my dear, you're evading the question. I must know what you yourself feel. I realize that innumerable other women might welcome such a marriage. But you, Clarice, may not be one of the innumerable throng. Are you? That is what I must know.

CLARICE   (*Aside*). Good heavens, he's insistent! (*Aloud*) Your Majesty, can you believe I'm the only one among them who's foolish enough not to seize an opportunity like this?

(*The* STATUE *remains impassive.*)

DERAMO.   You still speak ambiguously, Clarice. I am asking what your own feelings are. Would marrying me please you or would it not?

CLARICE   (*Aside*). Father, your cruelty forces me to lie. (*Aloud*) Yes, my king. It would please me.

(*The* STATUE *smiles faintly.*)

DERAMO.   I understand that you feel reluctant to say no. But let me beg of you this last time: respond without fear of giving offense. Are you in love with someone else?

CLARICE   (*Aside*). Oh, cruel father, I have to lie for you, or lose my life. (*Aloud*) No, Majesty, I love you and only you. I know that I am not a fitting consort for a king. But if I were, I'd want to be chosen by you, because I've never loved another man.

(*The* STATUE *smiles again, then composes its features.*)

DERAMO.   Good enough, Clarice. That's all. I won't encourage or discourage you. Now I must hear the others and make my decision.

(CLARICE *rises from her cushion and pays her respects.*)

CLARICE   (*Aside, as she leaves*). I can only hope he rejects me and lets me remain Leandro's.

(*The* GUARDS *enter, wait by the statues, and escort her out.*)

SCENE 9

DERAMO, *alone*

DERAMO.   I *thought* it was strange to find a woman who seemed to tell the truth. (*To the* STATUE) Thank you for that. Until you smiled, I was wondering whether you had lost your power.

SCENE 10

SMERALDINA *and* DERAMO. SMERALDINA *is escorted through the door by the* GUARDS, *who then leave. She pays her respects with ludicrous gestures.*

DERAMO   (*Aside*). And who is this? (*Aloud*) Please sit. (*Aside*) Isn't she my valet's sister?

SMERALDINA   (*Sits*). My gentle lord, I am the sister of Brighella. In Lombardy we were a family of consequence. Then ill-luck impoverished us, and so on and so forth. But poverty cannot undermine noble birth, can it?

(*The* STATUE *is already smiling.*)

DERAMO.   I understand. So, lady from Lombardy, you love me?

SMERALDINA.   Ah, tyrant, you can ask that? When I am utterly yours? (*She sighs noisily.*)

(*The* STATUE *is now chuckling.*)

DERAMO.   Tell me more, if you will. What if I chose you for my wife, and then died, and left you a widow? Would that make you sad?

SMERALDINA   (*With exaggerated gestures of sorrow*). Brutal man! What are you saying? Bite your tongue, you tiger in human form. Alas, help! Merely thinking about your death makes me want to swoon. (*She sinks to the floor.*)

(*The* STATUE *is now laughing helplessly.*)

DERAMO.   She's unwell, the poor lady from Lombardy. I'd better call in some servants to see her home. (SMERALDINA *promptly recovers.*) Dear lady, your affection for me is too intense. Only one more question: are you a widow or unmarried?

SMERALDINA   (*Waving her fan demonstratively*). If I were a widow, how could I have been brazen enough to offer myself to a handsome king like you who has no need of used merchandise? Your Majesty, I am an untouched maid.

(*The* STATUE *laughs grotesquely, its mouth wide open.*)

DERAMO.   Very good, Lombardy lady, you may go. I can assure you that, of the many women who graced this study before you, not one has given me so much delight. Now I must sit and ponder. Good-by.

SMERALDINA   (*Rising cheerfully*). You couldn't tell, Your Majesty, but I was choking back the most sweet, the most touching feelings, an ocean of devotion. I'm keeping it all in reserve until we consummate our marriage. Then you'll learn at first hand how much I love you. Farewell, farewell, farewell . . . (*Aside*) Done! He's cooked. I will be queen. (*Aloud*) Farewell, farewell . . .

(*She bows affectedly and sighs, turning this way and that. The* GUARDS *enter and escort her out. The* STATUE *freezes into stucco impassiveness.*)

SCENE II

DERAMO, *alone*

DERAMO (*To the* STATUE). Ah, my dumb, eloquent friend, how your laughter braces and cheers me! All you husbands, fathers, lovers: wouldn't you appreciate a helpful contrivance like this to let you know what your wives, daughters, and lady loves really think? No! That would be the worst fate for any man. Much better if, instead of questioning women, we could question men and protect ourselves from false friends, dishonest servants, and disloyal ministers. (*Glancing at the door.*) Angela's here. If she too is a liar or deceiver, I swear I'll give up this search. I hope she'll prove . . . But that hope is wild, after all the sickening flattery I've listened to so far. And yet I wish . . . No, stop! I'm dreaming, raving . . . Statue, tell me the truth about her!

SCENE 12

ANGELA *and* DERAMO

ANGELA (*With dignified directness*). I am here, my king, because of your order, which may be just or unjust.

DERAMO (*Aside*). Beautiful and bold! (*Aloud*) Be seated. I am never unjust.

ANGELA (*Sitting*). You are a king. Who would dare judge you to your face or question your orders?

DERAMO. Angela might: you don't strike me as being so short of courage that you would hesitate to reproach your king. But in case you have any doubts, I invite you to speak frankly. I shall not be offended.

ANGELA (*Aside*). Cruel man: he praises me only to reject me later. My heart aches. (*Aloud*) Is it justice, Majesty, to force unhappy young women to appear alone before you in this secret room and to compete for a throne—women of lesser rank whose humble state makes them hope for the impossible, and who are then dismissed, made ashamed and tearful at not having pleased you (*She wipes her eyes.*), perhaps because you rightly find them unworthy of you? Is it justice when I'm led here against my will, even though my father begged you to excuse me from the embarrassment of having to face your imposing person, your

88

severity, and even (forgive me) your whims? Those whims have hurt many unlucky women. Deramo, my king, heaven will in time avenge the defenseless. Put an end to all this. I know I am provoking you by speaking in this fashion, and I'm ready to risk the consequences, because I plead not for myself but for those other women outside who sadly await your repudiation. Let Angela be the last to know the agony of rejection. Pardon me, my lord. You granted me the freedom to speak, and I've spoken freely.

DERAMO   (*Aside*). Astonishing how she moves me! (*He looks at the STATUE, which remains straight-faced.*) No laughter yet. Could this mean she's sincere? I pray so, but I can't be sure. (*Aloud*) I do pardon you, Angela, and admire you. But if you knew the truth, you could never have said what you did. In the past I sought a wife who would love me sincerely, as long as I lived; but I didn't find her. Now my kingdom needs an heir to the throne, and I must continue to look, even though I fear the search is hopeless.

ANGELA.   My lord, why are you certain that, of all the women you have seen here, not one could truly love you?

DERAMO.   Why am I certain? I have my reasons. But certain I am. Are *you* certain, Angela, that you love me?

ANGELA   *Sadly*). I wish to heaven I did not love you, for then your rejection would not be the mortal wound I must now expect.

(*He glances at the STATUE, which doesn't change expression.*)

DERAMO   (*Aside*). Still no laughter. The joy I feel: it shakes my heart! Is it possible? Is Angela speaking the truth? (*Aloud, excitedly*) But would you love me, always, even if—yes, even if you outlived me?

ANGELA.   I would, my lord, if my feelings for you now are any guide. But oh, how you mix the sweet with the bitter in your questions, my king! Pleasantries, love, anguish—all invading one poor heart! (*She weeps.*)

(*Again he looks at the STATUE, which has not changed.*)

DERAMO   (*Aside*). Not even a smile yet. Is this Venetian woman honest, after so many others failed the test? (*He checks the STATUE once more.*) Can love have dazzled me and disguised the truth? (*He looks yet again at the STATUE, then speaks aloud in agitation.*) Angela, if you do not love me, if you love anyone else, if you are keeping anything back, please say so now. I implore you, before I make my choice. I can't hold this back any longer. I love you so much that if I discover you're deceiving me, I won't want to live.

(*She rises, then throws herself at his feet.*)

ANGELA.   Let me go! Your refusal will be easier to bear than this torture. No more, Deramo! What good can come from ill-treating me, from rending the heart of an innocent and miserable girl? I know I don't deserve you. Haven't I suffered enough? No more Deramo, no more! I'm heartbroken. Let me go, for pity's sake. No more of this mockery! (*She weeps violently.*)

(*He steals another glance at the unchanged* STATUE.)

DERAMO   (*Standing*). Don't cry, my dear lady, my rare gift. (*He lifts her to her feet.*) Rise. It would be a crime to lose a woman of your beauty and spirit. Ho there, ministers, guards! Come in, come in! The people can rejoice. I have found a wife who will love me always and whom I cherish.

(*The* GUARDS *enter.*)

ANGELA.   No, Deramo, don't shame me. I can bear to be turned away, but not to confront the people. Don't force me. That would be too harsh. I am not a suitable partner for you.

DERAMO.   You would suit the greatest ruler. My lovely Venetian, you love the truth and are true in love. You give the lie to lying tongues that call your city's women fickle and proclaim that their love is false . . . Come in, ministers, I have finally chosen a wife. I have chosen Angela.

## SCENE 13

TARTAGLIA, PANTALONE, GUARDS, ANGELA, *and* DERAMO

PANTALONE.   My girl, Your Majesty?

DERAMO.   Yes, your daughter. You're a fortunate parent, and more so for bringing such a treasure into the world than for becoming a king's father-in-law.

TARTAGLIA   (*Aside*). This is a terrible moment! I'm bursting. Angela lost to me and the throne lost to my daughter!

PANTALONE.   Your Majesty, haven't you already showered me with enough kindness, which I was never entitled to? And now you lift a girl who's not highborn to this dizzy height . . .

DERAMO.   Her virtue has earned her that place. I must marry for the sake of my succession. I found no more worthy bride than Angela.

TARTAGLIA   (*With overdone vivacity*). Long may you both reign! I'm overjoyed, Your Majesty. You couldn't have chosen better. Congratulations, Angela. And Pantalone, I cannot express my delight . . . (*Aside*) Because I'm choking . . . Death, hell, revenge!

PANTALONE.   My sweet child, never forget you're from a modest family. Don't get above yourself. Send a prayer every moment to heaven, from where all bounties flow—and all disappointments. That will do for the present. His majesty will grant me two private hours with you, I'm sure, so that I can advise you, heap on you the wisdom of a father who's had a long life. But it still seems impossible . . .

DERAMO.   Enough! Never doubt the king's word. Here: my right hand. Angela is my wife—so long as I have her consent.

ANGELA.   My king, you do. I give you my right hand, and with it, my love and everlasting fidelity.

(*They join hands.*)

TARTAGLIA   (*Aside*). I'm ready to explode with rage. (*Aloud*) Why, if I may ask, my most revered king, did it take you so long to decide? After those two thousand, seven hundred and forty-eight aristocratic ladies, this girl from Venice . . . ?

DERAMO.   Now I can tell you. Five years ago the magician Durandarte gave me two magic devices. One is this statue. The other I am keeping secret. Whenever a woman tells a lie, the statue detects her inner feelings, and laughs. Only one woman who appeared before me spoke honestly, and I chose her. Angela.

(ANGELA *gestures in wonder.*)

PANTALONE. Amazing.

TARTAGLIA (*In fury*). And that statue laughed at Clarice, pronounced my daughter a liar! Excuse me, I am going to skin her alive.

DERAMO. Restrain yourself. Clarice was already in love. I discovered it. She would not have been the right wife for me. And now, Angela, my pure one, I love you so deeply, I am so happy to have found you, and so convinced that I need never suspect your future love, that I am going to prove you own my confidence and my heart. (*Drawing his sword*) As an unmistakable sign that I will never look for anything flawed or ugly in you, I smash this infernal machine. (*He smashes the machine.*) Learn from me, all of you, how to end suspicion and jealousy, which do injury to faithful women and possibly—who knows?—cause them to be unfaithful. Let us celebrate. (*To* TARTAGLIA) Be satisfied, my honest adviser. Don't fret about your daughter. We will enjoy ourselves. Arrange for a hunting festival today. Angela: to the temple!

ANGELA. My king, let me follow you, thankful and confused.

(*Exit* DERAMO *and* ANGELA, *escorted by* GUARDS.)

PANTALONE. Great God, it's like a dream. Let me go write to my brother Boldo in Venice. Must let him know how happy I am. He'll probably read all about it in the Venetian Gazette, but if I want him to have the straight story, I'd better write a letter and rush it into the mail.[6] (*He skips off.*)

TARTAGLIA (*Alone*). My daughter spurned! And Angela, my Angela, snatched from me! I'm torn by rage, envy, ambition, love, jealousy . . . A cancer has attacked my heart, gnaws at me, devours me. A man of my caliber . . . There's no way I can clamp down on my feelings . . . My body boils in revolt, drives me to the limits. And this at a moment when I have to organize a hunting festival, a diversion! Damnation on my daughter, on Pantalone, the king, and that accursed statue! I must somehow hold myself back, remain alert, wait for the right time, and then exact the most terrible revenge ever enacted on a stage. When they hear the tale recited, my horrified descendants will fall flat on their fannies.

## Act Two

### SCENE 1

*A room in the palace.* TARTAGLIA *and* CLARICE

TARTAGLIA.  Torturer, murderess! I've lost everything, thanks to you. And you will not be queen. You told him you love Leandro. You ruined your own chances and dragged me down with you. A plague on you, a tumor, hoof-and-mouth disease . . .

CLARICE.  No, no, Father dearest. I said nothing, I swear. It was the statue; it looked into my heart.

TARTAGLIA.  Statue or no statue, heart or no heart, who gave you permission to fall in love with Leandro? If you hadn't been in love, you slut, you wouldn't have made the statue laugh.

CLARICE.  Leandro's good looks, his eyes, his enchanting words didn't give me time to think or ask permission. It happened before I realized—

TARTAGLIA.  Yes, if you pay attention to men's eyes and listen to their sugary speeches, you weak wanton, you'll fall for the entire male sex every day.

CLARICE.  Please don't shout at me, Father. Now that Deramo has his queen, couldn't you help me?

TARTAGLIA.  Help me, she says. Help you do what?

CLARICE.  Let me marry Leandro. After all, he's a gentleman of the court and the queen's brother now. He'll move up in the world.

TARTAGLIA  (*Furiously*). Listen to me . . . (*Aside*) Mustn't let my anger get the better of me. Tame it, put on a calm face, make sure of my revenge. (*Aloud, feigning*) Clarice my dear, ignore what I've been saying. That was my anger talking. Give me time to get over this setback. I need your understanding. Yes, I will help you. (*Aside*) I'd sooner see you hanged.

CLARICE.  Oh, thank you, Father, thank you!

TARTAGLIA.  Good. We've said enough. Now you may go to your room.

CLARICE.  I will. Please let me kiss your hand.

TARTAGLIA.  All right: here. Kiss it. Kiss whatever you want. That'll do. On your way. Let me pull myself together again (*Bustles her off-stage*). I could split you open, like a fish, like an eel. At this moment the king is whispering with Angela . . . I want to blow up, bang my head against a wall. This jealousy . . . hatred . . . I'll interrupt them with some false excuse, tell them the hunt is about to begin (*False exit*).

## SCENE 2

LEANDRO *and* TARTAGLIA

LEANDRO.  Signor Tartaglia . . .

TARTAGLIA.  What is it? I'm off to the hunt. (*Aside*) Another pest . . .

LEANDRO.  Fortune smiled on me when the king chose my sister, and not your daughter. If you find me worthy of Clarice, I wish to marry her.

TARTAGLIA.  "Fortune smiled on me when the king chose my sister," he says, "and not your daughter." What arrogance is this? (*Aside*) If fortune smiled on you, she frowned at me, and that's what is eating at my insides. (*Aloud*) I won't reject you as a relative. (*Aside*) I'd like to see you struck by lightning—you and your father. (*Aloud*) But give me three or four days, because I'm preoccupied with affairs of state. (*Aside*) And Satan willing, the affairs of state will shortly be a different state of affairs.

LEANDRO.  Dear Signor Tartaglia, you've made this a wonderful day for me, and—

(*Hunting horns call and the hounds bay.*)

TARTAGLIA.  The signal! His majesty must have mounted up already. Get ready yourself. Go on, now!

LEANDRO.  I will, instantly. Where will the hunt be?

TARTAGLIA.  They meet outside the gates, on that side, and then set off for the Forest of Roncislappe. (*Aside*) Where I hope to track down a big fox. (*Exit.*)

LEANDRO.   Obtuse man! He can't speak a civil word, but he *is* Clarice's father and the king's favorite. Best to handle him with kid gloves. (*Exit.*)

## SCENE 3

TRUFFALDINO *and* SMERALDINA. TRUFFALDINO *enters hastily, pursued by* SMERALDINA. *They both sink to the ground in exhaustion.*

SMERALDINA.   Stop!

TRUFFALDINO.   I've stopped.

SMERALDINA.   Truffaldino, listen for one minute.

TRUFFALDINO.   Not for one second.

SMERALDINA.   Don't leave me alone among these spooky trees. I love you.

TRUFFALDINO.   Oh sure, Smeraldina, with guns blazing. Now that you know the king doesn't want you.

SMERALDINA.   I always loved you.

TRUFFALDINO.   So why did you enter the queen contest?

SMERALDINA.   I had to. Brighella made me. He *is* my older brother.

TRUFFALDINO.   No use coming at me with that story. The king's statue showed you up. I don't want anything the statue said is defective.

SMERALDINA.   Me? Defective? How dare you! I'm completely un-defective. I'm perfect.

TRUFFALDINO.   Is that so? What about your dentures, your hidden scars, your wig, your dirty mind, your bunions, your greed, your ridiculous ambitions, your phony highfalutin accent, your—?

SMERALDINA.   That's all false.

TRUFFALDINO.   You bet. Most of it.

SMERALDINA.   You want to know the real reason why the statue made fun of me?

TRUFFALDINO.   Because you're the next best thing to perfect.

SMERALDINA.   Thank you.

TRUFFALDINO.   Imperfect.

SMERALDINA.   You swine! You—you lowbrow! No, it was because I'd been your mistress.

TRUFFALDINO.   Well, now you're not.

SMERALDINA   (*Weakly*). Please, Truffaldino, beloved, I feel faint. Help me.

TRUFFALDINO.   Not a hope!

(*He gets up, tries to scramble away. She seizes his sleeve. He drags her across the stage.*)

SMERALDINA.   I'll never let go.

TRUFFALDINO.   Keep the tunic. (*He slips out of it. She grabs his leg.*) Smeraldina! I'll take off my pants, too.

SMERALDINA.   Yes, please! Troofy-woofy, how can you treat me like this? After all those promises, those oaths?

TRUFFALDINO.   I'll give you oaths. I'll tell you a few more home truths.

SMERALDINA.   You do and I'll beat your brains in—or what passes for your brains.

TRUFFALDINO.   What would you know about brains?

(*He limps off with SMERALDINA clinging to his leg.*)

## SCENE 4

CIGOLOTTI *and the* PARROT. *The Forest of Roncislappe: a vast view; hilly woodlands with a waterfall that flows into a stream, and rocks for seating. Enter* CIGOLOTTI *holding the* PARROT.

CIGOLOTTI.    My lord Durandarte, this is the Forest of Roncislappe.

PARROT.    Yes, Cigolotti. Untie me.

CIGOLOTTI.    Farewell, Durandarte. Go back to working your magic for the benefit of all these deserving folk. I'll meet you tonight at the Inn of the Ape in your original human form, and we'll drink a respectful toast to the health of all noblemen. (*He releases the* PARROT *which flies off into the forest. Exit* CIGOLOTTI.)

## SCENE 5

DERAMO *and* TARTAGLIA. DERAMO *has an arquebus over his shoulder.* TARTAGLIA *carries his arquebus in his hand.*

DERAMO    (*Studying the location*). Here, Tartaglia, this is the perfect spot.

(*He turns away.* TARTAGLIA *aims his arquebus at* DERAMO. DERAMO *turns back again.* TARTAGLIA *quickly lowers the weapon. This* lazzo *is repeated several times during the following dialogue, but* DERAMO *never notices the minister's evil intention.*)

TARTAGLIA.    True, Your Majesty, the perfect spot. (*Aside*) He never gives me enough time.

DERAMO.    We're sure to see some game run by. (*He turns away.* TARTAGLIA *aims the arquebus again.* DERAMO *turns back.*) And provide some fun.

TARTAGLIA.    Definitely. (*Aside*) My hand is shaking. Soon as I cut him down—nobody's around—I'll toss him in the stream.

DERAMO.    It was here, as I recall, that I once cut down a stag.

(*Business as before, carefully timed*)

TARTAGLIA.   That's correct. So you did. I remember. (*Aside*) My soldiers are ready. I'll seize Angela first, then take over. But my heart won't stop pounding.

DERAMO.   Nobody's around. Where are the others?

(*Same business*)

TARTAGLIA   (*Raging*). Away over there. (*Aside*) Damn! I needed one more second.

DERAMO   (*Glancing at him inquisitively*). My dear Tartaglia, you look depressed, preoccupied. Has something made you sad, my friend? (*He sits on a rock.*) It troubles me to see you like this. You always cheered me up in the past, and if anything is bothering you now, let me know. I'll do anything for you. Come, sit here. Let's chat like good friends. I don't like to find you so gloomy.

TARTAGLIA   (*Aside*). That's that. I'll wait for the next chance. I've never been as much of a coward as I am today. (*Aloud*) Nothing is bothering me, Your Majesty.

DERAMO.   No? You look troubled to me. Perhaps you're upset about what happened earlier? Out with it now! Sit down. Remember, I'm your friend and I love you dearly.

TARTAGLIA   (*Aside, as he sits*). I'll mix truth and lies; he'll never catch on. (*Aloud*) Very well, Majesty, I won't suppress my indignation any more, my mortification.

DERAMO.   Over what? You're my most trusted associate. Your reasons! Speak up, speak freely.

TARTAGLIA.   I've served you without stint for thirty years, my king, and you know I've given you my best advice in time of peace and war alike. How often have I faced danger during the grim battles we got into because you refused the daughters of so many powerful rulers? I've spilled my blood, risked my life. I always came out victorious. But the wounds all over this body testify to the sacrifices I've made in upholding your honor and glory. It's true, I earned greater rewards than I deserved. But if I had died from those wounds I'd at least feel less insulted than I do today, and by you, the man I love as myself. (*He pretends to break down.*)

DERAMO.   How did I ever insult you? Tell me, Tartaglia, my faithful minister, how? Answer me.

TARTAGLIA.   How? I'd rather not say. I'm only hurt because of my devotion to you . . . Oh, I could weep like a boy who's had a jealous spat with his girl. (*He weeps.*)

DERAMO.   Please explain. I don't understand.

TARTAGLIA.   It's five years since you learned Durandarte's magic secrets. But you didn't share them with me, in spite of all I've done on your behalf. You might at least have spared my daughter the mocking laughter of that statue and spared me this humiliation. I've never sought medals or power, only your good will. Why do I feel distraught? Because I can't forget what you let happen to me or your accursed statue's mockery. And also because I have found that you don't love me as I hoped or consider me worthy of your entire confidence. Now you understand my grief. (*He weeps again.*)

DERAMO.   You are right, Tartaglia. I've been remiss. I could have confided in you and repaid your long service to me, or at least have excused Clarice from being embarrassed. But to make it up to you, to prove I value you above all other friends, before we leave here I am going to share the other secret, the greater one, with you, this spell from Durandarte: a verse of infernal power. (*He takes a small scroll from his tunic.*) If you recite the words over the corpse of an animal or a man, you die and your soul passes into the dead body, bringing it back to life, while your own body lies lifeless.

TARTAGLIA.   What? You mean, if I recite the spell over the dead body of a donkey, I give up my body in exchange for the donkey's! Is that an advantage? Poor Tartaglia! Your Majesty, feel free to make fun of me and humiliate me further. Even my life belongs to you.

DERAMO.   Tartaglia, you insult me. Let me finish. The animal with you inside it can speak the same words over your body and then it dies again, restoring you to life as yourself. (*He stands.*) So effective is the charm that I've passed from time to time into a dog, a bird, some other creature, or a dead human being in order to uncover the plot of a rebellion, lawyers' lies, disloyalty, and ugly misdeeds. I've rooted out crime and kept this kingdom free of evildoers. From now on you, Tartaglia, will share this rare charm. We'll use it together. Learn it by heart, my friend, and don't tell me any more that I don't love you. (*He embraces him.*)

TARTAGLIA  (*Aside*). If this is true, I see a way to work my revenge and win Angela back. (*Aloud*) My king, forgive my thoughtless outburst, which was purely the result of my love for you. The secret is a formidable one, and you've made it a token of your generous confidence in me. Permit me . . . (*He begins to kneel.*)

DERAMO.  Rise, my dear friend. I know your daughter loves Leandro. I am going to give him the Castle of Isola. Let Clarice marry him, to compensate her for the rejection.

TARTAGLIA  (*Aside*). And my desirable Angela? Who is still not mine? (*Aloud*) Magnanimous king, how can I ever show my gratitude?

DERAMO.  There's no need to. Learn the magic formula, and let's move on to a better place for game. (*Exit.*)

(TARTAGLIA *opens the scroll and goes off slowly after the king, as he reads aloud the magic spell of Merlin Cocai, in a stammering voice.*[7])

TARTAGLIA.  "Cra, cra, trif, traf, not, sgnieflet, canatauta riogna . . ." Horrible words, very difficult for me, but I now have an idea how to make use of them. (*Exit.*)

## SCENE 6

*We hear from the right the sound of hunting horns and the voices of several* HUNTERS, *among them* PANTALONE, BRIGHELLA, *and* LEANDRO. *A* BEAR *trundles into sight. The* HUNTERS, *armed with arquebuses, pursue him.* BRIGHELLA *takes a shot at the* BEAR, *which dodges.*

BRIGHELLA.  Missed by a mile! Now you, Signor Pantalone.

PANTALONE.  Out of my way, you good-for-nothing! He's mine.

(*He fires. The* BEAR *runs off.*)

BRIGHELLA.  Wonderful. Now he's getting away.

PANTALONE.  The firing pan was wet, you boob. Snap to it, boy, he's still in range—fire!

(LEANDRO *runs toward the wings, where the* BEAR *went.*)

LEANDRO.   He's mine, he's mine! (*He fires.*)

PANTALONE.   So he's yours, is he? Third place collects the prize. Look at him go, devil take him.

LEANDRO.   I hit him!

PANTALONE.   Hit him, my ass! Now, you two blockheads, bring him down!

(*The other two* HUNTERS *fire. A yelp.*)

BRIGHELLA.   The dopes! They shot one of the dogs.

PANTALONE.   Up the hill, after him, all of you . . . Brighella, that way. You, Leandro, take the long way. (*To the others*) Hurry, you beggars, run!

### SCENE 7

DERAMO *and* TARTAGLIA

DERAMO.   Did you hear that volley? Where is everyone?

TARTAGLIA.   I thought for sure they'd brought down a rhinoceros. There they go, running up the hill.

DERAMO   (*Peering into the distance*). Tartaglia, I see two stags heading this way. Under cover, fast! (*He hides.*)

TARTAGLIA.   By God, they're beauties. (*He takes cover elsewhere. Two* STAGS *approach.* DERAMO *shoots one* STAG, TARTAGLIA *the other* STAG.) Bravo, Majesty.

DERAMO.   We both did well. I'll send the stags as a gift to my darling wife.

TARTAGLIA   (*Aside*). What an idea I have . . . If I could manage it I'd get my revenge . . . then become . . . He'd never enjoy my Angela again. Let's try. (*Aloud*) These stags are certainly dead, Majesty.

DERAMO.   No doubt about it. Not a movement.

TARTAGLIA. Now, while we're alone and the others are far away, couldn't we experiment with the spell and take over the bodies of these stags? Trot up to the top of the hill, perhaps, and admire the view? Just for a moment, a quick moment? To tell you the truth, I can hardly believe it's possible. I'm dying to see whether it works.

DERAMO. Yes, we could do it. You'll see that I wasn't exaggerating. Hurry, then. Speak the magic words over one of the stags, and watch what happens.

TARTAGLIA (*Stepping back*). Ha, ha, ha. Well, I'm a little fearful, Your Majesty . . . put off by the sight of death, you know, ha, ha, ha. You'll laugh at me, ha, ha, ha, because I'm nervous . . .

DERAMO. I understand. You don't believe in it. I realize that what I said sounds unlikely. I'll go first. You'll see I was speaking the truth. Then, as soon as I've done it, you recite the spell over the other stag . . . "Cra, cra, trif, traf, not, sgnieflet, canatauta riogna . . ."

(*Gradually, while uttering the words, he collapses until he is lying motionless. The* STAG *revives and turns to look meaningfully at* TARTAGLIA, *then it swiftly canters off.*)

TARTAGLIA. It *is* a miracle. I'm beside myself. Courage, Tartaglia! At last: the moment for my revenge and happiness! I'll take over his body, the kingdom, and my precious Angela—in his likeness. But when I occupy that body, will I still stammer?[8] Nobody will notice. And once I'm king, what do I have to fear? No time to brood over it now . . .

(*He bends over the corpse of* DERAMO. *As he prepares to speak, we hear hunting horns, and the hunting party reenters, pursuing the* BEAR. TARTAGLIA *hides in fear. The* BEAR *and the* HUNTERS *go off. A figure closely resembling* TARTAGLIA *emerges from the hiding place and bends over the king's body. From a little way off,* TARTAGLIA *recites the spell while his double accompanies the words with appropriate movements and slowly collapses.*
*The body of* DERAMO *revives. The* BEAR *and the* HUNTERS *again cross the stage, in the opposite direction, and go off.* TARTAGLIA, *in the guise of the king, hides until they are gone. It is suggested that* DERAMO *wear a mask from the beginning of the play, so that when* TARTAGLIA *"changes" to* DERAMO, *he may simply put on a similar mask.[9]*)

## SCENE 8

TARTAGLIA, *alone*

TARTAGLIA.   Rest in grief, Deramo. (*He is stammering.*) Oh, this defective tongue! Is it still with me? Do I care, now that I'm king? Ruler of this realm—and Angela? What do I have to fear? Who is luckier? I can do away with everyone I suspect or dislike. As for you, old body (*To the Tartaglian corpse*), I must fix you so that Deramo, who's now a stag, can't use you and create confusion in my court. (*He cuts off the head with his sword and hauls the trunk into a thicket.*) Lie behind this bush, poor body of mine. I don't regret your fate or envy your state. (*He looks offstage.*) Here they come, the ministers, courtiers, hunters. Put on a regal pose. Our first command: to chase and slaughter that stag inhabited by Deramo's spirit. That's all I care about for now. He might still be able to do me some mischief. I've seen how effective that "cra cra trif traf" can be. Once he's dead, I'll have nothing to worry about.

## SCENE 9

PANTALONE, BRIGHELLA, LEANDRO, HUNTERS, *and* TARTAGLIA. *Later* DERAMO *as the stag. The courtiers bow obsequiously to the "king."*

TARTAGLIA.   Bestir yourselves, all of you! Two stags passed here. One, as you see, is slain. The other ran off somewhere. This is urgent: it must be destroyed. I'll give the man who shoots it whatever he asks for. Follow me!

PANTALONE.   Come on, lads. Bestir yourselves, as the king said. (*Exit.*)

LEANDRO.   Watch me handle this. If I kill the stag I'll ask for Clarice. (*Exit.*)

BRIGHELLA.   Go, go, go! This will end like the business with the bear—no one will be able to tweak his ass.[10] (*Exit.*)

(*The sounds of horns and arquebus shots from offstage, and voices shouting, "There he is, there he goes!" The* STAG *appears, running in terror from the hunting party, who are close behind him.*)

PANTALONE.   He's mine! (*Fires and misses*)

LEANDRO.   He's mine! (*Fires and misses*)

BRIGHELLA.  He's mine! (*Fires and misses*)

(*Exit the* STAG.)

TARTAGLIA  (*Enraged*). You clowns! Call yourselves marksmen?

## SCENE 10

*The same characters as in the previous scene and an* OLD MAN. *Enter an* OLD MAN, *an ugly, dirty, ragged peasant. The actor playing* DERAMO *assumes this role, miming gestures to an offstage voice. He walks leaning on a cane.*

TARTAGLIA.  You, old man! That stag that ran past—which way did he go?

OLD MAN.  I didn't see 'um.

TARTAGLIA.  Didn't see him? (*Incensed*) A curse on all of you! And you, you good-for-nothing old wreck, you'll pay for your insolence. You won't dream up any more plots in this world. (*He shoots him down with a pistol.*)

OLD MAN.  Aiee! He's killed me . . .

LEANDRO  (*Aside*). Why this sudden butchery?

BRIGHELLA  (*Aside*). I'm ready to scoot in half a sec.

PANTALONE  (*Aside*). I can't believe it. Is he drunk? (*Aloud*) Do you feel all right, Your Majesty? What's going on?

TARTAGLIA  (*Menacingly*). That'll teach you not to cross me. I'll gladly do the same to every other useless idiot here. Today we have no time left, but tomorrow I'll check up on you all. Surround the forest! I want that stag dead. I proclaim that whoever brings me that stag with a white mark on its forehead will have a reward of ten thousand gold pieces. Where is Tartaglia? (*He is stammering again.*)

PANTALONE  (*Aside*). Am I stupid or has he turned into a wild animal? I don't recognize him. His voice sounds different, and he's stuttering enough to make you puke.

TARTAGLIA    (*Stammering again*). I asked you: where's Tartaglia? What did you say about him?

PANTALONE    (*Fearfully*). Nothing, nothing. He was with Your Majesty.

TARTAGLIA.    Was he? I lost sight of him hours ago.

LEANDRO.    We're not far from the city. In case he hasn't gone back there already, he knows the route.

TARTAGLIA    (*His stammering accentuated*). Yes, but I'm aware of how everybody dislikes him because he's my favorite, and I don't want anything funny to happen to him.

PANTALONE    (*Aside*). God, will you listen to that stut-tut-tutter!

TARTAGLIA    (*Aside*). My tongue keeps tripping me. I wish I . . . But there's nothing to fear. (*Aloud*) You there, take this dead stag on your backs (*He beckons to the* HUNTERS). It's a gift for my dear Angela. I'm boiling with impatience to see her again. We'll take up the search early tomorrow. (*Exit.*)

PANTALONE.    Yes, let's go back now. I'm so worn out my legs hurt. But I'm also so scared of the change in him that, but for my daughter, on my honor as a royal minister, I'd scamper right off like a lackey to Venice. (*Exit.*)

LEANDRO.    Yes, if I'd killed the stag, Brighella, I could have asked for Clarice's hand. (*Exit.*)

BRIGHELLA.    Love is all that fellow has in his head, but mine hurts like it got hit by the musket ball that wiped out this poor old man. (*Exit.*)

### Scene II

DERAMO *as the* STAG. *The* STAG *enters, stops near the Old Man's corpse. Unseen by the audience,* DERAMO *speaks the stag's lines to sustain the illusion.*

DERAMO.    Jove, I thank you for saving me from a horrible risk. But oh, this misery . . . What am I reduced to? I wanted to know more than the gods permit man to discover. Heaven has punished me by turning me into an animal. Tormented by hunters and hounds, in danger of death at every second, the dry grass my diet, the rocks my bed, exposed to the wind, the rain, the tempest . . . But the most piercing anguish, the most cruel torment is that my Angela is cheated and preyed upon by a traitor she takes for her king and husband . . . Intolerable sorrow: how can I live with it? (*He notices the old man's body.*) And this? An old man, murdered. With the spell I can pass into his body and make my way back to her.

(*He bends over the corpse and recites the spell. The* STAG *dies as the* OLD MAN *revives.*)

## SCENE 12

DERAMO *as the* OLD MAN, *with a stick*

DERAMO.   Heaven has not abandoned me. I am restored to human shape. Now I can avenge myself. (*He looks at his reflection in the stream.*) But oh, that worn and wan face that looks back at me from the water . . . I am Deramo! But where is my real self? Am I Deramo? In this condition? And you, cruel traitor, is this how you repay me for raising you from the dirt and showing you so many favors? I was blind to trust you. I curse the moment when I shared the precious secret. All those years of loyal service tricked me. But one instant was enough to uncover the depths of evil you're capable of. Angela, I've lost you, my Angela! (*Longingly*) Oh, God, I seem to see her in that traitor's arms. (*About to leave*) I must hasten to . . . to the palace and tell her . . . (*He stops.*) But how? Can I make her believe I am her Deramo and that wicked minister has taken my place? Even if I could convince her, how could she love this wasted, helpless body? She is a woman, after all. She will prefer a wicked spirit that is outwardly fair to an honorable spirit that is outwardly repulsive, as women do. Courage, you tired old limbs! Perhaps Angela is not like other women. Legs, brace yourselves! Take me to the queen. Death comes to us all, but heaven never abandons us. (*Exit.*)

## SCENE 13

TRUFFALDINO, *later the* PARROT. *Enter* TRUFFALDINO *on the lookout for birds. He has his net slung around his neck and carries other bird-catching equipment.*

TRUFFALDINO.   This clearing looks fine. We'll set the net here. No, over there. No, in the middle. Oops, what's this? A stag? Dead? A real beauty! Aha, a white mark on the forehead. This is the one! The king's handing out ten thousand in gold coin for finding the stag with a white mark on its forehead. Whooee! I'll take it back, collect the reward, retire, buy a big house and a cozy wife—but not Smeraldina. (*Shouting*) I never want to see that (*Remembering not to startle the birds—in a whisper*)—never want to see that lump again. After all the birds I gave her for her nineteenth birthday, every year . . . This time I'm really giving her the bird . . .

(*Still muttering, he moves into hiding, crouches on one side of the stage, and blows his whistle to emit a variety of bird calls. The wizard DURANDARTE, let loose in his parrot form by CIGOLOTTI, flies into the clearing. TRUFFALDINO darts forward and tries to catch the PARROT, which evades him several times. He whistles to it. The PARROT flies voluntarily into the net.*)

TRUFFALDINO.   Got him! Smart work. He couldn't resist my special parrot whistle. This is my lucky day. What next? An albatross? (*He waits. The PARROT speaks in a parrot's voice.*)

## SCENE 14

DURANDARTE, *as the* PARROT, *and* TRUFFALDINO

DURANDARTE.   Truffaldino.

TRUFFALDINO.   Who was that? Smeraldina? Sounded like her croak. (*He looks around cautiously and comes across Tartaglia's head.*) T-t-tartaglia! Dead! D-d-did you call me? Where f-from? The back of b-b-beyond? (*He quietly gathers up his equipment.*) Er—nice talking to you—I mean listening to you. I have to t-t-take this k-k-king back to the palace and give it to the st-stag. So l-l-long . . . (*On the last syllable he is poised on one foot to flee when the PARROT speaks again.*)

DURANDARTE.   Truffaldino, don't be scared.

TRUFFALDINO.   Me sc-sc-scared? Hey, that wasn't Tartaglia. It's the parrot, thank God. A parrot I can handle. Hi, Polly. Awk, awk. Wanna cracker? A nut?

DURANDARTE.   Take me to the queen in the palace.

TRUFFALDINO.   Polly wanna crack—The palace? You? The queen?

DURANDARTE.   Yes, yes. You'll be rich, rich, rich.

TRUFFALDINO.   Me? Rich, rich, rich? Let's go. First stop, the palace. All of us—you, the stag, the cage, the net, and Tartaglia's—ugh!— head. (*He wants to shoulder everything at once, but one or another item is left on the ground or slips off his shoulder each time he tries to assemble them in a different order.*) It doesn't all fit. I'll *make* it fit. I can't. It won't. (*He spots two* PEASANTS *offstage.*) Hey, peasants, give me a hand here. Take these things to the palace for me. The stag and this head—what's the matter? Scared? Great louts like you scared of a dead head? Don't worry. It won't bite. Won't even talk. Very valuable. The king wants it for his head collection. He'll make you rich, rich, rich. And me . . . (*Rapid exit*).

## SCENE 15

TARTAGLIA, *now king, and* ANGELA. *A room in the palace.* TARTA-GLIA *enters behind* ANGELA, *who tries to keep her distance from him. He still has his old manner, awkward and boorish, and he stammers spitefully to himself from time to time.*

ANGELA   (*Sadly, as she enters*). Please let me go.

TARTAGLIA.   What the devil! My love, why have you changed? You were always so cheerful. I've been trying to fondle you for a whole hour. You're acting like a madwoman. Can't I even hold your hand? (*While he fumbles through his words,* ANGELA *looks bewildered and winces each time he stammers . . . Aside*) She's staring at me. Could she have guessed? Impossible. (*Aloud*) Come, dearest, calm down. Don't you love me any more?

ANGELA   (*In agitation*). Please, Deramo, don't be angry if I speak frankly. I can't bear this . . .

TARTAGLIA.   Be as frank as you damn please.

ANGELA.   Your Highness, perhaps it's only my imagination, but you don't appear to be my Deramo any more.

TARTAGLIA.   What do you mean? Why? (*Aside*) Another goddam snag in my plans.

ANGELA.   I don't know. (*Looking at him intently*) You don't look differ-ent. These are the same handsome features and form I fell in love with. But your manner, the feelings you express, your way of speaking—these don't belong to the high-minded and sensitive person who charmed me and made me confess my love and my hopes for our marriage. Forgive me, my king: it was not your outward looks that captivated me but your nobility, your delicacy, your imaginative play of thought, and your dignity. I see little trace of them in you now. That is why I am sad. (*She weeps.*)

TARTAGLIA  (*Aside*). Is it possible that I can't pass for Deramo, even though I'm wearing his body? (*Aloud*) Please don't weep, Angela.

ANGELA.  If I may speak with the same sincerity you once admired, I admit that, if I had seen you then as I see you now, I'd have told you, "My lord, I do not love you and do not want you for my husband."

TARTAGLIA.  These are stupid delusions, hysterical fancies. We'll call in the physicians, my love, and they'll give you a good bleeding.

ANGELA  (*Angrily*). Yes, perhaps I am losing my mind. But you are certainly not the person you were. Please let me leave, go to my room, and take refuge in my tears. (*Exit.*)

TARTAGLIA.  Of course, my darling. The illness will pass. You will soon love me again.

## Scene 16

TARTAGLIA, *alone*

TARTAGLIA.  Calm! I must calm down. This love has inflamed me. I'll work on her with sugar, soft soap, and entreaties: then, if necessary, force. And then—all-out vengeance. Arsenic? Why not? I must think of a way to terrorize her on the one hand and soothe her on the other—anything to get her to give in and quench my passion. I'm the king and I will remain king. I can dispose of everybody who annoys me or steps in my path. I'll imprison a hundred opponents—today. If she still resists me, there'll be blood, slaughter.

## Scene 17

CLARICE *and* TARTAGLIA

CLARICE.  My gracious lord, I come to you to plead for justice. (*She cries helplessly.*)

TARTAGLIA.  Clarice! What is wrong?

CLARICE. My father . . . found in the forest . . . his head struck from his body.

TARTAGLIA   (*Aside*). My heart goes out to her, the poor child. (*Aloud*) How can that be? Oh, my sorrow! Who could have deprived me of my truest servant? I knew it when he disappeared during the hunt . . . he had many enemies. Quickly, tell me who the traitors were.

CLARICE.   I know nothing more, only that I am the unhappiest woman alive.

(*She is still weeping desperately. Moved, he goes to embrace her, then catches himself.*)

TARTAGLIA   (*Aside*). What can I do to console her? If I could only reveal the secret and—No, I mustn't. (*Aloud*) Try to compose yourself, Clarice. In me, I promise, you will have a second father. And I assure you that blood and slaughter shall pay for the death of my devoted friend. I won't rest till I've tracked down the murderer. You may go now.

CLARICE   (*Still weeping*). Your Majesty's servant. I thank you. (*Exit.*)

## Scene 18

PANTALONE, LEANDRO, *and* TARTAGLIA

LEANDRO   (*Out of breath*). King Deramo, I have sad news for you . . .

PANTALONE.   Your Majesty . . . poor Tartaglia!

TARTAGLIA.   I already know. My unfortunate minister, my most trusted colleague . . . (*Feigning grief*) How did you hear about this?

PANTALONE.   From the bird catcher Truffaldino, Your Majesty. He discovered the corpse, with its head severed, in a clump of thorn trees.

TARTAGLIA.   Guards! (*The* GUARDS *enter.*) Have the body of my late minister cremated without delay, and the ashes placed in an urn. Bring the urn to my rooms; I want it near me. I want to remember that worthy man forever. Arrest Truffaldino and all those who took part in the hunt. Imprison them. Disarm Leandro immediately, and Pantalone. Take them down to the dungeons. Wait there. I'll begin the investigation with these two.

LEANDRO.   Disarm me?

PANTALONE.   And me, Your Majesty?

TARTAGLIA   (*To the* GUARDS). You have your orders. I know only too well how envy and treachery fester in the hearts of courtiers. Leandro, I realize that you wanted to marry his daughter, and that he would not allow it—that could have been your motive. Or you, old fossil, maybe you got him out of the way because he was my favorite. Take them to the tower. If they are proved innocent, they'll go free. (*Aside*) I must still reckon with the stag, but by tomorrow it will be dead. Now I feel more secure. The kingdom belongs to me.

LEANDRO.   I've lost all hope.

PANTALONE.   Is this the first profit I turn for becoming the king's father-in-law? Heaven will prove me innocent.

(*He and* LEANDRO *are marched out by the* GUARDS.)

## Act Three

*A room in the palace. In the background, a cage with the* PARROT *in it. The cage stands on a table or some other piece of furniture that will be needed for the magic transformation.*

SCENE I

DERAMO *as the* OLD MAN

DERAMO   (*Entering, weary and afraid*). No further! I'm so tired I can hardly stand. A few hours ago I ruled this palace. Now I must enter it by stealth, avoiding every official, every servant. My own dogs attacked me! But heaven saved me. Angela's room! I'll hide here until she comes in and we can talk privately. Will she believe my story? Can I blame her if she doesn't? (*He hides.*)

SCENE 2

ANGELA *and* DERAMO

ANGELA   (*Entering*). Tartaglia killed . . . and my father and brother locked up—what next? What insanity, what new wickedness can we expect from my tyrant of a husband? All this confirms that he's not the man I married.

DERAMO   (*Emerging from hiding*). She's here. (*He sees someone approaching*.) Fate keeps tricking me. A servant's coming. (*He hides again*.)

## SCENE 3

TRUFFALDINO *and* ANGELA

TRUFFALDINO   (*With clumsy humility*). My lady, with my uppermost respects for your queenliness, I ask you to be kind enough to overlook my awkward and impudent courage in daring to address you as I tender you the most priceless item—well, anyway, one of the most priceless—

ANGELA.   Please, Truffaldino, I'm too preoccupied with serious matters to think about your awkwardness or listen to your effusions. What kind of "priceless" gift could you possibly come up with? Stop pestering me.

TRUFFALDINO.   It's that parrot. Look at him. A more talented parrot, a more scholarly parrot never graduated from college. I had him especially transported here by my two trained assistants to submit him for your inspection and approval, and to collect the ten thou—

ANGELA.   No more of that. Go, and take your parrot with you.

TRUFFALDINO.   My lady, you must know that this parrot has more eloquence in him than all the women in the world. I'll get him to talk. Awk! Hey, parrot! Say something fascinating to the queen. Don't be bashful. (*To* ANGELA) He's bashful, as parrots go. Are you listening, my queen? Did he speak? No, I didn't hear him, either. Parrot, if you know what's good for you . . . He's talking under his breath. Parrots have shy voices. Speak up, parrot, or I'll kick you one in the tail. No, I won't. I'll make him laugh. He has a tinkling laugh. (*He pulls faces, blows his pipes, performs comic* lazzi. *Not a peep comes from the* PARROT.) This parrot is an ungrateful dog, a pig, after all I did for him. I'll pull out his plucking feathers one by one—

ANGELA.   I asked you to go, Truffaldino. If you don't, I'll have you thrown from the balcony.

TRUFFALDINO   (*To the* PARROT). It was your idea. (*Imitating the* PARROT) "Take me to the queen in the palace, Truffaldino. You'll be rich, rich, rich."

## SCENE 4

*A* GUARD, TRUFFALDINO, ANGELA, *and the* PARROT

GUARD.   Excuse me, my lady.

ANGELA.   Who called for you?

TRUFFALDINO.   Please don't lose your temper, your queenship. This man comes from the king to pay me the ten thousand gold pieces, my reward for bravely killing the stag with the white mark on its head. (*To the* GUARD) You have the money with you? I'll take it and be off.

GUARD.   By the king's command, this man is placed under close arrest and confined to the dungeons. He's suspected of having murdered Tartaglia. My lady, I apologize for this intrusion. Let's go, scum. (*He tugs* TRUFFALDINO *by the arm.*)

ANGELA.   An arrest? In my rooms? Is this the place to—?

GUARD.   I'm only obeying orders. (*To* TRUFFALDINO) Out of here, clown. No more funny business for you.

TRUFFALDINO   (*As he is dragged off*). The parrot, the king, the queen, the stag, the white mark, the gold pieces—you know what you can do with them all—?

## SCENE 5

ANGELA, *alone*

ANGELA.   More of his tyranny! I see that my misfortunes will pile up until they bury me. My dear father and brother—is it your fault that Tartaglia was murdered in the forest, or that I can't love my husband as I did at first? (*She weeps.*)

## SCENE 6

DERAMO *and* ANGELA

DERAMO   (*Hidden*). Don't cry, my beloved, my sweet wife. No more tears!

ANGELA   (*Startled and fearful*). What was that? The king's voice?

DERAMO.   The voice of your true husband.

ANGELA.   Or was it the parrot? Is it possible?

(DERAMO *reveals himself and holds out a trembling hand to her.*)

DERAMO.   Try not to be repelled or frightened, my dearest soul. (*He steps forward slowly.*)

ANGELA.   Who let you in here? Who are you? How dare you enter my rooms! (*Aside*) He stole in to eavesdrop on me and report back to Deramo. (*Aloud*) Leave this instant or I'll have my servants—(*She is about to call them.*)

DERAMO.   Wait, for God's sake! Angela, listen. (*Aside*) She finds me repulsive, and rightly so. She'll never recognize me as her Deramo. (*Aloud*) Angela, tell me: do you detect anything familiar in this old body? Anything that doesn't repel you?

ANGELA.   A question like that from a foolish old man like you . . . ? What are you really asking?

DERAMO.   Foolish? I certainly am. Tell me, my love: don't you find the king unlike what he was this morning?

ANGELA.   Good God, how could you know? Who told you to ask me that, you miserable wretch?

DERAMO.   Yes, it's true: I am wretched. Do you remember, only this morning, when your Deramo smashed the magic statue that laughed at lies, so as not displease his dear Angela, how he said the statue was the first of two wondrous secrets given him by a magician? But he could not tell you about the second secret?

ANGELA.   How did you find this out? I'm so confused.

DERAMO  (*Aside*). She's doubtful, suspicious: keep trying. (*Aloud*) Angela, do you also remember that this morning, in the intimacy of your room, your Deramo . . . (*He strikes his chest*) . . . your Deramo joked about an almost invisible birthmark on your breast and said it was your only imperfection? (*She listens, extremely surprised.*) Now there are a thousand imperfections on your husband. His wife doesn't know him. He is no longer young or respected or a king. (*He weeps.*)

ANGELA  (*Going toward him nervously*). Old man, do you mean that . . . ? No, finish what you were saying.

DERAMO  (*Summoning all his strength*). Angela, you must know that— O heaven, lend me your strength! Make my words ring true! Angela, I am your Deramo—in this crippled body. Tartaglia used a spell to take my place as king; I trusted him too far; I'll repent that fatal weakness as long as I live.

ANGELA.  An old man? Deformed . . . ?

DERAMO.  If you loathe the sight of me and refuse to believe me and no longer love me, take my life. I can't endure any more of this misery. (*He weeps again.*)

ANGELA.  You speak with Deramo's voice—with his words and feelings. It's true! You *are* my Deramo. (*She takes his hand.*)

DERAMO.  Then you still love me, in spite of this ruined body? Oh, the greatness of your soul! (*He kisses her hand, still weeping.*)

ANGELA.  But how did you come to be so deformed? And what of Tartaglia? You say he is king; but he is dead and his corpse is now being cremated. I don't understand any of this. I knew that Deramo's body no longer held his spirit, which I love so deeply. (*She weeps.*)

DERAMO.  Don't weep, my Angela; your tears sharpen my misery. Has that traitor who took your husband's form tried to—? No, I won't ask. Don't tell me if he did. If his crimes, and my misfortunes, have gone that far, then live, Angela, if you have the heart to—but let me die.

ANGELA.  My king, I could never love the body of Deramo while your spirit is absent from it. And while it's governed by Tartaglia, he behaves like a madman. He flies into rages and bouts of cruelty. He has imprisoned my father and brother. He has threatened everyone in the palace. Quickly! I must run, reveal his deception, make the people rebel against him. Perhaps they'll tear him to bits . . . (*She moves toward the door.*)

DERAMO.  Don't go, Angela. That would cause a massacre. How will you convince them? Our only hope is for you to remain calm. We're in danger here; the life of the palace goes on around us. There's a small room nearby where we can talk quietly. I'll tell you what to do. I will need all your love and help.

ANGELA.  My feelings have not changed. Together we'll restore your kingdom and youth—and our happiness. (*They go out.*)

### SCENE 7

SMERALDINA *and* BRIGHELLA. *Another room in the palace*

BRIGHELLA  (*Trying to get away from* SMERALDINA). Will you stop hounding me! They say a guard is after me, to take me prisoner. I can't stop to listen to your rubbish. Get away from me or I'll land you outside with a couple of heavy boots in the butt.

SMERALDINA.   It's all your fault: you and your ambitions. I'm ruined. You kept at me to go before the king, and I was laughed at. Now Truffaldino doesn't want me. I've lost my reputation and all my best chances, so you'd better find me a husband, or I'll make your life hell. I'll drive you out of your mind until you hang yourself.

BRIGHELLA.   You didn't want it? You didn't want me to introduce you to the king? Just like a woman to say that now. Find you a husband? Ha! You go to hell. Sell yourself at an auction. Find a husband for yourself—if you can.

SMERALDINA.   I've done everything I could to find one, you stuck-up ass. I'm not wasting any more effort. I've held hands with every footman in the palace, made eyes at the scullions in the kitchen, sighed my heart out in front of all the drudges on the back stairs and the boys in the stables. Not one would look at me. It's as if I give them nausea or something. They grin and turn up their noses. And all this because the word got out that the king turned me down. Which was all your fault.

BRIGHELLA.   Oh? You want me to tell you why they're grinning and why they won't have anything to do with you?

SMERALDINA.   Why? I'll tell you why. You and no one but you murdered my reputation and my standing at court.

BRIGHELLA  (*Heatedly*). They won't touch you because you have forty years or more on your elderly ass. And you're uglier than a dead tree. And—I may as well say it—you try to pass yourself off in these parts as a virgin, but everyone knows that back in Lombardy you played around like a tart. So stop hounding me, you crazy old witch! (*Exit.*)

SMERALDINA.   Yokel, riffraff, lowlife! (*She runs out after him.*)

## SCENE 8

ANGELA, DERAMO *as the* OLD MAN, *and* DURANDARTE *as the* PARROT. *The same room as before (scenes 1 to 6), now prepared for the transformation*

ANGELA. Don't worry, my darling. I'll follow your instructions to the letter. Even if the plan fails, Tartaglia will die. Whatever happens, you'll be yourself again.

DERAMO. No, dearest. Keep to our plan of action. Violence would be dangerous. Hush, I can hear the impostor's voice out there. Oh, where is my former strength? My anger is overwhelming, but this body is too weak to work my revenge . . . Angela, concentrate on that one task: to bring back the Deramo that was. Please, Angela . . . (*Taking her hand*) Play up to him but, I implore you, don't show him any affection; don't let him near you. Go only as far as . . . No! Don't listen, for I'm nearly blind with jealousy. (*He hides.*)

ANGELA. He's coming. You'll see everything I do. Hurry—hide!

## SCENE 9

TARTAGLIA, GUARDS *behind him, and* ANGELA

TARTAGLIA (*To himself*). The stag is dead. I recognized the white mark. But Truffaldino's story is all mixed up. He couldn't have killed him. I'm full of doubts. I wouldn't want . . . But there's nothing to fear. I'm king. Everyone else fears me.

ANGELA (*To herself*). Bold heart, brave front. Pretend you can stand the sight of him.

TARTAGLIA (*To himself*). I need to win her heart, that's all, and I'll be happy. This love is driving me wild! Now for the last attempt. (*Aloud*) Angeletta, my angel, you don't mean to let me die of love, do you? Have you recovered from the hysteria that made you dislike me? (*Aside*) Well, I couldn't be nicer than that.

ANGELA. My lord, I've prayed to heaven to lift this illusion from me, and I am now a little less repelled. After reflecting for a long time I said to myself, "He's the same man I've always loved. Will I let this madness ruin the rest of my life? No, Angela," I decided, "cast this cruel delusion out of your heart and mind. Requite the love of this great man, and let your wretchedness melt into married bliss." I am sane once more, Deramo, and my tender feelings for you are returning.

TARTAGLIA   (*Seizing her hand*). My own! Wonderful woman . . . I'm overjoyed! Come with me . . .

ANGELA   (*Aside*). Heathen! Felon! (*Aloud*) But there is still one obstacle to our happiness. You have imprisoned my father and brother and a hundred others. Please, my Deramo, revoke the order or I shall never get over my grieving, my tears. (*She weeps.*)

TARTAGLIA.   Don't weep, my sun, my moon. (*Aside*) It worked! The old soft-soap treatment unhardened her heart. (*Aloud*) I imprisoned them, Angela, to protect them from the rebellious anger of the mob, after the news of my poor Tartaglia's death. But once the formal investigation is completed, your father and brother shall be released, even if they took part in any criminal activities.

ANGELA   (*Aside*). Hypocrite!

TARTAGLIA.   And if freeing them will make you love me now, they shall be released at once. (*To a* GUARD) Leandro and Pantalone are to be set free immediately. (*The* GUARD *hurries out.*)

ANGELA.   Ah, Deramo, you know how to revive my devotion. I feel it growing again, flowering, nurtured by your great mercy. I am . . . falling in love with you again.

TARTAGLIA   (*Ecstatically*). Beloved, ask anything of me, whatever you desire. Everything. I adore you.

ANGELA.   My dear husband, I have one more tiny favor to ask. My brother Leandro loves Clarice. Let them be married.

TARTAGLIA.   Oh, yes, yes, certainly yes. I'll give her to Leandro and throw in the Castle of Isola, too. Come, Angela. (*He takes her arm.*)

ANGELA.   Dearest Deramo, not yet. There is still one little thing you could do to make me love you completely.

TARTAGLIA   (*Even more excited*). Ask, ask, my dove, for God's sake. Don't keep me hanging like this . . . (*He tugs at her arm.*)

ANGELA   (*Quietly*). Dismiss the guards.

TARTAGLIA   (*To the* GUARDS). Outside! Come back when I call you. (*The* GUARDS *leave.*)

ANGELA.   This morning, to prove your love, you told me about a magic spell; with it you can change places with a corpse and then return to your own body. Show me how you perform this marvelous trick.

TARTAGLIA   (*Aside*). What? Deramo told her the secret?

ANGELA.   You seem unwilling. It would please me so immensely. But perhaps you don't feel you can trust me?

TARTAGLIA.   I do. (*Aside*) This is too much. I'm beginning to think . . . No, I won't let her see I'm suspicious. (*Aloud*) Very well. If it means so much to you, dearest. But after all I've done to gratify you, what will you offer from your side? I am your husband, after all.

ANGELA.   I swear, Deramo, that after you satisfy this last wish, you'll learn how bountifully I can love my husband.

TARTAGLIA   (*Aside*). This is too dangerous, I'm sure of it. Now I'm really suspicious. I won't give in. I'll use force. After all, what do I have to fear? (*Aloud*) Angela, there's a dead stag lying outside. I'll have it brought in, and you shall see how the spell works. But first, come!

ANGELA.   No, first show me the spell. Then . . . I'll be yours.

TARTAGLIA   (*Dragging her*). Enough of these delays! If I have to force you . . .

ANGELA   (*To herself, agitated*). I've failed . . . I've lost . . . (*Aloud*) Deramo, I beg of you—

TARTAGLIA   (*Struggling with her*). No more begging. You're coming with me.

ANGELA   (*Trying to fight him off*). Oh, God, Deramo, Deramo, help me!

## Scene 10

DERAMO, TARTAGLIA, ANGELA, *and* DURANDARTE

DERAMO   (*Still hidden*). Stop, villain, impostor! Stop!

TARTAGLIA   (*To himself*). The king's voice! I'm caught. (*Dismayed, he lets go of* ANGELA—*aloud*) You betrayed me . . . You have assassins hidden here? I'll flush them out. They'll pay for this, and so will you.

(*He draws his sword and strides across to where* DERAMO *is hiding.*)

ANGELA.   Help, save us! (*She collapses in a faint.*)

(TARTAGLIA *seizes Deramo's arm and drags him out.*)

TARTAGLIA   (*Furiously*). Who's this old fool? How did you get in here? Answer, or I'll slit your throat.

DERAMO.   Traitor, on your knees! I am Deramo, your king. Remember all I've done for you, villain. Kill me if you like, but heaven will destroy you.

TARTAGLIA   (*Confused, to himself*). Now I recognize him: the peasant I struck down in the forest. I was careless to leave the body there, but as the proverb says, crime makes us blind . . . This time, once and for all . . . (*Aloud*) This time, you old pretender, you die forever, and go straight down to—

(*He raises his sword. There is an explosion of noise and light.* DERAMO *and* TARTAGLIA *move apart in terror and stand transfixed in their new positions.* ANGELA *regains consciousness.* DURANDARTE *is now in the guise of a giant parrot.*)

DURANDARTE.   Providence, let your miracles now take place! Protect the innocent, while I cast off these plumes . . .

(*He is transformed from a parrot to a man.*)

DERAMO   (*Astonished*). A miracle! Heaven answered our prayers with its exquisite timing.

TARTAGLIA   (*Bewildered, aside*). What should I do? Flee, or brazen it out? I can hardly think. I'm confused, trembling . . .

DURANDARTE   (*Holding a wand*). Deramo, you are innocent and have nothing to fear. Tartaglia, you are a traitor and have everything to fear. Angela, you are virtuous and will now witness your revenge.

DERAMO   (*In a tearful voice*). Angela, beloved, the miracle has saved me, but saved me as an object that is loathsome in your eyes.

ANGELA.   In my eyes, your soul gilds your body, makes you handsome and undeformed.

TARTAGLIA.   Who is robbing me of my power to fight back? Ministers, guards, servants! Rescue your king!

DURANDARTE.   They are deaf to your cries. Heaven bestows its aid only on the pure in heart. The evil are punished—and when they least expect. You will serve as a warning to those who would take the form of a king and make monarchs into your subjects, as you did to Deramo—seizing his power, his reputation, his kingdom. A man is set apart from others by the quality of his soul. But if Deramo must appear fair to his subjects (*Raising his voice*), so be it! All his degradation and ugliness—and more—now alight on you! And Deramo, you good and intrepid king, let heaven return you to your proper form. Gnash your teeth, Tartaglia. Deramo, give thanks.

(*He strikes the floor with his staff.* DERAMO *now wears his royal garb from the thighs down. Tartaglia's bare legs are covered with sores.*)

ANGELA.   This miracle . . . !

DERAMO.   Old friend . . . this fortune . . . !

TARTAGLIA.   Oh, God, this misery . . . Stop, no more!

DURANDARTE.   Follow your bitter fate. Angela, rejoice: your Deramo is again king.

(*He strikes the floor with his staff.* DERAMO *is now royally attired.* TARTAGLIA *wears a ragged cloak with his skin visible through the rents.*)

ANGELA   (*Exultantly*). Heaven completes its blessings . . .

DERAMO.   My recovery . . . thanks to my friend . . .

TARTAGLIA.   This hideous shape . . . No more!

DURANDARTE.   There will be more, and it will hurt. You others, be happy in your fulfillment.

(*He strikes the floor with his staff.* DERAMO *now wears a jeweled turban, while Tartaglia's head is changed to the snout of a horned animal.*)

ANGELA.   Deramo!

DERAMO.   Angela! (*They embrace.*)

TARTAGLIA.   My luck be damned—and my ambition and betrayal! Where can I hide? (*He is about to flee.*)

DURANDARTE.   Stop, traitor! You are condemned to die of shame. Let this room become a public square, where the crowd may heap ridicule upon you.

(*He strikes the floor with his staff. The room turns into a vast, outdoor perspective, a piazza, as magnificent as the stage and playhouse allow.*)

### SCENE II

*All the principal actors, the* GUARDS, *and the* PEASANTS

TARTAGLIA   (*Frantically, in all directions*). Kill me, I entreat you! Will nobody put an end to me? Friends, I'm Tartaglia, reduced to this condition by the will of heaven. I am evil.

(*People move away from him, stupefied.*)

CLARICE   (*Going to him, weeping*). My father . . . my poor father!

TARTAGLIA.   No tears, my child. I don't deserve them. You must forget your father and his sins. Let all of you forget his ugliness and ugly deeds. Shame and remorse have piled up so much sorrow in my heart that they are darkening the day and draining my life away. King Deramo has had ample revenge. Your Majesty, don't let my innocent daughter suffer because of me. Let her marry Leandro. Guide her, protect her. She has no one left for a father but you. Ambition, love, jealousy drove me into evil and I became a monster. I am sinking: my pain bears me down . . . (*Fearfully*) The rage . . . Death has arrived . . . the terrifying demon . . . Aiee! He's taking me. (*He falls dead.*)

PANTALONE.   I don't know which is strongest in me: fear or relief or the longing to understand this mystery.

LEANDRO.   I feel numb. I understand nothing.

(CLARICE *still weeps. The others stand around in fear and wonder.*)

DERAMO.   Friends, I sympathize with your confusion. At some later time I'll relate the whole story of the miracle. Clarice, look beyond this sad moment. Soon you will be married to Leandro. As for you, illustrious magician, my dear friend and benefactor, I put myself and my kingdom into your charge.

DURANDARTE.   Durandarte has no need for kingdoms, for magic spells do not exist any more. I am no longer a wizard. These days, science is your magic. So let the industrious physicist make war on tiny particles that pass from one body to another without ever changing. And may this learned speech of mine put an end to all those scholarly disputations.[11] Let the wedding be celebrated with the usual turnips and the usual mice; and may the happy couple live happily ever after.[12] And as for you . . . (*Turning to the audience*)

> If, dear patrons, we've befriended
> Most of you as we transcended
> Normal boundaries, and blended
> Men and beasts, we feel contented.
> Home you go—our tale is ended.
> Now it's your turn: recommend it!

The end of

# The King Stag

# Notes

1. Other than Gozzi's assertion, I know of no record of Goldoni's having made such a statement.

2. Gasparo Gozzi reviewed the production in *L'Osservatore Veneto* on 9 January, 1762.

3. Cigolotti was a well-known "character" of eighteenth-century Venice. According to Chasles, he was a public storyteller and poet-for-hire, often seen drunk, who dressed in a ragged black cassock with a red beret and red stockings full of holes. See Philarète Chasles, *Études sur l'Espagne et sur l'influence de la littérature espagnole en France et en Italie* (Paris: Amyot, 1847), 543.

4. The date is that of the play's first performance.

5. Smeraldina has supposedly modelled her seductive behavior on two of the most famous "vamps" of Italian literature: Armida of Torquato Tasso's *Gerusalemme liberata* (Jerusalem Delivered), canto 4, and Corisca in Battista Guarini's pastoral drama *Il pastor fido*. The lines from Ariosto refer to Orlando's love-inspired madness (*Orlando furioso*, canto 1, lines 11–12). According to contemporary testimony, the poetry of Ariosto and Tasso was often sung by the common people of seventeenth- and eighteenth-century Venice.

6. This satirical remark is directed at Pietro Chiari, who followed Gasparo Gozzi as director of *La Gazzetta Veneta* from 7 February 1761 to 10 March 1762. Even when personal and artistic enmity was not involved, however, Gozzi's attitude to the newspapers of his day was far from complimentary: see *The Serpent Woman*, 3.5.

7. Merlin Cocai is the pseudonym of Teofilo Folengo (1491–1544), one of the inventors of macaronic poetry. The incantation that follows is taken from his *Baldus*.

8. Tartaglia is traditionally a stutterer. See *The Raven*, note 20.

9. Gozzi's directions for this substitution are not entirely clear. In the production directed by Andrei Serban for the American Repertory Theatre in Cambridge, Massachusetts, a false head with Tartaglia's mask on it was used. Deramo, who had worn a mask from the beginning, here switched to a different one: a contorted Deramo face with aspects of Tartaglia's features in it. Deramo went on to play Tartaglia in a growling, stammering voice. The old man was not played by the Deramo actor, but by a puppet, as were the parrot and the stags. The puppet handlers were visible on stage.

10. That is, to catch up to him.

11. Durandarte's final remarks equating modern science with fairy-tale magic reflect Gozzi's polemic against the culture of the Enlightenment, in which the rational activity of science had an important place.

12. "The usual turnips and the usual mice" is a reference to a common formula found at the end of many folktales. See *The Raven*, note 17.

# Turandot

## A Tragicomic Tale of China
## for the Theatre
## in Five Acts

### Preface

A great many people confessed that *The Raven* was an intrinsically power-ful play. Many others, however moved they had been by it, and although they had seen it more than once with pleasure, refused to say that it had any real worth. They chattered on about it without any convincing proof, insisting that the play's successful run was due only to the skill of the comic actors (though the masks had in fact had quite small parts), to the wonder-ful scenery, and to the transformations of a man into a statue, and a statue into a man.

In reality, the puerile title and unrealistic plot were the sole reasons why these people wouldn't give any credit to the poor *Raven*.

It was because of these ungrateful people that I based my next play on a Persian tale, the ridiculous story of Turandot.[1] I used the commedia dell'arte characters very little, just enough to continue my support of them, and the play was almost entirely devoid of magic and miracles.

I wanted the three riddles of the Chinese princess, artfully situated in a tragic context, to give me material for two acts of the play. The difficulty of guessing two names, and the important consequences of success or failure, provided me with the theme for three more, to create a seriocomic work in five acts.

Three riddles and two names are truly a large foundation on which to construct a play that must hold a cultured audience's attention for three hours, and keep them in a serious frame of mind at odds with the plot. If my critics, with their rare talents, had had such a beautiful plot on their hands, they would have created a famous and fabulously successful piece of work, and one far better than mine. I concede it.

The simplicity of this nonsensical tale, lacking magic and transforma-tions, allowed me to counter what my critics said about the worth of such transformations, although I knew from the outset that their objections had no basis in fact.

The transformations I used in my tales for the theatre were for the most part painful afflictions, and consisted of nothing more than the final out-come of dramatic circumstances prepared and developed long before the physicai changes occurred. They always had the power of holding the audience's attention for as long as I wished, and of maintaining a convincing and varied illusion, even during the transformation itself.

This artistic aim, for which I strove with all the strength of my weak intellect, was well understood by perceptive people. And if my stupid critics had observed that, after my foolish tales, the old-fashioned "magical" scenes of the commedia dell'arte fell entirely out of use, that objective fact would have convinced them of the truth, without requiring them to use the intelligence that they either do not have, or else use only for cheap, malicious remarks.

The tale of Turandot, constructed around the impossible occurrences that you will see, with sparing use of the commedia dell'arte characters, and without showy magic effects or transformations, was brought onto the stage of the San Samuele Theater of Venice by Sacchi's company on the twenty-second of January, 1761.[2] It was repeated for seven nights to the applause of full houses, which somewhat reduced the previous criticism.

This work of theatrical fantasy did not die after its birth. It is still performed every year, and its success is the only reason for the anger of its enemies.

# *Turandot*

TURANDOT (TOO-rahn-DOHT), princess of China,
daughter of
ALTOUM (ahl-TOOM), emperor of China
ADELMA (ah-DEL-mah), princess of Tartary, Turandot's
favorite slave
ZELIMA (zay-LEE-mah), Turandot's servant
SCHIRINA (skee-REE-nah), Zelima's mother, wife of
BARACH (bah-RAHK), under the name of Hassan,
former tutor of
CALAF (kah-LAHF), prince of the Tartars, son of
TIMUR (tee-MOOR), king of Astrakhan
ISHMAEL, former tutor of the prince of Samarkand
PANTALONE, Altoum's secretary
TARTAGLIA, lord high chancellor
BRIGHELLA, master of the pages
TRUFFALDINO, chief eunuch of Turandot's seraglio
Eight SAGES of the Chinese high council
SLAVEWOMEN, EUNUCHS, SOLDIERS, PRIESTS, and an
EXECUTIONER

*The scene is in Peking and nearby. All characters wear Chinese garb, except for Adelma, Calaf, and Timur, who are dressed as Tartars.*

## Act One

*A view of the city gate of Peking. Above the gate are many iron spears. On each, a severed head is impaled.*

### Scene i

CALAF, *then* BARACH

CALAF   (*Entering from the side*). I knew I could find one good-hearted person, even in Peking.

BARACH   (*Entering from the city*). No! Can it be . . . ?

CALAF   (*Surprised*).   Barach!

BARACH.   Your Highness . . .

CALAF.   You, in Peking?

BARACH.   You alive? Here?

CALAF.   Hush! For heaven's sake don't give me away. How did you come here?

BARACH.   When King Carizmo destroyed your army under the walls of Astrakhan, I saw the defeated Turks flee and the barbarous sultan Carizmo usurp your throne and overrun the realm. I went back, wounded, into the city. There I heard that you and your father, King Timur, had died in the battle, and I wept. I ran to the palace to save your poor mother, Elmaze, but I could not find her. The enemy and his troops

129

were already entering Astrakhan unopposed. I had to escape. Months later, my wanderings brought me to Peking. I changed my name to Hassan, and pretended to be Persian. I met a poor widow who was down on her luck. With good advice and some gems I sold for her, I soon improved her fortune. I liked her, and she was grateful. In the end she became my wife, and to this day she thinks I'm Persian and calls me Hassan, not Barach. I am a poor man now, but at this moment I am wealthy beyond imagination at seeing my dear Prince Calaf, whom I raised almost like a son and had mourned for dead. How do you come to be alive, and here in Peking?

CALAF.   Don't mention my name. After that terrible battle, my father and I ran to the palace. We quickly packed up the best of the jewels, and with my mother we fled, disguised as peasants. Oh, God, Barach! What sufferings and hardships! At the foot of Mount Caucasus thieves stripped us of everything save our lives. Hunger and thirst were our constant companions. On we went. I carried my old father and mother on my back by turns, first one, then the other. Time and again I had to prevent my father from killing himself in desperation. I had to keep reviving my mother when she fainted from weariness and sorrow. One day we reached the city of Jaich. At the mosques and in the bazaar I begged for coins and crusts of bread. The shame! But that was not all. The savage tyrant Carizmo had not found our bodies and was not satisfied with the rumor of our deaths. He promised fat rewards to anyone who brought him our heads. You know how much people fear that ferocious man, and fallen kings have little influence when it comes to diplomacy. By chance, I discovered that the king of Jaich was secretly searching for us through the city. I ran to my parents, urged them to flee. They wept, they wanted to die. At last I calmed them, reminding them of heaven's secrets and its decrees, and we ran away—to undergo new hardships . . .

BARACH   (*Weeping*). Stop, Your Highness, my heart is breaking. The bravest, most merciful, the wisest of royal families reduced to beggars! Please answer me now: is my king still alive, and his wife?

CALAF.   Yes, Barach, both he and my mother are living . . . But let me tell you the trials a man may be subjected to, although he is born to high station. A strong soul must bear good and harm alike. Compared to the gods, a king is nothing: only obedience to heaven's decrees gives a man his true worth. We found ourselves at the court of Cheicobad, the king of Carazani. I took on the most menial jobs to support my parents. The king's daughter, Adelma, took pity on me—and I think she felt something beyond mere pity. Her penetrating glances told me that she suspected I was more than a servant. But her father declared war on Altoum, the emperor of China—I don't know why, and I never believed the stupid stories told by the rabble. All I know is that the emperor defeated him, sacked his city, and put his entire family to the sword, except for Adelma, whom they drowned in a river. Or so the story goes. We took off again, to escape the slaughter and the raging war. After a long and painful journey, we came, ragged and barefoot, to Berlas. And there I provided for my poor parents for four years by working as—don't be shocked—as a humble porter. Yes, I bore burdens on my back like a peasant.

BARACH.   No more, Your Highness, say no more. Since I see you now in royal dress, please put this unhappiness aside, and tell me how fortune smiled upon you at last.

CALAF.   Smiled? Wait. One day Alinguer, the emperor of Berlas, lost a precious falcon. I caught it and returned it to him. He asked me who I was. I told him only that I was a poor man and provided for my parents by carrying burdens. The emperor commanded that my mother and father be brought to the poorhouse, and that they be well served and looked after there. (*Weeping*) Barach, that is where your king and queen are . . . My mother and father live in constant fear that they will be discovered and beheaded.

BARACH   (*Weeping*). Oh, God! Such an unfair punishment!

CALAF.   The emperor gave me this gold (*Drawing a purse from his robes*), a good horse, and these fine clothes. In desperation, I embraced my parents, and told them I was going to seek my fortune. Either I'd lose my life or they could expect great things from me, for I could not bear to see them in such poverty. They wanted to stop me, follow me. Heaven keep them from doing so. I changed my name and came to Peking to join the emperor's army. If I can raise myself to a higher rank, Barach, if fortune favors me, I will take my revenge. But I don't understand why the city is so full of foreigners. I couldn't find lodgings. A kind woman in that house took me in and stabled my horse . . .

BARACH.   Your Highness, she is my wife.

CALAF.   Your wife! You are fortunate to possess such a gracious woman. (*Ready to leave*) I will return, Barach. I want to see this ceremony, which has drawn so many people to Peking. Then I will present myself to the emperor, and ask to be accepted as a soldier. (*He goes toward the city gate.*)

BARACH.   Stop, Calaf! Don't be drawn into this grisly spectacle. Peking is a theatre of atrocities.

CALAF.   What do you mean?

BARACH.   Haven't you heard of Turandot, the emperor's only daughter? She is as cruel as she is beautiful. She brings us slaughter, tears, and mourning.

CALAF.   I do remember hearing some foolish stories about her among the Carazani. They even said that King Cheicobad's son died in some horrible way here in Peking, and that was why the king declared war on China. But the ignorant common folk make these things up. They think they know their masters' business, but the sensible man listens to them and laughs.

BARACH.   Turandot is as wise as a sage, and so lovely that no painter can do her justice. Portraits of her have passed from hand to hand in foreign courts, and great princes have asked to marry her—all in vain, for the heartless creature hates men.

CALAF.   Yes, that's the tale I heard. I laughed at it. Go on, Barach.

BARACH.   It's not a tale. Her father tried to marry her many times. She will inherit the empire, and he wished to find a royal husband who'd be capable of governing it. The obstinate woman refused, and her loving father would not force her. He has had to fight wars because of her, and though he is powerful and has always won, he is growing old. Finally, he spoke to her firmly, trying to reason with her: "I am an old man," he said, "and I have angered too many monarchs by promising your hand in marriage, only to find you opposed. Either take a husband, or tell me how to avoid these wars you have caused by your unjust refusals. Then you may live and die as you wish. My request is fair, and my love for you has never faltered." The proud Turandot begged him over and over to change his mind, but he would not. Finally the viper fell ill from sheer rage. On the point of death, she asked her saddened but steadfast father to grant one diabolical request . . .

CALAF.   Yes, that's the story I heard before. I know what you are about to say. She wanted her father to issue an edict that any prince could ask for her hand, but on this condition: that in the imperial council, before the sages, she would present the candidate with three riddles. If he solved them, she would accept him as a husband and heir to her empire. If he failed, the emperor Altoum, by solemn vow, would have him beheaded. Isn't that the same fairy tale, Barach? Tell me the rest, because I bore myself reciting it.

BARACH.  Fairy tale? If only it were! The emperor rebelled when he heard that, but the tigerish woman drove the poor, weak man nearly out of his mind. Sometimes she stormed at him, sometimes she pretended to be dying, and at last the emperor agreed. "No men will dare attempt it, and I will live in peace," she told her father. "And if any try, my father will not be blamed for carrying out a sworn public edict." This cruel law was sworn and publicly proclaimed, and I wish I could say it was a fairy tale, whose effects are no more than a dream.

CALAF.  I believe it, since you are the one who is telling me. But certainly no prince can have been fool enough to take up the challenge.

BARACH.  No? Look. (*He points to the skulls above the gate.*) Those are the heads of the young princes who have tried to solve Turandot's riddles.

CALAF  (*Shocked*). Monstrous! How can they have been so stupid? Throwing away their lives for such a bloodthirsty woman!

BARACH.  You wouldn't say that, Calaf, if you had seen her portrait. It has such power of fascination that young men who glimpse it rush blindly to their death.

CALAF.  A madman might do that.

BARACH.  Even a wise man would. The crowds are here in Peking today to watch the beheading of the prince of Samarkand, the most handsome, intelligent, and gracious young man this city has ever seen. Altoum regrets his vow and weeps, while his prideful, inhuman daughter gloats in triumph. I left the city so as not to see it. (*The sorrowful sound of a drumroll is heard.*) Listen! That dreary sound is the signal for the ax to fall.

CALAF.  These are strange events you've described, Barach. How could nature give birth to a woman so incapable of loving, so stripped of compassion?

BARACH.  My wife's daughter is one of Turandot's servants. Now and then she tells my wife things. Turandot is a tigress, Your Highness, and her greatest sin is her unrelenting pride.

CALAF.   To the devil with that inhuman abomination! If I were her father, I would burn her at the stake.

BARACH   (*Looking toward the city*). There is Ishmael, the tutor of the prince they have just executed. Oh, my poor friend—he's weeping!

SCENE 2

ISHMAEL, CALAF, *and* BARACH

ISHMAEL   (*Enter, weeping*). My prince is dead, Barach. Why didn't they behead me instead?

BARACH.   But how could you let him take the chance of solving the riddles?

ISHMAEL.   Don't add insult to my injuries. I did my duty, Barach. If I'd had time, I'd have told his father. But I had no time, and the boy wouldn't listen to reason. A tutor is only a servant, and cannot command his prince.

BARACH.   Don't grieve for him, Ishmael. Try to take this calmly, like a philosopher.

ISHMAEL.   Don't grieve for him! I loved him, Barach, and he wanted me by his side until his final moments. The memory of his last words will be a knife in my heart as long as I live. "Don't weep for me," he said, "I die willingly, since the cruel woman cannot be mine. Tell my royal father I beg his pardon for leaving his court without saying good-by. I disobeyed him because I was afraid he would not let me go. Show him this portrait. (*He draws a portrait from his robes.*) When he sees her beauty, he will forgive me, and pity my fate." After that, he kissed this loathsome portrait a hundred times, and drew his robes back from his neck. Then—ghastly sight!—I saw his blood spurt, and his body fall to the ground as the executioner clutched my dear master's severed head. I fled, blind with grief and horror. (*He throws the portrait to the ground and stamps on it.*) A curse on the foul, hellish portrait. If I could only trample on Turandot like this. (*To the portrait*) Take you back to my king? No, I'll never return to Samarkand. I'll go into the desert and weep away my life. (*He rushes out.*)

## SCENE 3

CALAF *and* BARACH

BARACH. You heard that, Your Highness?

CALAF. Yes, and I pity him. But how can this painting have such unheard-of power? (*He is about to pick up the portrait;* BARACH *stops him.*)

BARACH. Your Highness! What are you doing?

CALAF (*Smiling*). Picking up the portrait. I want to see this enchanting beauty. (*Again he goes to pick up the portrait, and* BARACH *holds his arm.*)

BARACH. It would be like looking at the Medusa. I won't let you.

CALAF. Don't talk rubbish. (*He shakes off* BARACH *and picks up the portrait.*) You may believe that foolishness, but I don't. I have never come across a woman who could make me look twice at her, much less one who could cut me to the heart. And I mean a living woman, Barach. Let's see if a few signs daubed by a painter can have such a dramatic effect. What a silly story. (*Sighing*) I have gloomier things to think about than love. (*He is about to look at the portrait, when* BARACH *puts his hand in front of Calaf's eyes.*)

BARACH. Close your eyes, for pity's sake!

CALAF (*Pushing him away*). Show some respect, you blockhead!

(*He looks at the portrait, is visibly startled, and gradually, with a sequence of serious and dignified* lazzi, *shows that he has fallen under its spell.*)

BARACH (*Brokenly*). I foresaw this disaster!

CALAF (*Amazed*). Look, Barach! This sweet image, these gentle eyes, this soft breast—they could never conceal the stony, tyrannical heart you described.

BARACH. How do you mean, Your Highness? Turandot is even more lovely than her portrait. No painter has captured all her beauty. I won't hide the truth. But neither could the highest eloquence of the finest speaker succeed in describing her pride, her ambition, the rancor and perversity in her heart. I beg you, my lord, throw that poisonous image away, far from you. Its beauty is deadly, a plague.

CALAF    (*Still contemplating the portrait*). Don't try to frighten me. The curve of those blushing cheeks, the smiling lips and eyes! How blessed a man would be to possess such harmony, perfection, here on earth, in a living, speaking form. (*Resolutely*) Barach, do not reveal my identity to anyone. I must grasp at my destiny. I will solve the riddles. I will win the most beautiful woman alive, together with her empire, or else give up a life I could not endure without her. (*To the portrait*) Most dear one, I will unravel your enigmas or become your victim. Have mercy on me. (*To* BARACH) If I fail, Barach, will they let me see her living beauty before I die?

(*A harsh drumroll is heard offstage, nearer than before. A Chinese* EXECU-TIONER, *with bare, bloody arms, is seen above the gate, carrying a severed head.* CALAF *watches attentively as he affixes the head to a pike above the battlements and goes off.*)

BARACH.    Look at that before you try the riddles. The prince of Sa-markand's blood-soaked skull is still warm with his blood and steaming in this cold air. That man is his executioner, and will be yours as well. Your death is certain. The riddles cannot be solved. Tomorrow your head will sit on a pike, with your face frozen and contorted, up there next to his, as an example to other brave fools.

CALAF    (*To the prince's head*). Unfortunate boy, what destiny drives me to become your companion? Barach, you have mourned my death once; why mourn again? I must take the chance. Don't tell anyone my name. Perhaps heaven is tired of inflicting misfortune on me, and will now make me happy. Perhaps I will save my parents. If I solve the riddles, I will reward your concern for me. Farewell. (*He tries to leave.* BARACH *restrains him.*)

BARACH.    I can't let you . . . For pity's sake . . . My dear boy . . . Wife, come here, my friend hopes to solve Turandot's riddles!

### Scene 4

*Enter* SCHIRINA.

SCHIRINA.    What do you mean? Who? My guest? Who has persuaded you to go to your death?

CALAF   (*Showing her the portrait*). This beautiful face. She summons me.

SCHIRINA   (*Shocked, weeping*). Who gave you that damnable painting?

BARACH   (*Weeping*). A chance encounter.

CALAF.   Good woman, and you, Hassan, I leave my horse with you, and this purse . . . (*He takes the pouch out of his robes and gives it to* SCHIRINA.) a mere token of gratitude. If you are willing, use some of the gold for sacrifices—ask the gods to help me. Give some to the poor. Let everyone pray for this unfortunate man. Farewell. (*Exit, into the city.*)

BARACH.   My lord . . .

SCHIRINA.   Stop, boy . . . He won't listen. The poor, generous man! He's hurrying off to his death. Who is he, Hassan?

BARACH.   Don't be so inquisitive. He has a sharp mind. Perhaps there is hope for him. Wife, we must give every scrap of this gold to the poor and the priests. They'll pray for him. But we will have to mourn his death. (*He hurries off, grief-stricken.*)

SCHIRINA.   I'll give all this gold to charity for him, and all the money of my own I can scrape together. His handsome face, his elegant manners mark him as a noble-hearted soul. And he is a friend of my dear husband. We'll do all we can. We'll sacrifice three hundred chickens to mighty Berginguzino, and three hundred fish from the river, and huge quantities of beans and rice. May Confucius listen to our prayers!

## Act Two

*The hall of the high council. There are two large doors on opposite sides of the stage. One leads to the quarters of* TURANDOT, *the other to the emperor's apartments.*

### SCENE 1

TRUFFALDINO *and* EUNUCHS, *later* BRIGHELLA, *all dressed in Chinese style*

TRUFFALDINO   (*Enters running, sweeping the* EUNUCHS *before him with a gigantic broom*). Sweep! Swash! Swish! . . . No, just sweep. I don't want you eunuchs to start swishing on me. Get this council room cleaned up! It's got to be spic and span before the crowd gets here. Look at these cobwebs. (*He swings the broom around in a huge arc to point at them, accidentally decking a* EUNUCH.) And the dust in that corner!

(*Same business. Other improvised* lazzi *as desired. As the scene continues, the* EUNUCHS *set up two Chinese-style thrones on opposite sides of the stage, and eight chairs for the* SAGES.)

BRIGHELLA.   Hey, you! Head eunuch! What's all this?

TRUFFALDINO.   Emergency meeting of the imperial council in five minutes: the emperor, the judges, my darling little princess, the whole gang. Business is booming! Another prince begging to be barbered— down to the collarbone.

BRIGHELLA.   You beheaded one an hour ago! What is this, two heads are better than one? What are you tickled about?

TRUFFALDINO.   Nobody makes these princes take the risk. But when they see my cute little mistress, they . . . lose their heads. Fine by me. Whenever a new one gets it in the neck, the princess gives me a healthy tip.

BRIGHELLA.   Parasite! Sucker-up! If you love your princess so much, why don't you marry her yourself?

TRUFFALDINO.   Don't make me sick. A wife? Women! Every one of them's a pain in the acid. And princesses are the worst.

BRIGHELLA.   Of course! You're the number one eunuch. You gave up the equipment. That was reckless. Left you rockless. You'll never know what you're missing.

TRUFFALDINO   (*Getting angry*). I'm not missing a thing! Marriage is disgusting! You know why? Because it produces little Brighellas like you, who grow up to spurt out more little Brighellas.

BRIGHELLA.   You don't realize what you're saying. If your mother hadn't married, you'd never have been born.

TRUFFALDINO   (*Shouting*). That's a stinking lie! My mother was never married a day in her life, and I did get born. Didn't I?

BRIGHELLA.   Sure, you got born—against the rules.

TRUFFALDINO.   Don't tell *me* rules, lover-boy—or should I say boy-lover? I've heard you teach your pages all there is to know about marriage.

BRIGHELLA.   Why you dirty . . . I'll scar your cheeks for you—all four of them!

(*They begin to fight, but the squabble is interrupted by a blast of brassy music from offstage.*)

TRUFFALDINO.   Watch it! The emperor's processional.

BRIGHELLA.   Let's get out of here! Back to the servants' quarters.

TRUFFALDINO.   Back to the harem. (*Exeunt.*)

### Scene 2

*To the sounds of a march, enter* SOLDIERS *armed in oriental fashion. They are followed by the eight* SAGES, *then* PANTALONE *and* TARTAGLIA *and finally* ALTOUM. *The emperor is a venerable old man, richly attired. When he appears, the others prostrate themselves, foreheads to the ground.* ALTOUM *climbs the stairs and sits on one of the thrones.* PANTALONE *and* TARTAGLIA *flank him. The* SAGES *sit on their chairs, as the march ends.*

ALTOUM.   My faithful subjects, how long must I put up with this vile responsibility? One funeral is barely over, I have hardly finished weeping over the death of one unlucky prince when another appears to renew my anguish. Cruel daughter, you were born to torture me! I curse the day I swore that solemn vow to sacred Confucius. Ah, what good does cursing do me? My daughter will not yield. And this stream of insensate wooers never ceases. Who can advise me how to break this desperate stalemate?

PANTALONE.   My dear Majesty, I don't know what to say. In my country, there aren't any laws like that. Princes don't fall in love with portraits of girls—at least not enough to lose their heads over them. And we don't have girls like your daughter Turandot, who hate men. Not on your life! Before my bad luck made me leave my country, and good fortune rewarded me more than I deserve by making me your secretary, I didn't know a thing about China. I thought it was one of those powders you take for tertian fever.[3] I still can't believe all these vows and beheadings. If I told them about it back in Venice, they'd say, "Come off it, you old line spinner, you windbag, what are you trying to put over on us? Go tell your fairy tales to the kids." Then they'd laugh in my face and turn their backsides on me.

ALTOUM.   Tartaglia, did you speak with the new candidate?

TARTAGLIA.   Yes, Your Majesty. He's here in the palace, in the rooms we give the foreign princes. He is so handsome and has such a noble way of speaking—I could hardly believe it. I never saw a worthier man. I liked him right away. It breaks my heart—an attractive youngster like that, come to be slain like a lamb . . . (*He weeps.*)

ALTOUM.   The misery of it! Have the sacrifices been performed? Perhaps this time the heavens will help a prince solve my daughter's riddles. A vain hope.

PANTALONE.   We sacrificed, all right: a hundred bulls to the sky, a hundred horses to the sun, and a hundred pigs to the moon. (*Aside*) But I don't see the good of all that imperial slaughter.

TARTAGLIA   (*Aside*). They should have sacrificed that virginal vixen of a Turandot. That would solve *our* riddles.

ALTOUM.   Very well. Bring in the new prince. (*One of the* SOLDIERS *leaves.*) We will try to dissuade him. You, my faithful ministers, and you judges, help me convince him if words fail me in my sorrow.

PANTALONE.   We've been through plenty of experience, Your Majesty. We'll wear out our lungs talking, then he'll go off and get his throat cut like a turkey.

TARTAGLIA.   Listen, Pantalone, he seemed bright. Don't give up hope yet.

PANTALONE.   You think he can handle that bitch's riddles? Not a chance.

## SCENE 3

*Enter* CALAF, *with a* SOLDIER.

CALAF ⸱ (*Kneels and touches a hand to his forehead*).

ALTOUM.   Rise, you rash young man.

(CALAF *rises and goes to stand proudly in the middle of the council hall between the two thrones, facing the audience.* ALTOUM *looks closely at him, then continues in an aside.*)

What a noble bearing! It makes me pity him all the more. (*To* CALAF) Where are you from, you misguided man? What king is your father?

CALAF   (*A little surprised; then with a dignified bow*). My lord, may it please you to let my name remain unknown.

ALTOUM.   You dare aspire to my daughter's hand, without telling me who you are?

CALAF   (*Grandly*). I am a prince. If heaven wishes me to die, before the executioner's ax falls I will reveal my name and my nation. Then you will know that I did not aspire to the princess's hand without having royal blood in my own veins. (*He bows.*) But for now, may it please you to let my name remain unknown.

ALTOUM   (*Aside*). Nobly spoken! I pity him more than ever. (*Aloud*) But if you solve the riddles and I find you are not of noble birth, how . . .

CALAF   (*Boldly interrupting him*). The law applies only to princes! My lord, if I solve the riddles and cannot prove my blood noble, then strike my head from my shoulders and throw my body to the dogs and crows. There is someone in Peking who knows me and can tell you who I am. (*He bows.*) But for now, may it please you to let my name remain unknown.

ALTOUM.   I will permit it. I can deny nothing to such a fine-looking young man, who speaks so exaltedly. If only you were as eager to grant the wish of an emperor . . . Draw back, young man, draw back from this frightful trial. You have made such a strong impression on me that I will offer you anything within my power. Join me now in ruling my empire, and after my death you will be royally rewarded. If you have any pity, brave man, do not force me to be a murderer against my will and to weep over your corpse. My subjects call me a weakling for having sworn such an unwise vow. They despise my daughter's vain, cruel obstinacy. And I despise myself for having given birth to her. Draw back from this trial, prince. Do not increase my misery. (*He weeps.*)

CALAF.   Sire, the gods know how much I pity you. Your daughter could not have learned cruelty from such a father. Your only faults—if they *are* faults—were to bring into the world a woman whose beauty enthralls men, and to love your only child. I thank you for your generous offer, but I cannot accept. Heaven will make the empire mine by allowing me to possess your daughter, or I will die, unable to survive her loss. This is my choice: death or Turandot.

PANTALONE.   But my dear young prince, you must have seen all the skulls posted above the city gates. Do I have to say more? I don't know why you want yourself slaughtered like a goat, without a hope of winning. Why make us weep? Listen, that princess will whip up three riddles even the astrologer Cingarello couldn't deal with. These judges here have studied for years, worn out their eyes poring over riddle books, and even they have a hard time figuring them out. They're tricky, not easy, not like "Why did the chicken swim the Grand Canal?"⁴ They're brand-new ones, and damned hard. And if the judges weren't given the right answer in sealed scrolls, even they probably wouldn't know what was going on. My dear boy, pull out of this mess while you can. Watching you there as handsome as a painting, I feel sorry for you. I like you, boy, but if you insist on going through with this trial, I'd give no more for your head than for a radish from the imperial gardens.

CALAF.   You're wasting your time, old man. Your advice does not disconcert me. This is my choice: death or Turandot.

TARTAGLIA.   Turandot! Turandot! My dear young fellow, you're as stubborn as the devil. Now, listen. You're not betting a cup of hot chocolate or a coffee and cake on this, you know: we're talking about your brain-box, boy. Isn't that enough for you? His Majesty is practically on his royal knees; he's gone and sacrificed a hundred horses to the sun, a hundred pigs to the moon, and a hundred bulls to the sky to bring you luck. But you, you lump of ingratitude, you're going through with this no matter how much pain you cause him. Even if Turandot were the only woman on earth, your stubbornness would make no sense. Excuse me, my dear prince. It's my affection for you talking. Don't you understand—you'll lose your top! I can't believe this.

CALAF.   You speak disrespectfully. I will not listen. This is my choice: death or Turandot.

ALTOUM.   Then your cruelty shall be satisfied. Go forward to the death you desire, and leave me to my grief. (*To the* SOLDIERS) Bring the princess to the council hall to meet her new victim. (*A* SOLDIER *leaves.*)

CALAF  (*Aside, passionately*). Heavenly gods, inspire me! Don't let me be overwhelmed by her beauty. My mind falters, my heart is racing. (*To the whole assembly*) Members of the high council, sages, wise judges of my answers and my life, I beg you to pardon my daring. Have mercy on a man who is blinded by love, doesn't know where he is or what he's doing, and abandons himself to his destiny.

### SCENE 4

*March music, with tambourines. Enter* TRUFFALDINO, *his scimitar at his shoulder, followed by a file of* EUNUCHS. *After them, a file of* SLAVE WOMEN *playing tambourines. Next, two slaves, veiled. One is dressed richly, after the fashion of the Tartars: this is* ADELMA. *The other is dressed less richly, in Chinese style: this is* ZELIMA. *She also carries a small tray on which are scrolls, sealed: the answers to the riddles. As they pass the emperor's throne,* TRUFFALDINO *and his* EUNUCHS *prostrate themselves. The* SLAVE WOMEN *kneel and place a hand to their foreheads. Enter* TURANDOT, *richly dressed in Chinese fashion; her manner is grave, but confident. The* SAGES *and ministers prostrate themselves.* AL-TOUM *stands.* TURANDOT *bows to her father, placing one hand to her forehead, then climbs to her throne and sits. She is flanked by* ADELMA *and* ZELIMA. CALAF, *who has knelt at Turandot's entrance, rises and stares at her as if enchanted. When everyone is in place,* TRUFFALDINO *takes the tray from* ZELIMA *and, after a few improvised* lazzi, *gives the sealed answers to the* SAGES. *After many bows, he retires. During all of this pantomimed ceremony, the march music is played. At Truffaldino's exit, the council chamber remains in silence.*

### SCENE 5

ALTOUM, TURANDOT, CALAF, ZELIMA, ADELMA, PANTA-LONE, TARTAGLIA, SAGES, *and* SOLDIERS

TURANDOT  (*Scornfully*). Who dares the secret of my riddles, after so many others have failed? Who wishes to throw away his life?

ALTOUM.  Here, Daughter. (*He points to* CALAF, *who is standing as if enchanted in the center of the council hall.*) This man is worthy to be your husband. Take him, end these trials, and stop tormenting your father.

TURANDOT  (*To* ZELIMA, *softly, after having looked at* CALAF *for some time*). Zelima, this is the first time a prince has made me feel sorry for him.

ZELIMA   (*Softly*). Then give him easy riddles, Your Highness, and end your cruelty.

TURANDOT   (*Softly, but with arrogance*). What? And lose my reputation? How dare you suggest it?

ADELMA   (*Aside*). God in heaven! I can't believe this: the man who was a servant in my father's court. And a prince? I knew it in my heart. I was sure of it.

TURANDOT.   Prince, do not attempt this fatal trial. Whatever lies you have heard about me, the gods know that I am not heartless. But I abhor your sex, and I defend myself in the only way I know, so that I may remain free from men. Why should I not be as free as you are? Who forced you to come here, to make me be cruel against my will? If prayers can convince you, I will beg you humbly to withdraw. Do not try to pit your skill against mine. My skill is the only thing I am proud of. God gave me intelligence and ability. If my ingenuity were beaten in this contest, I would die of shame. Go! Do not oblige me to put the riddles to you, or you will die.

CALAF.   All this beauty of voice and face . . . all this spirit and discernment in a woman! How could a man be at fault in risking his life to possess you? Turandot, you boast of your intelligence—and yet you do not see that the greater your merits, the more men will yearn for you. If I had a thousand lives in this poor body, cruel princess, I would risk them all for you.

ZELIMA   (*Softly, to* TURANDOT). For pity's sake, make your riddles easy. He is worthy of you.

ADELMA   (*Aside*). How sweetly he speaks! If only he could be mine! Why didn't I realize he was a prince, before my fate turned me from a princess into a slave? My heart is alight with love, now that I know he is of noble birth. That love will give me courage. (*Softly, to* TURANDOT) Turandot, don't forsake your glory.

TURANDOT   (*Aside, perplexed*). How does this man weaken me with compassion? No! I must be strong. (*To* CALAF, *vehemently*) Foolhardy prince, prepare yourself for the contest.

ALTOUM.   Prince, do you still insist?

CALAF.   My lord, I do. This is my choice: death or Turandot.

ALTOUM.  Let the fatal decree be read aloud. Listen, and tremble.

(PANTALONE *takes the Book of the Law from his robes, kisses it, and presses it first to his breast, then to his forehead. He presents it to* TARTAGLIA, *who prostrates himself, then accepts the book, and reads.*)

TARTAGLIA.  It is written: "Any man of royal blood may vie for the hand of Turandot. Before the sages of the high council, she will ask three riddles. If he can answer them, she will become his wife. If he fails, let him be bound over to the executioner, his head to be struck from his body. To holy Confucius, Altoum, emperor of China, so solemnly swears."

(*When he has finished reading, he kisses the book, presses it to his breast and his forehead, and presents it to* PANTALONE, *who receives it after prostrating himself, and then presents it to* ALTOUM, *who raises a hand and places it on the cover.*)

ALTOUM  (*Sighing*). This tormenting law . . . I swear that I will faithfully execute my vow. So be it.

(PANTALONE *returns the book to his robes. The council hall is silent as* TURANDOT *rises to her feet.*)

TURANDOT  (*Solemnly*). Listen well, stranger.

> We notice her presence in lands high and low,
> In cities, the country—wherever we go . . .
> In war, as in peace, she is safe in her place
> And everyone living has looked on her face.
> She is friendly to all and she strives for our gain,
> Yet her unequalled splendor can drive men insane.
> You know who she is, but don't know that you do—
> Now answer me, stranger—my riddle is through.

(*She sits.*)

CALAF  (*He looks heavenward for a moment, lost in thought, then bows to the princess with a hand to his forehead and responds*). I shall be a happy man, princess, if none of your riddles is more obscure than this.

> That presence we notice in lands high and low,
> In cities, the country—wherever we go;
> Who in war, as in peace, remains safe in her place
> And whom everyone living has seen face to face;

That friend of all creatures, who strives for our gain
But whose unequalled splendor can drive men insane
Has a name that I know, and your riddle's undone,
My princess. I give you my answer: the sun.

PANTALONE   (*Overjoyed*). Tartaglia, he got it!

TARTAGLIA.   Bull's-eye!

SAGES   (*Opening the first riddle, then in unison*). Correct. It is the sun, it is the sun, it is the sun.

ALTOUM   (*Ecstatic*). My boy, heaven help you with the remaining riddles.

ZELIMA   (*Aside*). O gods, give him the correct answers.

ADELMA   (*Aside, agitated*). Heaven forbid! He must not become Turandot's husband! I feel faint.

TURANDOT   (*Aside, arrogantly*). Could he outwit and defeat me? Never! (*Aloud, rising to her feet*) Listen well, and riddle me this.

> The tree in which the hours
> of human life are told
> Is as young as a newborn infant,
> Yet infinitely old.
> Its leaves are white on one side,
> On the other, black as sable.
> Tell me what this tree is,
> Prince, if you are able.

(*She sits.*)

CALAF   (*After a moment's thought, he bows and answers*). Do not be distressed, princess, if I succeed in solving your riddles.

> The tree in which the hours
> Of human life are told,
> As young as a newborn infant,
> Yet infinitely old,
> Whose leaves, like days, are white,
> And make your riddle clear
> By being black as night below,
> This tree must be: the year!

PANTALONE   (*Overjoyed*). Tartaglia, that's it!

TARTAGLIA.   Another one smack on target.

SAGES   (*In unison*). Correct. It is the year, it is the year, it is the year.

ALTOUM.   How happy this makes me! Great gods, help him with the last riddle.

ZELIMA   (*Aside*). If that had only been the last one!

ADELMA   (*Aside*). Must I lose him? (*Softly, to* TURANDOT) One more riddle, Your Highness, and you will be shamed before the assembled high council. He will defeat you.

TURANDOT   (*Aside, angrily*). Never! The heavens will fall and the human race perish first. (*Aloud*) Fool! Can't you see that I hate you more, the more you hope to defeat me? Leave this council, escape this last riddle, and save your life.

CALAF.   Princess, your hatred saddens me. If I am not worth your compassion, then let them strike my head from my shoulders.

ALTOUM.   Stop, my dear son. Stop, Daughter. We have no need for a final riddle. He is worthy to be your husband: accept him.

TURANDOT.   Never! The law must take its course.

CALAF.   My lord, don't be distressed. This is my choice: death or Turandot.

TURANDOT   (*Scornfully*). Then take death! (*She rises to her feet and solemnly intones the last riddle.*)

> Tell me the name of the kingly beast
> Who makes the world tremble and ruins his foes,
> Still mighty today as he was in the past,
> Winged and four-footed, in active repose.
> His hindquarters rest on the restless seas,
> His breast and his forepaws cover the sand.
> His untiring wings will never cease
> To cast their protection over the land.

(*After reciting the riddle,* TURANDOT *rips the veil from her face to dazzle* CALAF.)

Look at my face, and try not to tremble. Who is the beast, prince? Answer, or die.

CALAF.    That beauty! Radiant! (*He hesitates, standing with his hands to his eyes.*)

ALTOUM    (*Agitated*). No! His mind is wandering. My son, don't be afraid. Come back to your senses.

ZELIMA    (*Aside, breathlessly*). I feel faint.

ADELMA    (*Aside*). Stranger, you're mine! Love will show me how to rescue you.

PANTALONE    (*Agitated*). Come on, boy, come on! Oh, if I could only help him! I'm so afraid for him, my guts are quivering.

TARTAGLIA.    If I weren't in the royal presence, I'd run for the smelling salts.

TURANDOT.    You have lost, prince! You shall have the death you asked for.

CALAF    (*Coming to his senses*). Turandot, the sight of your beauty stunned and confused me. But I have not lost. (*To the audience*)

> The four-footed beast endowed with wings,
> Who lives on land and sea, and brings
> Protection to a lucky nation,
> The mightiest power in all creation,
> Who wards off every harm and menace:
> I know his name, the lion of Venice! [5]

PANTALONE    (*Jumping for joy*). Oh, bless you, boy, I'm bursting with happiness.

TARTAGLIA.    Your Majesty, he made it all the way!

SAGES    (*They open the third riddle, then in unison*). The lion of Venice. He's right! He's right!

(*Cheers from the assembled populace, and a noisy burst of music.* TURANDOT *faints and is assisted by* ZELIMA *and* ADELMA.)

ZELIMA. He has won, princess. It's over.

ADELMA (*Aside*). I've lost you, my love . . . But I can't give up yet.

(*Joyfully,* ALTOUM *descends from the throne, assisted by* PANTALONE *and* TARTAGLIA. *The* SAGES *retire upstage in single file.*)

ALTOUM. Daughter, you can no longer rule me with your whims. Come to me, prince.

(*He embraces* CALAF. TURANDOT, *who has regained consciousness, sweeps down from her throne.*)

TURANDOT. Stop this! He is not my husband yet—nor will he be. I must ask him three more riddles tomorrow. I demand it. I did not have time to prepare or time to think. Stop . . .

ALTOUM (*Interrupting*). Senseless, coldhearted woman! No more tolerance from me! The brutal law has been followed to the letter. My ministers will now pronounce your sentence.

PANTALONE. Pardon me, princess. We don't need any more riddles, or any more heads chopped off like pumpkins. This boy came up with the answers, the law was followed, and by God we're going to enjoy your wedding cake. What do you say there, chancellor?

TARTAGLIA. It's an open and shut case: I sentence her to marriage. What do you say, judges?

SAGES (*In unison*). The law is clear: the vow to Confucius has been fulfilled.

ALTOUM. Let us go to the temple. The stranger will tell us who he is, and the priests—

TURANDOT. Father, have mercy, postpone—

ALTOUM. No more delays. I will not give way.

TURANDOT (*Falling to her knees*). Father, if you love me, if you value my life, let me pose new questions. I could not endure the shame. I'll die before you can subject me to this arrogant man and before I consent to become a wife. The thought of it, the very word "wife" is enough to kill me.

ALTOUM.    I refuse to heed your stubborn, fanatical brutality. Ministers, precede us to the temple.

CALAF.    Rise, Turandot, my beloved tyrant. My lord, I beg you to revoke your orders. I cannot be happy so long as she hates me. I love her too much ever to cause her pain. What is my affection worth, if it receives in return only hatred? Ruthless woman, if I cannot soften your heart, then you shall remain free. I will not be her husband. But, Turandot, if you felt my pain, you would feel for me. Do you want me to die? If so, my lord, I agree to a new contest because I no longer value my life.

ALTOUM.    No. No more concessions. No more contests. To the temple!

TURANDOT    (*Violently*). To the temple then . . . and your daughter will die at the altar.

CALAF.    Die? My lord, my princess, I beg of you to grant me this much. Tomorrow, here in the council hall, I will ask Turandot a riddle.

> Who is the prince who fed his father
> By carrying burdens and begging his bread?
> Who is the prince who loved a princess,
> And answered her riddles while risking his head?
> The prince whose bad fortune gave way to his fame,
> Yet still is unfortunate—what is his name?

Tomorrow, in the council hall, you must tell me the name of that unlucky prince and of his father. If you fail, torture me no longer! Give me your hand: become my devoted wife. If you succeed, let me die. Be satisfied with my blood.

TURANDOT.    I accept your offer, stranger.

ZELIMA    (*Aside*). A new danger.

ADELMA    (*Aside*). I can hope again.

ALTOUM.    I do *not* accept this offer. The law must take its course.

CALAF    (*Kneeling*). Your Majesty, if I deserve anything from you, if you have any mercy, concede this favor to your daughter and to me. I do not wish her to be dissatisfied. She is intelligent: let her answer my riddle tomorrow in the council hall.

TURANDOT   (*Aside*). I'm suffocating with anger. He is mocking me!

ALTOUM.   How can you make that request, you imprudent man? You don't appreciate this woman's cunning . . . But as you insist, I will agree to another contest. If she answers your riddle, she need not become your wife. But I will not allow her to put you to death. Altoum will never again weep over a murdered prince. (*Aside, to* CALAF) Follow me. You fool, why did you do that?

(*The processional march begins again.* ALTOUM *and the* SOLDIERS, *the* SAGES, PANTALONE, *and* TARTAGLIA *leave through the door lead-ing to the emperor's quarters.* TURANDOT, ADELMA, ZELIMA, EU-NUCHS, *and* SLAVE WOMEN *leave through the door leading to the princess's apartments.*)

## Act Three

*A room in Turandot's seraglio*

### Scene 1

ADELMA *and a* SLAVE WOMAN

ADELMA.   I forbid you to say another word. I can't follow your advice. Too much is weighing on my heart. I love this nameless prince, and hate the evil princess and my condition as a slave. For five years I have kept my hatred a secret and have pretended to be devoted to her and resigned to my own slavery. But I too am of royal blood, at least her equal. How long must I serve her? I'm withering away with hatred I dare not express. I must strike back and throw off my slavery or die.

SLAVE.   No, my lady. It's too soon . . .

ADELMA   (*Angrily*). Don't ask me to bear it any longer. Not another word! (*The* SLAVE WOMAN *bows with her hand to her forehead, and leaves the room.*) She is coming—my enemy, her heart overflowing with anger and shame, almost demented. Time to risk everything or die. I must listen to her. (*She hides.*)

### Scene 2

TURANDOT, ZELIMA, *later* ADELMA

TURANDOT.   Zelima, I can't bear it. My shame scorches my heart.

ZELIMA.   But my lady, how can such a handsome, generous man provoke your hatred? He loves you so much!

TURANDOT.   Stop tormenting me! I am ashamed to admit . . . he made me feel . . . as I've never felt before. Feverish . . . ice-cold . . . It can't be true! Zelima, I hate him, I wish him dead. He humiliated me in front of the high council. Soon everyone in the empire will know how I was overcome. They'll laugh at me. Laugh! At my ignorance. Help me, Zelima. I must not give the wrong answer tomorrow and be forced to marry him.

> Who is the prince who fed his father
> By carrying burdens and begging his bread?
> Who is the prince who loved a princess,
> And answered her riddles while risking his head?
> The prince whose bad fortune gave way to his fame,
> Yet still is unfortunate—what is his name?

He means himself, but who on earth can tell me his name? The emperor says he may keep it secret until the moment of the trial. I accepted the challenge only to gain time. I will never be able to guess it. What can I do, Zelima?

ZELIMA.   Aren't there magicians here in Peking or a soothsayer to consult?

TURANDOT.   You may be credulous, Zelima, but I am not. Only the ignorant rabble believes in those frauds. Have you no better suggestion?

ZELIMA.   Do you remember how he sighed, how much pain there was in his voice when he spoke to you? When he went to his knees and begged your father to let you ask more riddles?

TURANDOT.   Stop! I feel . . . No! I won't give in. I wish he were dead. Men are liars, cheats, incapable of loving any woman. They pretend to love only in order to seduce us. And when they have us, not only do they not love us, but they also disregard their marriage vows and skip from woman to woman. They lust shamelessly after the vilest woman, a slave or prostitute will do. Don't speak in his favor, Zelima. If he wins tomorrow, I will hate him more bitterly than death itself. If I let myself think of it, if I see myself as a wife, subjected to a man, if I imagine how I can be defeated . . . I will go insane!

ZELIMA.   You are young and proud, my lady. But an unhappy time will come: there will be no more suitors. Your regrets will then be unavailing. What do you lose by being defeated? What fanatical glory, what honor?

ADELMA  (*Little by little she has crept up on them, listening. She interrupts*). Those are the questions of a lowborn woman. Zelima, you have no conception of what a princess feels—the agonizing shame in being publicly debased after so many victories. I saw the eyes of those men—more than a hundred of them—shining in triumph. They sneered, they laughed at her riddles, as if an idiot child had asked them. How can you feel for what she feels when she may become a wife against her will and her instincts?

TURANDOT.  Stop! I don't need to hear . . .

ZELIMA.  In what way does it hurt her to become a wife?

ADELMA.  Please! How can you understand a noble heart? I am no flatterer. Do you think it is easy to accept the challenge, guess the prince's name, and stand up before the high council tomorrow, in front of the nobles and the rabble? And if she answers incorrectly, or if she can't answer at all . . . I seem to hear a thousand men laughing, and making rude remarks, as if she weren't a princess, but some poor actress who muffed her lines.

TURANDOT  (*Wildly*). Adelma, if I cannot announce his name tomorrow in the council hall, I will stab myself.

ADELMA.  No, princess. You will solve the riddle, by wit or by slyness.

ZELIMA.  Very well, you understand the princess better than I do. You help her.

TURANDOT.  Yes, my dear Adelma. How will I learn his name, and his father's name too, if I don't know where he comes from?

ADELMA.  He said in the council hall that someone in Peking can identify him. Search every corner of the city, offer gems and gold . . .

TURANDOT.  Take gold and gems. Spend them as you will. Take all my treasure, but I *must* know that name!

ZELIMA.  How will you spend her treasure? Whom will you search for? And how will you disguise her cheating? How will you hide the fact that she has discovered his name not by her own wits, but by fraud?

ADELMA.   Who would know, unless *you* betrayed her . . .

ZELIMA.   You go too far. Princess, keep your treasure. I hoped to calm you and reconcile you to a worthy husband. But since I cannot, I will be ruled by my duty to my mistress. My mother, Schirina, told me she was delighted that the riddles had been solved. She did not know about the new trial, but she said the prince was staying at her house, and that my stepfather Hassan knows him. I asked her his name, but Hassan will not tell her. She promised she would try to find out. Now, princess, you cannot doubt my love for you, or my obedience. (*Exit, angrily.*)

TURANDOT.   Stay with me Zelima, don't go . . .

ADELMA.   Turandot, Zelima may have given you a lead, but she is only a silly girl. It is senseless to think her stepfather will reveal the name, now that he has heard about the new trial. There is no time to lose. Let us retire, and I will give you my advice in secret.

TURANDOT.   Yes, my friend, come. I will do anything to keep the stranger from winning. (*Exit.*)

ADELMA.   Gods of love, help me to throw off this slavery. My enemy's pride will become my ally. (*Exit.*)

SCENE 3

*A room in the palace.* CALAF *and* BARACH.

CALAF.   But you are the only man in Peking who knows my name. Our kingdom is far from here, and it fell to the invader over eight years ago. We hid our identities, and there were rumors that we had died. A man who falls into poverty is quickly forgotten, Barach.

BARACH.   Forgive me, my lord. You were unwise. Men who have been ill-used must learn to fear even the impossible. Walls, trees, inanimate objects denounce them, everyone is against them. I can't understand it. You were lucky enough to outdo that supremely beautiful woman; you won an empire at the risk of your life. And then suddenly, out of pity for her, you threw it all away.

CALAF.   Barach, my love for her cannot be measured by material gain or loss. You didn't see my Turandot's anger, there in the council chamber, her desperation.

BARACH.  As a son, you should have thought first of your parents' poverty, not of a beaten woman's anger.

CALAF.  Do not scold me, Barach. I wanted to please her. I am trying to soften her heart. Perhaps she feels a spark of gratitude for what I did.

BARACH.  Who? Turandot? You are dreaming.

CALAF.  I cannot lose her now. Barach, did you reveal my name? Did you tell your wife?

BARACH.  No, my lord. I know my duty toward you. And yet . . . this disturbing presentiment . . . I don't know why I'm trembling.

## SCENE 4

*Enter* PANTALONE, TARTAGLIA, BRIGHELLA, *and* SOLDIERS.

PANTALONE  (*Bustles in*). Here he is, here he is, by jingo.

TARTAGLIA  (*To* CALAF). Your Highness, who is this man?

PANTALONE  (*To* CALAF). Where did you run off to? Who's this fellow?

BARACH  (*Aside*). More trouble! What are they after?

CALAF.  I don't know him. I met him just this minute. I was asking him about . . . ah . . . the city, the people . . .

TARTAGLIA.  Excuse me, my lord, but you've got a screw loose under your turban. You're too trustful, I saw that in the council hall. How the devil could you do such a dumb thing?

PANTALONE.  Come on, what's done is done. Your Highness, you may not know it but you're in way over your head. If we weren't here to watch out for you, you'd pull some stupid stunt and let that girl string you up like a salami. (*To* BARACH) Hey, soup strainer, you there with the mustache, you can run along now. Your Highness, please go back to your room. Brighella, the emperor has mobilized two thousand soldiers, and you are to take all your pages and guard the prince's door. Nobody gets in, you hear that? Emperor's orders. He likes you, Your Highness, he wants you for a son-in-law, and he'll die of heartbreak if anything goes wrong. But listen, Your Highness, that was a crazy give-away in the council hall. (*Softly, to* CALAF) For heaven's sake, don't let your name slip—unless maybe you want to whisper it to me, you know, as a special favor?

CALAF.   Is that how you obey your emperor, old man?

PANTALONE.   Bravo! All right, Brighella, he's all yours.

BRIGHELLA.   I've been ready for half an hour. Sure you're finished talking?

TARTAGLIA.   Guard him well, Brighella, if you're fond of your head.

BRIGHELLA.   Don't worry about my head. I'm very attached to it.

TARTAGLIA   (*Softly, to* CALAF). I'm dying to know who you are, Your Highness. You can tell me. I know how to keep a secret.

CALAF.   Don't try to wheedle me. You'll know my name tomorrow—not before.

TARTAGLIA.   Excellent. That's the ticket, don't tell a soul.

PANTALONE.   Farewell, Your Highness. (*To* BARACH) And you, mustache-face, why don't you get out of the palace? Go smoke a pipe in the square, and mind your own business. (*Exit.*)

TARTAGLIA.   And keep your mind on minding it. I don't like your looks, fellow. (*Exit.*)

BRIGHELLA.   Excuse me, Your Highness. Emperor's orders. Shall I show you to your room?

CALAF.   Yes, I'll come with you. Farewell, my friend, we'll meet again when all this is resolved for the best.

BARACH.   Good-by, my lord.

BRIGHELLA.   Come on, that's enough. Haven't you finished yet?

(*He orders the* SOLDIERS *to surround* CALAF, *and they march off.*)

## SCENE 5

BARACH, *then* TIMUR. TIMUR *is a feeble old man dressed in rags.*

BARACH (*After the departing* CALAF). Heaven help you to guard your tongue, my foolhardy prince. I will certainly guard mine.

TIMUR (*Seeing his son surrounded by guards*). Can it be? My son, surrounded by soldiers. Have the troops of Carizmo, that tyrant who stole my kingdom, arrived in Peking as well? At least I can die with him. (*Trying to follow him*) Calaf! Calaf!

BARACH (*Surprised, he draws his sword and grabs* TIMUR *by the arm*). Stop, old man. Keep silent or I'll kill you. Who are you? Where have you come from? And how do you know that name?

TIMUR. Barach! Alive, and here in Peking? And with your sword drawn against your sovereign!

BARACH (*Amazed*). Timur!

TIMUR. Yes, you traitor. Go on, kill me—I'm weary of life. If my most trusted minister has turned his coat, if foul Carizmo has captured my son, then I have no reason to live. (*He weeps.*)

BARACH. Your Majesty . . . I recognize you. (*He kneels.*) Pardon, sire, my anger sprang from my affection for you and for your son. I beg you, my lord, if you love him do not let his name or your own pass your lips. Here I am called Hassan, not Barach. (*Rising and looking anxiously around*) I hope we have not been overheard. Tell me, sire . . . Is the queen with you?

TIMUR (*Weeping*). Must you remind me of my dear wife? There, in our poor refuge in Berlas, tormented by past troubles and present anguish, clasped in these weary arms, with my son's name the last word on her lips—she died.

BARACH. Oh, my poor queen!

TIMUR. In desperation, I came to Peking seeking my son, and my death too. This past moment, as I arrived, I saw him surrounded by soldiers—captured!

BARACH. We must not dawdle here, Your Majesty. Do not fear for your son. Perhaps tomorrow he will be a happy man, and you will be happy too—so long as you tell no one his name or yours.

TIMUR. What is this mystery?

BARACH. Come. When we are far from the palace, I will explain it all. (*He looks around suspiciously.*) What's this? Schirina, coming out of Turandot's rooms? We're lost! Where have you been? What were you doing?

SCENE 6

*Enter* SCHIRINA

SCHIRINA. I was glad that the stranger had solved the riddles, and I wanted to find out whether that tiger of a Turandot could stand to become a wife. So I went to see Zelima.

BARACH (*Angrily*). Foolish woman, before taking note of dangers, you run to your daughter and gossip! I was looking for you to forbid what you have just done—but the stupidity of women outruns the wise man's caution. Now I am too late. What did you tell her? I can almost hear it—you told her the stranger, the prince, is our guest, and I know who he is. Didn't you?

SCHIRINA (*Mortified*). But . . . would it be bad if I had said that?

BARACH. Did you say it?

SCHIRINA. Yes. And afterward she wanted to know his name. I didn't know, and to tell you the truth I promised . . .

BARACH. Idiot! Quickly, we must escape!

TIMUR. I don't understand this mystery.

BARACH. We must leave the palace and the city. Now! (*He looks off.*) No! It's too late. Here come Turandot's eunuchs. (*To* SCHIRINA) Chatterbox! Thoughtless creature! They're after me—quickly, run, hide. Take this old man with you.

TIMUR. But can't you tell me . . .

BARACH    (*Softly, to* TIMUR). Be silent. Don't let your name cross your lips. (*Hurriedly, to* SCHIRINA) Wife, if you are grateful for all I have done for you, if you want to make up for the tragedy you have set in motion, run now and hide until tomorrow.

SCHIRINA.   Husband . . .

TIMUR.   Can't you come with us? I don't understand . . .

BARACH.   Don't talk back to me, Schirina. They've found me out, I have to stay. Now hurry. Go, hide!

TIMUR.   But why . . .

BARACH    (*Uneasy*). God, what agony. (*Looks off.*)

SCHIRINA.   What did I do wrong?

BARACH    (*Pushing them off*). Go! Tell no one your name. Stupid wife! Poor old man! Very well, then we will flee together. (*Looks off.*) No! Too late.

SCENE 7

*Enter* TRUFFALDINO *and* EUNUCHS, *armed.* TRUFFALDINO *and the* EUNUCHS *surround them, hedging them in with their weapons.*

BARACH.   You are looking for Hassan. I am he.

TRUFFALDINO.   Shut your trap. I've come to do you a favor. A big favor.

BARACH.   Yes, I know. Come, take me away.

TRUFFALDINO.   A favor like you never dreamed of. Nobody gets into the harem, into Turandot's rooms. Why, if even a fly tries to buzz in there, we check if it's male or female. And you, you lucky dog . . . Hey, who's the old geezer?

BARACH.   A beggar. I don't know him. Shall we go?

TRUFFALDINO.   Well, I'm in a generous mood. I'll do him a favor too, and bring him along. Who's the woman?

BARACH. Your mistress is searching for me, no one else. Leave the poor woman alone—I've never seen her before.

TRUFFALDINO. What are you, blind? I know who she is. Your wife— though you never saw her before. I'm not stupid. You crooked-mouth . . . I ought to give you a fat lip. (*To his* EUNUCHS) Grab them, boys, and let's move.

TIMUR. What do you want with me?

SCHIRINA. What's going on?

BARACH. What will they do with us? Whatever it is, we will have to be strong. (*To* TIMUR) Remember what I told you. (*To* SCHIRINA) Now, woman, you'll pay for your flapping tongue.

TRUFFALDINO. All right, all right, shut your faces and get the lead out. *Hup,* two, three, four . . .

(*The* EUNUCHS *frog-march them off.* TRUFFALDINO *supervises officiously.*)


## Act Four

*A vestibule with columns. On a table there is a huge bowl full of gold coins. It is night.*

### Scene i

TURANDOT, BARACH, TIMUR, SCHIRINA, ZELIMA, *and* EU-NUCHS. *The* EUNUCHS *tie* BARACH *and* TIMUR *to different columns. They have been stripped to the waist.* ZELIMA *and* SCHIRINA *stand to one side, weeping. On the other side is* TURANDOT.

TURANDOT (*Fiercely*). You still have time to save yourselves. I repeat my offer: that pile of gold is yours. But I tell you again, if you refuse to confess the name of the prince and his father, my servants will whip you to death. Slaves!

(*The* EUNUCHS *make a deep bow, then pick up whips and clubs.*)

BARACH. Are you satisfied, Schirina? Do you understand your mistake? (*Crying out*) Kill me or torture me, Turandot. I am ready to die. I know the names of the prince and his father, but I will suffer torment and death sooner than tell you. To me, your gold is less than dirt. Don't grieve for me, wife. Save your tears for this poor old man; beg the princess to spare his life, not mine. (*Weeping*) His only fault is that he is my friend.

SCHIRINA    (*Pleading*). Have mercy . . .

TIMUR.    Stop. Do not beg for the life of an old man who wishes for death to ease his misery. My friend, I will die, but you must live. I will tell you, tyrant . . .

BARACH.    No, for pity's sake! Don't let the stranger's name pass your lips or he will be lost.

TURANDOT.    So you know his name, old man?

TIMUR.    Do I know it? You cruel woman! (*To* BARACH) Explain this mystery, my friend. Why can I not tell her?

BARACH.    Because you would seal his death. And ours.

TURANDOT.    Old man, he hopes to frighten you. Whip him, slaves!

(*The* EUNUCHS *make ready to whip* BARACH.)

SCHIRINA.    Husband! My husband!

TIMUR.    Stop! This is torture! Princess, swear that his life and the prince's will be safe, and I will tell you the name. Let the punishment fall on me, I won't seek to escape it.

TURANDOT.    I swear upon my head to dread Confucius that I will spare your lives and that of the unknown prince. (*She places a hand to her forehead in token of sincerity.*)

BARACH    (*Shouting*). Liar! Say nothing, old man. There is poison hidden in that oath. Turandot, swear that when you know the two names, you will marry the stranger, and not let him die of heartbreak. Swear that we will be safe, that you will spare our lives and not keep us in a dungeon to rot forever, so that no one will ever know that you cheated in the contest. If you swear all that, Turandot, I will gladly tell you the prince's name.

TIMUR   (*Astonished*). What mysteries are these? Heaven, enlighten me.

TURANDOT.   I am tired of this resistance. Slaves! Kill them both.

(*The* EUNUCHS *step forward.*)

SCHIRINA.   Mercy, Your Highness.

BARACH   (*To* TIMUR). Now you see what she is like.

TIMUR.   My son, I surrender my life for you. Your mother is dead, and now I follow her. (*He weeps.*)

TURANDOT.   Your son! Stop, slaves. You are a king? You are the prince's father?

TIMUR.   Yes, I am a king . . . a father . . . a pauper.

SCHIRINA.   A king! Reduced to this?

TURANDOT   (*Aside, moved*). A king, so abject, in such poverty! The father of the prince I am trying to hate, although . . . in my heart . . . (*Resolutely*) No, what am I thinking? The father of the man who put me to shame, who tainted my glory. There is not much time left. (*Aloud*) Tell me more, old man. At once!

TIMUR.   What should I do, my friend?

BARACH.   Suffer, and remain silent. Turandot, he is a king. If you harm him, you disgrace your own nobility. Take your inhumanity out on me. But you will never know the prince's name.

TURANDOT   (*Furiously*). Yes, I will respect the old king, but you—you will feel the brunt of my anger. You prevented him from answering me, and now you'll pay for your folly. (*She gestures to the* EUNUCHS, *who pick up their whips and make ready to strike him.*)

SCHIRINA.   My husband! Oh, gods, my husband!

SCENE 2

*Enter* ADELMA.

ADELMA.   Stop, my lady. I overheard what was said here. Quickly, have your slaves hide these two prisoners. Altoum will be here in a moment. Schirina, give me that gold. I have bribed the prince's guards, and we may enter his rooms and speak with him. It is my doing. If you all follow my advice, Turandot will be free, happy, and victorious again. Schirina, if you love your husband, and you Zelima, if your mother is dear to you, do exactly as I say. Carry out my plan, and you will be rich. Quickly—and before long we will all rejoice.

TURANDOT.    My friend, do as you see fit. Take the gold. Schirina and Zelima will go with you. You three are my only hope.

ADELMA.    Schirina, Zelima, follow me. (*Aside*) If only I can find out his name! Turandot will reject him. And then perhaps he will be mine— if I can convince him to leave this land, and take me with him.

(*Exeunt* ADELMA, SCHIRINA, ZELIMA, *and a* EUNUCH *with the gold.*)

BARACH    (*Calling after them*). Wife, Daughter, do not betray me. Do not obey these evil women. (*To* TIMUR) My lord, now the worst can happen to us.

TURANDOT.    Slaves, put these prisoners under lock and key. Quickly.

TIMUR.    Turandot, do what you like with me, but spare my son.

BARACH.    This savage creature spare him? Your son will be betrayed, and we shall rot in the perpetual night of her dungeons so that no one knows of her deception. Vile woman! Heaven will avenge us.

(*The* EUNUCHS *drag them off.*)

## Scene 3

TURANDOT.    What will Adelma do? If this venture succeeds, no woman's name will be more celebrated than mine. No fool will ever again dare the riddles. I will revel in telling him his name, there in the council hall before the sages. I'll shame him, and reject him. (*Hesitating*) And yet, am I sure that I will enjoy it? . . . I can almost see his sadness. It distresses me, I don't know why. Ah, Turandot! What are you thinking? Did he care how sad he made *me* when he solved the riddles? Heaven, please help Adelma. Let me defeat the prince and remain a free woman— free to despise marriage, and men, who want to keep women weak and useless.

## SCENE 4

ALTOUM, PANTALONE, TARTAGLIA, SOLDIERS, *and* TURAN-
DOT

ALTOUM (*Aside, thoughtfully*). So, the usurper Carizmo was fated to
die. And Calaf, Timur's son, was meant to come to Peking and make his
fortune in the contest. Heaven, your ways are unaccountable. Who can
penetrate your mysteries? Who dares ignore your will?

PANTALONE (*Softly, to* TARTAGLIA). What the devil is wrong with
the emperor? Look at him muttering to himself.

TARTAGLIA (*Softly, to* PANTALONE). He just received a secret message. Something's in the wind, for sure.

ALTOUM. Daughter, dawn is near, and here you are: still awake, nervously pacing your room, trying to guess the unknowable. And while
you rack your brains, chance has brought me the names you seek. (*He
takes a slip of paper, folded, from his robes.*) They are here. A secret messenger from a far land has just arrived. He spoke to me, then I had him
put under guard until the morning. He gave me proof that the stranger
is a king, the son of a king. You cannot dream who they are, for their
realm is very distant. I have come here out of pity for you. What satisfaction can you take in becoming a mockery for the second time in
the council hall, before the people? The rabble will howl and whistle at
the merciless princess they hate, happy to see her pride humbled. The
people cannot be controlled when they are angry. (*He makes a dignified
gesture to* PANTALONE, TARTAGLIA, *and the* SOLDIERS. *They
bow low and leave.*) Daughter, I can protect your honor.

TURANDOT. My honor? What do you mean? Thank you, Father, but I
need no help or protection. I will protect myself tomorrow in the council hall.

ALTOUM. No, Daughter. Believe me, this riddle is beyond you. I can
see the desperation on your face. Come, I am your father. You know I
love you. There is no one here to listen. Tell me now—do you know
those two names?

TURANDOT. You will hear them tomorrow, in the council hall.

ALTOUM. No, Turandot, you can't know them. If you do, I entreat you
to tell me. I ask it as a favor. If you know who he is, I will tell him he is

defeated and allow him to leave the empire a free man. I will make it known that you won, and that, in your mercy, you spared him a public defeat. That will save you from my subjects' hatred, and it will please your father. I have been a loving parent, Turandot. This is so little to ask. Can you refuse it?

TURANDOT. I know the names . . . That is, I don't, but . . . Father, the prince thought nothing of how I felt when he triumphed over me in public. He deserves to suffer in the same way. Tomorrow you will see if I know the names.

ALTOUM (*Impatient, he tries to force a reasonable tone*). He made you suffer because he loves you, and because his life was at stake. Conquer your anger for at least one moment, Turandot. I want you to realize how much your father cares for you. I would wager my head that you do not know those names. I do know them, and I will tell them to you. Tomorrow, I will summon the council. The stranger will appear before it, and will suffer when you defeat him in public. Let him feel shame and anguish. Let him weep and despair because he has lost you, whom he loves more than his own life. All I ask is that, after his torment, you give him your hand in marriage. Daughter, swear to do this, and I will tell you the names. No one else will know, and your reputation will remain unblemished. My subjects will begin to love you. You will have as your husband the most worthy man alive, and you will please your aged father after causing so much suffering.

TURANDOT (*Aside, hesitant*). How persuasive he is! Should I trust Adelma, and hope to win by myself? Or ask my father the names, and consent to the repugnant bonds of marriage? If the prince were to win . . . it would be less shameful to give in to my father's request. But Adelma was sure of herself. What if she discovers the names, after I have promised . . . ?

ALTOUM. What are you thinking, Daughter? What makes you hesitate? I can't believe that you have really learned those names. Come, give your father his wish.

TURANDOT (*Aside*). No, wait. See what Adelma can manage. My father is too anxious. He must be afraid that I can come by the names on my own. He likes this stranger. Perhaps the prince himself gave him the names. Perhaps they planned this offer together, as a temptation.

ALTOUM. Come, Turandot, you must make up your mind. Calm your rebellious spirit. Stop tormenting yourself.

TURANDOT.  I have decided. Let the sages be assembled tomorrow in the council hall.

ALTOUM.  So, you are determined to be mocked in public? To yield to force rather than to a father's prayers?

TURANDOT.  I insist. The trial shall be held.

ALTOUM  (*Angrily*).  Fool! Most ignorant of women! You will be a laughingstock, I assure you. You will never guess the names. Hear me now: the council hall will be prepared for tomorrow's trial. When you have lost, you will be married there, immediately, against your will, while everyone mocks you. I will not forget that you refused to make your father happy. (*Exit, angrily.*)

TURANDOT.  Adelma, my loving friend, my father is angry with me. You are now my only hope. (*Exit.*)


## SCENE 5

*The scene changes to a magnificent room with several doors and an oriental sofa, center. It is the middle of the night. Enter BRIGHELLA, carrying a torch, and CALAF.*

BRIGHELLA.  Your Highness, it's three o'clock in the morning. You've paced the room exactly three hundred and sixteen times. To tell you the truth, I'm bushed. If you want to get some sleep, don't worry, you're safe here.

CALAF  (*Preoccupied*).  I'm restless, too nervous to sleep. But you may go, if you like.

BRIGHELLA.  My dear Highness, can I ask a favor of you? If, ah . . . a ghost or two strolls by, don't lose your temper.

CALAF.  Ghost? What do you mean?

BRIGHELLA.  It's like this, Your Highness. We have orders to keep everyone out of your rooms, on pain of death. But . . . poor ministers . . . ! The emperor is the emperor, but the princess, you might say she's the empress. You know what she's like. Poor ministers! It's tough to decide between them . . . If you only knew . . . We're between the devil and the deep blue sea. I wouldn't like anyone to get upset, if you know what I mean. Poor slobs! If we want to put anything aside for old age . . . well, we're in a hell of a fix.

CALAF   (*Surprised*). What do you mean? My life is not safe here?

BRIGHELLA.   Well, I wouldn't say that. But you know how curious everybody is to know your name. Some little imp could slip in through the keyhole to tempt you. All you have to do is keep your wits about you. Don't give anything away. You know what I mean? Poor ministers! Poor beggars!

CALAF.   No need to worry, I'll be careful.

BRIGHELLA.   Good. And please . . . don't give me away. I'm counting on you, Your Highness. (*Aside*) Could I refuse a bag of gold coins? I tried, but no luck. It's like being tickled—some people feel it, some don't. (*Exit.*)

CALAF.   This is very suspicious. Who did he mean by "imps"? Well, let the whole of hell pour in. They'll never get me to tell them my name. Winning Turandot matters too much to me. But dawn is near, and my anxiety and waiting are almost over. Will she still despise me? I must try to rest if I can. (*He is about to lie down on the couch.*)

## SCENE 6

*Enter* SCHIRINA, *dressed as a soldier.*

SCHIRINA.   Boy . . . (*She looks around.*) My lord—(*Looking around again*). My heart is racing.

CALAF.   Who are you? What do you want?

SCHIRINA.   I'm Schirina, the wife of Hassan—poor Hassan! I disguised myself as a soldier and mingled with your guards. When I saw my chance I slipped into your room. I have terrible things to tell you, Your Highness, but fear . . . doubts . . . sorrow clog my throat.

CALAF.   What is wrong, Schirina?

SCHIRINA.   My poor husband has gone into hiding. Someone told Turandot he knew you, and she ordered her men to search for him in secret. He is in danger, if they catch him he'll be tortured, and he has sworn to let them kill him before he reveals your name.

CALAF. My poor servant! Turandot is ruthless . . .

SCHIRINA. But there is more. Your father is at my house. He says your mother is dead . . .

CALAF. What are you saying? My God!

SCHIRINA. That isn't all. He knows that they are looking for Hassan, and that you are surrounded by soldiers. He is worried, afraid, tearful. He wants to come to the palace and tell them who he is. He keeps crying, "I want to die with my son!" I tried to stop him by telling him what you did today. He thinks I'm making it all up to keep him calm. The only thing that will stop him is a note from you, in your handwriting and signed with your name, telling him you are safe. That is why I took the frightful risk of coming here—for that note.

CALAF. My father, here in Peking! My mother, dead! Schirina, you are lying.

SCHIRINA. May Berginguzino blast me if I lie!

CALAF. My poor mother! Father, I am so sorry for you . . .

SCHIRINA. There is no time. Send the letter right away, or there will be worse trouble. Here, I brought pen and ink with me. (*She takes pen, paper, and inkwell out of her robes.*) Let your poor father see a few words from you, and he'll be happy. If not, he'll come to the palace and your name will soon be known.

CALAF. Yes, hand me that paper. (*He begins to write.*) No, what am I doing? (*He thinks for a moment, then throws the letter to the floor.*) Schirina, tell my father that I said he should go to the emperor and ask for a private audience. Altoum will tell him enough to set his mind at ease. That's the best way.

SCHIRINA (*Confused*). You don't want to write? A line or two would be enough . . .

CALAF. No, Schirina, I will not write. No one will know my name until tomorrow. I am amazed that Hassan's wife would try to betray me.

SCHIRINA (*Still more confused*). Betray you? What do you mean? (*Aside*) I pray Adelma's other plans don't go awry like this. (*Aloud*) Very well, Your Highness, I will tell your father what you have said. But I never expected to be called a traitor after all my efforts and risks on your behalf. (*Aside*) Adelma is smart, but this prince is no idiot either. (*Exit.*)

CALAF. Brighella was right. A ghost did appear. But Schirina swore a sacred oath that my father is in Peking, and my mother dead. It must be true, alas. The blows of misfortune fall on me like hail . . . (*He looks toward another door.*) Another ghost.

SCENE 7

*Enter* ZELIMA.

ZELIMA. Prince, I am one of the slaves of Turandot. Her influence has made it possible for me to enter your room. I have good news.

CALAF. I wish that could be true, but I doubt it. Your princess is still angry, and her heart is hard.

ZELIMA. That is so, I can't deny it. But Your Highness, you are the first to make an impression on that heart. It seems impossible, and I know you will call me a liar, but though she says she hates you, I can tell that she's really in love. May the earth open and swallow me if I lie.

CALAF. Very well, I believe you. That is indeed good news. Do you have anything more to tell me?

ZELIMA. My lord, she is still desperately miserable. Her ambition makes her so. She knows she will be unable to reveal your name tomorrow in the council hall. She fears that after so many ugly victories, the people will mock her unmercifully when she loses. May hell open and swallow this slave if she lies.

CALAF. There is no need to take such a heavy oath, slave. I believe you. Tell Turandot that the trial can be cancelled. The people will hate and mock her less if, instead of riddling, she shows herself capable of mercy, and takes pity on a lover's pain and a father's anguish by agreeing to become my wife. Is that what you were sent to tell me?

ZELIMA. No, Your Highness. You must excuse the weakness of women. The princess begs a favor of you. She wants to save appearances, and to be able to announce the names. After she does, she will descend from her throne and offer you her hand in marriage. We are alone here. It will cost you so little. A few words will win her heart, and make her your loving bride—not a wife by force.

CALAF (*Smiling*). You left out a few words at the end of that speech, didn't you, slave?

ZELIMA. What words, Your Highness?

CALAF. "May hell open and swallow this slave if she lies."

ZELIMA. Do you think I'm not telling the truth?

CALAF. Perhaps not the whole truth. And my doubt is so strong that I will not do what you ask. Go back to Turandot and tell her to love me. Say that I refuse to reveal my name, not to cause her pain, but because I love her so much.

ZELIMA (*Angrily*). Foolish man, you have no idea what your defiance will cost you.

CALAF. I do not care if it costs my life.

ZELIMA (*Fiercely*). Good. Then may you get what you ask for. (*Aside*) Useless! (*Exit, infuriated.*)

CALAF. Go, foolish ghosts. And yet somehow Schirina's words—they unsettle me. I wish my poor mother . . . my father . . . No! Be strong. Only a few hours, and you will know whether what she told is the truth. I must rest, if I can. (*He sits on the sofa.*) My churning mind . . . it needs some respite. Perhaps I'll sleep. (*He falls asleep.*)

## SCENE 8

TRUFFALDINO *enters on tiptoe, virtually on point, and cases the room fearfully, exploring its perimeter until he stumbles into the sleeping* CALAF.

TRUFFALDINO. Great, he's snoring. (*In a whisper*) Or pretending? (*He retreats rapidly, trips, falls.*) No damage, luckily. I only hit my head. Where did I put that magic mandrake? (*He frantically searches his pockets.*) Truffaldino, don't say you lost it! After you paid cash! Did I leave it somewhere? If one of my eunuchs picks it up, puts it under my pillow . . . disaster! I'll lose the reward: two bags of gold for his name. Think back, Truffaldino! You took it in your left hand for safety. It was clammy. Why didn't you keep it there? I did! It's here! Still clammy. Magic mandrake, the root of truth. Now . . . I slide it under his pillow, like so. (CALAF *grunts.* TRUFFALDINO *goes into a swift crouch. A bang*) Only my head again. Did he wake? Where's the mandrake? Truffaldino, you didn't drop it? I did. (*He scrabbles around on his hands and knees.*) There you are, you rotten little root. Get under that pillow! Now . . . Give it about a minute to work. The mandrake dealer said you could ask questions and it makes a person reply in his sleep. A general told an enemy spy a load of military secrets. A merchant told his son where he'd stashed away his savings. A minister told his wife about an affair he was having with her sister, the bastard. Talk about the immorality of our times! Times? Time's up: put the question. Stranger, for two bags crammed with gold, what's your name? I want the straight answer. (CALAF *moves restlessly.*) That was a signal. He's spelling it out, letter by letter. I wish I could spell. That looked like a *T.* (CALAF *continues to turn over, roll his head, stretch his arms, change his sleeping position, as* TRUFFALDINO *counts off his interpretation, letter by letter.*) So *T*—an *R*—a *U*—an *F*—another *F*—an *A*—an *L*—*D*—*I*—*N*—*O* . . . Who'd have believed it? He has the only name I can spell. Race away, tell the princess, collect two bags of gold. Wait, Truffaldino! Don't forget your mandrake. (*He recovers the mandrake gingerly from under Calaf's pillow.*) You clever little, clammy little root! You'll make me rich. Tonight I'll tickle you under the king's pillow . . . You're the best thing that ever hap—(*As he kisses the root he bangs into the door.*) No damage. Only my head again. (*Exit.*)

## SCENE 9

*Enter* ADELMA, *veiled and carrying a small torch.*

ADELMA  (*Aside*). My first plans failed and I could not discover the names, but perhaps I can now induce him to love me and take me away from the city. This is the moment. Gods of love, lend me strength and ingenuity. Fortune, make my plot succeed, and break the chains of my slavery. (*She holds her lamp over* CALAF.) My beloved is sleeping; he is so handsome. I wish I didn't have to wake him. But there is not a moment to lose. (*She puts the lamp down, and speaks aloud.*) Stranger, wake up.

CALAF  (*Startled awake, he rises*). Who woke me? Another ghost? What do you want? Won't you leave me alone?

ADELMA.  Angry? How can an unhappy woman harm you? I have not come to fish for your name. Do you want to know what brings me here? Listen.

CALAF.  What are you doing in this room, woman? I warn you, don't try to betray me.

ADELMA   (*Gently*). I, betray you? Ungrateful man! Tell me, stranger, didn't Schirina come? Didn't she try to convince you to write a letter?

CALAF.   She did.

ADELMA   (*Anxiously*). You didn't write it?

CALAF.   I am not a fool. No.

ADELMA.   Thank heaven. Didn't a slave come with another story to find out your identity?

CALAF.   Yes, but she went away without discovering it, exactly as you will.

ADELMA.   If you knew me, my lord, you would not have such suspicions. First sit and listen to me. Then, if you think I'm betraying you, condemn me. (*She sits:* CALAF *sits next to her.*)

CALAF.   Very well, tell me what you want.

ADELMA.   Look at me first. Do you recognize me?

CALAF   (*Examining her*). There is an air about you, woman . . . your bearing, your behavior are noble. From your dress, you seem to be a slave. Didn't I see you before in the council hall? I felt sorry for you.

ADELMA.   As I felt sorry for you five years ago, when I saw you as a humble servant, and even more when I saw you today in the council hall. I knew in my heart that you were not of low birth. I did all I could for you then. You must have known, from the way I looked at you, how I felt. (*She removes her veil.*) Haven't you seen this face before?

CALAF   (*Surprised*). Adelma, the princess of Carazani! I thought you were dead.

ADELMA.   Yes, Adelma, daughter of the king of Carazani—born to a throne—and now a miserable slave. (*She weeps.*)

CALAF.   Everyone thought you were dead. Poor princess! A slave!

ADELMA.   Let me describe my sad plight. I had a brother who was as mad with love for Turandot as you are now. He attempted the riddles.

(*Weeping*) You have seen his skull, there with all the others above the city gates.

CALAF.  Poor woman! I heard this once before, and I thought it was a story, a lying fairy tale. Now I know better.

ADELMA.  My father was a brave man, who raged at the death of his son, and sought revenge. He led his army against Altoum's empire— but fate frowned on him. He lost the battle and was killed. One of Altoum's ministers, a pitiless man jealous of our royal titles, attempted to wipe out every member of my family. He slew my three remaining brothers, then threw my mother, my sisters, and myself into a river to drown. Just then the merciful Emperor Altoum arrived at the river-bank. He was angry at his minister's cruelty, and had his soldiers pull us out of the water. Too late! My mother and sisters were already dead. I was less fortunate. I lived, and the emperor gave me as a slave to his daughter. Prince, if you have human feelings, you will pity me. Think of how it feels to be a slave to the cruel Turandot: the cause of all my troubles, the fountain of my misfortune. (*She weeps.*)

CALAF  (*Moved*). I do pity you, princess. But your brother was the first cause of your misfortunes, and after that your father's rashness. What can I do for you now? I am helpless. If tomorrow I reach the pinnacle of happiness, I can give you your freedom. Until then, your story can only make my own sorrows harder to confront.

ADELMA.  I revealed my identity by showing you my face. You know my lineage and my wretched history. I hope you will believe a princess's word when her compassion—I dare not say "her love"—forces her to tell you a secret. You are blindly in love with Turandot. May heaven help you to believe what I must tell you about her.

CALAF.  Come, Adelma, what is it you want to say?

ADELMA.  I want to say . . . But you will tell me that I came here to deceive you, you will think that I am like those lowborn women. (*She weeps.*)

CALAF.  Adelma, don't keep me in suspense. What do you want to tell me about my beloved?

ADELMA  (*Aside*). Heaven, make him believe my lie. (*Aloud, forcefully*) My lord, Turandot—depraved, vicious, infamous Turandot—has given orders to have you murdered at dawn. That is how the woman you love will treat you.

CALAF  (*Surprised, jumping to his feet*). Orders to kill me!

ADELMA  (*Rising*). Yes, to kill you. When you leave this room tomorrow, twenty swords will plunge into your body.

CALAF  (*Agitated*). I must call the guards (*Heading for the door*).

ADELMA  (*Holding him back*). No! What are you doing? If you hope to save yourself by warning the guards . . . Poor man, you have no idea how influential the princess is, how far her power extends.

CALAF  (*Desperate, he is raving*). Oh, poor Calaf! And Timur, Father! Is this how I have helped you? (*He buries his face in his hands.*)

ADELMA  (*Aside, surprised*). Calaf, the son of Timur! My lie brought me luck! He told me his name without meaning to. Now, gods of love, help me convince him to hate Turandot.

CALAF  (*Continues, desperately*). Fortune, what more can you do to a desperate, forsaken man—to an innocent and devoted prince? After so much misery, you add this final blow, that Turandot could commit such a murder? No, unthinkable. So lovely a face cannot mask a heart so evil. (*Scornfully*) Princess, you are lying.

ADELMA.  That is an insult, but I will not be offended. I knew you would not believe me. Stranger, the riddle of your name has driven Turandot nearly mad. She knows that she will never solve it. (*Mockingly*) She paces back and forth like a madwoman, she shakes herself like a dog, and howls, and grimaces. Her face is pale and sickly green with fear, her eyes red and swollen, her expression clouded. She would look horrible to you now, not like the beauty you saw in the council hall. I told her how handsome you are, described you in the most convincing words, and argued that she should accept you as a husband. I failed. She gave her eunuchs orders to kill you secretly. A more infernal woman was never born. She repays your love with death. I know you don't believe me, and your distrust does not wound me—but I weep for the fate that hangs over you. (*She weeps.*)

CALAF.  I am surrounded by an emperor's army, put there to protect me, and I am in danger of betrayal? That foul minister was right to say that self-interest and fear can make any man unfaithful. Ah, Turandot!

Is this how you repay a lover who in his mad passion for you tries to be generous to the limit and give you all you desire? I do not wish to live. Let my callous destiny overtake me.

ADELMA.   Stranger, Adelma will find a way for you to flee your fate. I pitied you, and so I bribed your guards with Turandot's gold. In a cave in my former kingdom an immense treasure is buried. Alinguer, the king of Berlas, is linked to me by both blood and friendship. Some of the guards will be our escort. Horses are ready for us. Let us escape from this ugly city. Together with Alinguer, we will have the strength to regain my kingdom, which will be yours, along with my gratitude, my love, and if you wish, myself. If you do not want me as your wife, there are many other princesses more beautiful than I among the Tartars. You may have my kingdom, I wish only to save you from death and myself from slavery. If that could come to pass, I could even suppress my love for you—a love that is tearing me apart, a love I am embarrassed to confess so openly. But if my love means nothing to you, at least think of your life. Daybreak is near . . . Come, stranger, we must hasten away.

CALAF.   You are a generous woman, Adelma. I am deeply sorry that I cannot free you from your slavery and escort you to Berlas. What would Altoum say about my flight? He would call me a traitor, and he would be right, since in freeing you I would violate the sacred laws of hospitality.

ADELMA.   Say rather that his daughter violates them.

CALAF.   She will never be my wife now, Adelma. I have lost hope of that. Yet I will be happy to die at the hands of a woman I adore. Escape if you wish: I will remain here. Without her, my life is worthless, no better than a living death. Let her murder me.

ADELMA.   You're serious? Has love driven you into delirium?

CALAF.   Love or death: my only choice.

ADELMA.   Stranger, I know very well that she is more beautiful than I am, but I hoped you would at least be grateful to me. I can bear the shame of this rejection. It is your life that matters to me. Let us go together. Save your life, I beg you.

CALAF.   Adelma, I have made up my mind. I will die.

ADELMA.   Thankless man! If you will not escape, neither will I. I will remain a slave, but not for long. We shall see which of us can give up life, and scorn the punishment of adverse fortune more heroically. (*Aside*) Perseverance is often successful in love, Calaf, son of Timur. (*Aloud*) Stranger, farewell. (*Exit.*)

CALAF.    Has any man ever passed a night of more torment? In love with a woman who hates me, surrounded by plots, my mother reported dead and my father fearful for me. And just when I hope that I am about to reach true happiness, I find that Turandot wants to murder me. Merciless woman! Her slave told me it would cost me dear when I refused to tell her my name. She was right. There, the sun is rising. (*The room lightens.*) It is time. Let the serpent drink my blood, if she thirsts for it so badly, and end my misery.

## SCENE 10

*Enter* BRIGHELLA *and* SOLDIERS.

BRIGHELLA.    Your Highness, it's time for the trial.

CALAF  (*Agitated*).  So, minister, are you the one? Carry out your orders. Kill me if you will. I don't care.

BRIGHELLA  (*Thunderstruck*).  Orders? My only orders are to bring you to the council hall, because the emperor is almost ready.

CALAF.    Good, we'll make for the council hall, though I know I'll never arrive there. You will see that I can die with dignity. (*He throws down his sword.*) I will not defend myself. That spiteful woman will hear that I die for her of my own will. (*Exit, angrily.*)

BRIGHELLA  (*Amazed*).  What the hell's got into him? Damned women! They wouldn't let him sleep, and he's gone off his rocker. All right, boys, we'll follow and make sure he's safe. Present arms! *Hup* two, three, four . . .

## Act Five

*The scene returns to the council hall. Upstage, behind a curtain, an altar with a Chinese idol and two* PRIESTS. *As the scene opens,* ALTOUM *is seated on his throne and the* SAGES *are in place.* PANTALONE *and* TARTAGLIA *flank* ALTOUM, *and the* SOLDIERS *are placed as in act 2.*

## SCENE 1

ALTOUM, PANTALONE, TARTAGLIA, SAGES, SOLDIERS, *then* CALAF. CALAF *enters as if agitated, looking around suspiciously. He comes center and bows to* ALTOUM.

CALAF   (*Aside*). What is going on? All the way here I imagined that I was about to be attacked, but no one bothered me. Either Adelma was deceiving me, or Turandot has discovered the names and countermanded her orders to kill me. Is she lost to me, then? If that is true, I would rather die. (*He remains preoccupied.*)

ALTOUM.   My son, you seem upset. You should be happy. There is nothing to worry about. Today your misfortunes come to an end. What I have learned will give you great joy. My daughter will be your wife. Three times she has sent me messages, begging me to delay the trial and prevent the marriage. Do you see? Your victory is sure.

PANTALONE.   It's a safe bet, Your Highness. Twice I was called to the door of the harem to receive her commands. I dressed in a hurry and ran to obey. It was so cold my beard is still shivering. But I didn't care— I got a kick out of seeing her so desperate. It warmed my heart just to think of all the happiness in store for us.

TARTAGLIA.   I was there at six o'clock. The dawn was breaking. She kept me there for half an hour, begging. Between the cold and her anger, I lost my patience. I may have let a bad word slip. (*Aside*) I could have spanked her pretty behind.

ALTOUM.   Do you see how late she is? I have sent strict orders for her to come; if she refuses I will have her dragged here by force. I have reason to be angry with her. Here she comes, with a sadder face than she has ever worn. Let her be sad, since she wouldn't let me help her. My son, rejoice.

CALAF.   Pardon me, my lord. I thank you for your kind words, but certain fears are tormenting me, and I am distressed to cause her pain. I would rather . . . No, I cannot say that. I could never live without her. In time, my tenderness will make her forget her hatred of me. My whole heart will be dedicated to her. I will desire what she desires. When I am king, anyone who needs a royal favor will not need to seek out flatterers and court cronies. I will favor only those for whom my wife intercedes. I will always be faithful to her, and will never give her cause to distrust me. Before long, I hope, she will requite my love and regret her former hatred.

ALTOUM.    Ministers! We are ready. Open the curtain and let her see that all is prepared for her to be married immediately, here in the council hall. She will see that I mean what I say. Let the people enter. It is time for my ungrateful daughter to pay in some small measure for what she made her father undergo. Let everyone rejoice. Let the wedding take place. Prepare the altar.

(*The upstage curtain opens, revealing altar and* PRIESTS.)

PANTALONE.    Here she comes, chancellor. Seems to me she's crying.

TARTAGLIA.    Her escort is pretty melancholy. This wedding looks more like a funeral.

### Scene 2

*Enter* ADELMA, ZELIMA, TRUFFALDINO, EUNUCHS, SLAVE WOMEN, *and* TURANDOT. *The sound of a funeral march announces Turandot's entrance. She is preceded on stage by her usual escort, dressed in mourning. The ceremonies of act 2 are repeated. As she ascends her throne,* TURANDOT *is clearly surprised to see the altar and* PRIESTS. *All characters are placed as they were in act 2.*

TURANDOT.    Stranger, I know that in your heart you are glad to see my servants' mourning clothes and their sad expressions. I see the altar prepared for my wedding, and I too am sad. I used all my skill to avenge the shame you put upon me by defeating me. But in the end, I had to yield to my destiny.

CALAF.    Princess, I wish I could show you my heart, so that you could see how my joy is made bitter by your unhappiness. How can you regret making me happy when I adore you? Let us be united by mutual love. I beg to be forgiven, if a lover need ask forgiveness for loving.

ALTOUM.    My son, she does not deserve such consideration. It is at last time for her to be humiliated. Let the music play, and the wedding proceed.

TURANDOT.    No, it is not yet time for that. I could have no greater revenge than this: after lulling you into happiness with the appearance of sadness and defeat, I now shrivel you from joy to anguish. (*She rises.*)

Calaf, son of Timur, leave this hall. Those are the two names you challenged me to guess. Look for another bride, and learn how easily Turandot unravels your feeble mysteries.

CALAF    (*Astonished and dismayed*). I have lost her.

ALTOUM    (*Surprised*). Gods, is it possible?

PANTALONE.    By the blood and bones of Bacchus, she's given it to us. In the nose.

TARTAGLIA.    Oh, Berginguzino! This is a knife in my heart.

CALAF    (*Desperately*). I have lost everything. Who can help me now? No one. I am my own murderer. I have lost my beloved by loving her too much. If I had not solved the riddles yesterday, my head would now be cut off, and I would have avoided this pain, which is worse than death. Altoum, why did you not agree to let her kill me if she revealed my name? If you had, I would now be more fortunate. (*He weeps.*)

ALTOUM.    Calaf, I'm overcome . . . This unforeseen stroke grieves me deeply.

TURANDOT    (*Softly, to* ZELIMA). I'm sorry for the poor man. I can no longer defend my heart from him.

ZELIMA    (*Softly*). Then yield to your heart, Your Highness. Listen, the people are murmuring against you.

ADELMA    (*Aside*). What she decides now means life or death for me.

CALAF    (*Raving*). Is this a nightmare? Am I losing my mind? (*Angrily*) Tell me, you tyrant, are you unhappy that the man who adores you is still living? Then let your triumph include my death. (*Furious, he approaches Turandot's throne.*) Here is your victim at your feet: Calaf, whose name you know and curse. And I, Calaf, curse heaven, and earth, and my own destiny. Here, in your presence, I die. (*He draws a stiletto and is about to stab himself.* TURANDOT *rushes down from the throne and prevents him.*)

TURANDOT    (*Tenderly*). No, Calaf, I will not let you.

ALTOUM.    What is this miracle?

CALAF (*Surprised*). Turandot—why have you prevented my death? Are you capable of mercy? No, you woman of marble, you want to force me to suffer more by living without you. Do not carry your revenge so far. At least, let me escape my misery. If you wish to be truly merciful, help my father Timur who is here in Peking, poor, ragged, and persecuted. But let me die. (*He tries to stab himself. TURANDOT prevents him.*)

TURANDOT. No, Calaf. You must live for me. You have won. Listen . . . Zelima, run and give this happy news to the poor old man and his faithful minister. Go, and comfort your mother.

ZELIMA. Yes, Your Highness, I'll do so with pleasure.

ADELMA (*Aside*). There is no more hope. Her choice is my death.

TURANDOT. I won the trial unfairly, Calaf. You revealed the names to Adelma last night, carried away by I don't know what outpouring of grief. She told them to me. Let the world know that I am incapable of a dishonest act. And let them know as well that your own merits, your generosity, and your handsome features have softened my heart. Live, Calaf! Turandot is your bride.

ADELMA (*Aside, softly*). Oh, my misery!

CALAF (*Throwing down the knife*). You are mine! I could die of joy!

ALTOUM (*Descending from his throne*). Daughter . . . my dear daughter. I forgive all the pain you gave me, all your former cruelty.

PANTALONE. Time for the wedding! Time for the wedding! Make way there, sages.

TARTAGLIA. Withdraw to the rear of the hall.

(*The SAGES move to the rear.*)

ADELMA (*Coming forward angrily*). Live then, you stubborn man, live with my enemy. Princess, I hate you. All my plots were aimed at winning this man, whom I have loved since I first saw him, five years ago, at my father's court. I pretended to help you while I was telling him you were wicked and asking him to flee with me. He accidentally revealed the names you sought. I told you, hoping you would reject him. I thought I could then convince him to escape with me, but he loves you too much. All my plotting was useless. My hopes have died. I have one choice left. I was born to royalty, and am ashamed to have lived as your slave. I abhor you and your wickedness. You took my family from me— my father, my brothers, my mother and sisters. You have taken my kingdom and the man I love. I am the last of my family—now slay me, too, if you wish. My blood will wash away that shame from the past. (*She picks up Calaf's knife.*) You drew this knife back from your lover's heart. Now it will pierce mine. Let the people see how I free myself from slavery. (*She tries to stab herself. CALAF prevents her.*)

CALAF.   Stop, Adelma!

ADELMA.   Let me go, oppressor! (*Weeping*) Let me go, thankless man. I want to die. (*She tries again to stab herself. CALAF takes the knife away from her.*)

CALAF.   I will not let you. I received nothing but good from you. Your betrayal made me a happy man. The torment it aroused in me moved a woman who hated me but is now in love. Pardon me if my love for her was too great to overcome. I am not thankless. I swear to the gods that if I could love any other woman, it would be you.

ADELMA   (*Breaking into tears*). No, I am unworthy of you.

TURANDOT.   Adelma, what is this madness?

ADELMA   (*To* TURANDOT). Princess, you have heard my grim story. Now you are stealing the man I love. I became a traitor for his sake, and now he robs me of my revenge. But give me my liberty, at least! Let me leave the city as a wandering beggar. Do not make me stay to see Calaf in your arms: that would be too cruel. Remember, a jealous heart dares anything for revenge. You will always be in danger if Adelma is near. (*She weeps.*)

ALTOUM   (*Aside*). Poor princess, I pity you.

CALAF.   Adelma, do not weep. I can now repay you in part for all you have inadvertently done for me. Wife, Altoum, if a request from me has any influence on you, give this princess her freedom.

TURANDOT.   I ask it too, Father. I know she sees me as a bitter reminder of her misfortunes. My love and complete trust in her were misplaced. She hated me secretly all along, and will never believe that I could wish to be more her friend than her superior. Let her go free. And if the prayers of Calaf and your daughter can sway you, then we beg you to be still more generous.

ALTOUM.   On such a glad day as this I cannot stint in my generosity. Adelma must be happy too. The princess shall have her kingdom back and choose a husband who will rule more prudently than her rash father.

ADELMA.   My lord . . . remorse . . . love . . . my emotions oppress me, and I cannot appreciate your liberality. Time will clear my mind. But for now I can only feel sad and not hold back my tears.

CALAF.   Is my father in Peking? Where can I find him and embrace him?

TURANDOT.   He is in my care, and by now he has heard the joyful news. Please do not force me to confess my folly in public. I am too ashamed. I will tell you everything when we are alone.

ALTOUM.   Timur in your care! Rejoice, Calaf. My empire is yours already. And let Timur rejoice as well, for his kingdom is freed. The tyrant Carizmo, whose savagery made him hated, has been assassinated by your subjects. A faithful minister holds the scepter, awaiting your return, and has sent secret messages to kings and emperors describing you and your father, and recalling you to the throne, if either one of you remains alive. This message will inform you of the usurper's death. (*He gives* CALAF *a message.*)

CALAF   (*After reading it*). Gods in heaven, can it possibly be true? Turandot . . . My lord . . . But my thanks should go to heaven, not to mortals. Gods, I raise my hands to bless and thank you, asking you to visit even greater misfortunes on me, to prove that your power to redeem us goes beyond all human expectation and understanding. I humbly beg your pardon for my complaints, and if my desperation made me give up all hope of aid from an omnipotent hand, I ask your forgiveness, and repent my error.

(*The onlookers are visibly moved.*)

TURANDOT.   Let no one else trouble my wedding day. (*Thoughtfully*) Calaf risks his life out of love for me. A faithful minister scorns death to make his lord happy. Another minister, who could proclaim himself king, holds the throne for his rightful monarch. I saw an old man ready to die for his son, and a woman I regarded more as a friend than a servant betrayed me. Heaven, I have indeed been brutal and stubborn in my hatred of men, and now I ask your pardon. (*She advances and addresses the audience.*) Gentlemen, I once hated your sex, but I have repented. Pray, give me a sign of your forgiveness. (*She mimes applause.*)

The end of
*Turandot*

## Notes

1. In preparing the first edition of his works (1772) from which this preface is taken, Gozzi mistakenly situated *Turandot* after *The Raven* and before *The King Stag*. In fact, it was fourth in the chronological order of his *Tales*.

2. Actually 1762.

3. A pun in Italian: *china* (quinquina) was a common medicine in the eighteenth century.

4. The riddle Gozzi gives in the original, probably well known at the time, is no longer comprehensible.

5. The solution to the final riddle is a blatant appeal to the patriotism of Gozzi's audience, and obviously clashes with *Turandot*'s oriental setting. The symbol of Venice was the lion of Saint Mark: a winged lion, bearing in its paws a book inscribed "Pax tibi, Marce evangelista meus."

# The Serpent Woman

## A Tragicomic Tale for the
## Theatre in Three Acts

### Preface

My new genre of the fairy tale for the theatre was going well, as may be seen from the plain truth of the preceding prefaces.

By now, the claque supporting Signors Goldoni and Chiari was very weak.[1] Their mockery was nothing less than an insult to the theatre-going public, which was very enthusiastic about my *Tales* and anxious to see new ones.

My new genre was so different from the plays of the above-mentioned authors that it should have done no harm to their so-called reformed and learned works. However, I couldn't guarantee anyone against competition. In a war between playwrights, it is the audience that determines losses and victories.

The most difficult thing in this new genre (among the many difficulties it presents) was avoiding repetition, and inventing new and effective situations.

The "marvelous" is a paltry source for poor talents, such as my own.[2] However, when a writer has sufficient intelligence to prepare a plot the function of which is to criticize, and which contains a clear allegory on the customs of men and the false studies of the times; when he can do so with truth, decorum, and wit; when he can treat his subject with eloquence, situating the marvelous in its rightful place; then he will find that the marvelous is far from artistically sterile, and that such a playwright is the most effective and useful sort of author for the theatrical companies of Italy.

I assure you that I have tried in every way to make my ten *Tales* different from each other in their plots and their circumstances.

*The Serpent Woman* was my fifth Tale for the theatre. Produced by the Sacchi company at Venice's Sant'Angelo Theatre, it opened on 29 October 1762, and between the autumn and the following spring season, it had eighteen very successful performances.

The fifth scene of the third act is one of those inventions that foolish, "serious" newspaper critics called boring trivialities and silly, awkward satires.[3]

The plot of the play was full of miracles. To save time, and to reduce the company's production expenses by freeing them from the necessity of staging such marvels, which the audience still had to know about in order to understand the plot, I wrote a scene for Truffaldino in which he imitated those ragged rascals who go though the city selling newspapers, shouting out their contents with all sorts of ridiculous exaggerations.[4]

Sacchi entered in a short, ragged coat and a moth-eaten hat, with a huge bundle of papers under his arm. Imitating those rascals, he shouted out the events that had happened offstage, pretending that such was the content of his papers, and offering to sell copies for a copper apiece.

This unexpected imitation, performed with accuracy and wit, was one of those scenes that are particularly fortunate in the theatre. The audience burst into laughter again and again, and people in the boxes threw Sacchi food and money to buy his papers.

This invention, however trivial it may seem, was presented in the free and frank style I always undertook in my *Tales,* and was well appreciated by intelligent people. Indeed, it gave rise to a prank that made the whole city laugh, and made everyone want to see the play.

When the newspaper sellers heard how successful the scene had been, they got together outside the door of the theatre with a huge bundle of musty back issues that had nothing to do with the performance. When the audience emerged, they began to shout out the plot of *The Serpent Woman.* In the dark of the night, they fooled a great many people into buying their papers, and then went off to the tavern to drink toasts to Sacchi. The episode became the talk of the town, causing the sort of gossip so favorable to a theatrical troupe.

When a "low" scene is developed on the stage with all the hallmarks of truth, and when it arouses interest and enthusiasm, causing people to attend the performance, it is no longer low. Rather, it is a useful and entertaining invention. To see if it is entertaining, you need only ask the audience. To see if it is useful, ask the actors, and you will find that such a scene is perfectly in keeping with the precepts of Horace.[5]

It is superfluous to add that this *Tale* is revived annually for an audience which every year is kind enough to bear it.

# The Serpent Woman

FARRUSCAD (fah-roos-CAHD), king of Tiflis
CHERESTANÌ (kay-ray-stah-NEE), a fairy, queen of Eldorado,
Farruscad's wife
REZIA (RAY-tsyah), their daughter
BEDREDINO (bay-dreh-DEE-noh), her twin brother
CANZADE (kahn-ZAH-day), Farruscad's sister, warrior,
and lover of
TOGRUL (toh-GROOL), grand vizier, a faithful counselor
BADUR (bah-DOOR), another counselor, and a traitor
SMERALDINA, Canzade's lady-in-waiting
PANTALONE, Farruscad's old tutor
TRUFFALDINO, Farruscad's huntsman
TARTAGLIA, minor counselor, who stutters
BRIGHELLA, servant of Togrul
FARZANA (fahr-TSAH-nah) and
ZEMINA (zay-MEE-nah), fairies
A GIANT
A BULL
SOLDIERS and LADIES-IN-WAITING
A SERPENT
OFFSTAGE VOICES

*The play is set partly in an unknown desert, partly in the city of Tiflis and nearby.*

## Act One

### Scene 1

*A wood.* FARZANA *and* ZEMINA

ZEMINA    (*Sadly*). Farzana, you're not weeping.

FARZANA.    Why should I weep, dear Zemina?

ZEMINA.    Have you forgotten our Cherestanì? Her father, a human being, the king of Eldorado, wed the beautiful fairy Zebdon. Cherestanì, you remember, also married a mortal, Prince Farruscad. She pleaded to give up her immortality for his sake. Our king, Demogorgon, angrily refused, but she . . .

FARZANA.    Yes, Zemina, I recall what Demogorgon demanded. She must reach sundown on the second day of the sun's transit of the Dog constellation without being cursed by her husband. If she can do that, she will become a mortal like him, and that is what she hopes for.

ZEMINA.    Oh, God! Tomorrow at sunrise the fatal day will begin. We are losing Cherestanì, our most lovable, most beautiful fairy, in the flower of her youth.

FARZANA.    But you remember the conditions our king imposed? For eight years she has had to hide her identity and reveal none of her mysteries. And tomorrow she must treat Farruscad with unheard-of cruelty. Have no fear! He will damn her before the day is out, and she'll still belong to us.

ZEMINA.   But Farruscad must swear never to curse her, and then break his vow.

FARZANA.   In that case, he'll take the vow, then break it, and she'll be ours forever.

ZEMINA.   He'll never promise that.

FARZANA.   He will.

ZEMINA.   If he swears the oath, he'll keep it.

FARZANA.   No, Zemina, he'll curse her, and she'll return to us.

ZEMINA.   How cruel you are! You know what a horrible punishment she'll suffer if he does. For the next two hundred years her beauty will be transformed into the body of a revolting serpent.

FARZANA.   What of that? She must pay some price for her mad request. Two centuries will quickly pass, and in the meantime her rash husband will die. In the end Cherestanì will once more be ours.

ZEMINA.   But he has one way to save her from that punishment. If he succeeds, she'll become mortal, and we will have lost her.

FARZANA.   You're dreaming! He'll die first. My task is to guard our condemned companion. Then, tomorrow, I am to kill her husband. She will not turn mortal—all danger of that will die with him.

ZEMINA.   But Farruscad's friend, the magician Geonca—aren't you afraid of what he may do?

FARZANA.   No. Come, we must not tire an audience that is waiting for miracles, or reveal too soon the secret workings of our tale.

ZEMINA.   Heaven forbid! May Farruscad and Cherestanì both perish before we bore our patrons.

## SCENE 2

*A forbidding desert with cliffs in the background. Scattered rocks which can be used as seats. Enter* TRUFFALDINO *and* BRIGHELLA, *arm in arm.*

BRIGHELLA.  Truffaldino, my old pal! How you doing? How the hell did you get here? What's up with the prince? Where did he get to? Is he all right? Why did you—

TRUFFALDINO.  Hold it. I'll tell you everything. It's an amazing tale. (*He sits down as if about to tell a children's story. His following narration is much in the style of an oral fairy tale.*) So, my friend, eight years back on April the twelfth—remember?—Prince Farruscad and Pantalone, the royal tutor, and a lot of huntsmen and me took off on a hunting trip. We left Tiflis and traveled for miles. And miles. And so, my friend, far away from the city we came to a tremendous forest, and saw a doe standing between two trees. A doe as white as snow, flowers all over her, gold chains and jewels hanging around her neck, rings on her hooves and diamonds glittering in her mane. The most gorgeous creature, the most *gorgeous* creature any two eyes could ever see. The prince fell madly in love with her, just like that, a doe! He ran toward her. She skipped off, disappeared among the trees. A very dainty doe. He raced after her. Pantalone raced after him. I raced after Pantalone. And so, my friend, we ran and ran, past maybe a hundred thousand trees. Every so often we could see the doe flitting ahead of us. She left the forest and stopped for a couple of seconds at a riverbank. The prince almost caught up. He almost grabbed her by the tail. Almost. But she jumped into the river. And vanished. And then—a miracle!

BRIGHELLA.  She drowned?

TRUFFALDINO.  Don't interrupt. This is important. The prince was desperate, in a frenzy. He made us drag the river. We had to find her, he said, dead or alive, because he was so crazy about her. And so, my friend, we fished for her and we fished for her, hours and hours it must have been. Didn't come up with a thing. When—

BRIGHELLA.  Another miracle?

TRUFFALDINO.  A wonder of wonders! All of a sudden the sweetest voice any two ears could ever hear came out of the water. It said, "Farruscad, follow me." The prince went berserk, plunged right into the river. Pantalone jumped in behind him, holding onto that beard of his. I would have gone too, except I didn't want to get wet. Not scared, mind you, just cautious. As I looked in the river, I saw a table loaded down with a big dinner, eighteen courses. Well, I thought, caution is one thing; loyalty to my prince is another. In I went. And then—another miracle. On the riverbed I found—

BRIGHELLA.   More food than any mouth could ever taste.

TRUFFALDINO.   No. The doe. But she'd turned into a princess, the most gorgeous creature, the most *gorgeous* creature any two eyes could ever see. A princess with her ladies-in-waiting. Delectable? Um-m-m. The prince was kneeling in front of her, and Pantalone was standing there like a dummy watching him. I heard Farruscad say, "O rare beauty! Who are you? Tell me and take pity on this poor heart, which has never before burned so fiercely."

BRIGHELLA.   And did she?

TRUFFALDINO.   Did she what?

BRIGHELLA.   Show any pity.

TRUFFALDINO.   I don't know what you'd call it. She replied, "You must not try to learn my name. In time, all will be revealed. Your loving impetuosity pleases me, and your heart is strong enough to bear terrifying trials. I accept you as my husband. Take my hand." The prince didn't give a hoot about the future. He swore he'd marry her. Pantalone argued, but they went into a palace with diamond columns, ruby doors, gold beams, you know the sort of thing. And so, my friend, the wedding took place, with Pantalone still arguing against it. Nine months later the princess had twins, a boy and a girl. The most gorgeous, the most *gorgeous* kids any two eyes could ever see. They named the boy Bedredino and the girl Rezia. That was, I guess, seven years ago. I had a great life in that palace, always plenty to eat and plenty of delicious ladies-in-waiting just, well, waiting. Pantalone never stopped worrying. He didn't know who the princess was or what country she came from. Every so often the prince would repeat, "O rare beauty! Who are you? Tell me and take pity on this poor heart, which has never before burned so fiercely." And the princess would reply, "You must not try to learn my name. In time, all will be revealed. Your loving impetuosity pleases me, and your heart is strong enough to bear terrifying trials. You are my husband—but all too soon there will come a time of terror for both of us." What a woman! All secrets, all mysteries! Three days ago, when the prince was forcing her desk to find a letter with her signature— she caught him at it. She went wild. Cried and told him off furiously for being so disobedient. Then she stamped her dainty little foot on the ground and—a miracle! The princess, the two kids, the ladies-in-waiting, the whole palace—gone. Not a trace. And this is where we found ourselves, in the desert.

BRIGHELLA   (*Ironically*). A miracle!—I don't believe a word of it.

TRUFFALDINO.   On my oath. On my mother's—no, leave my mother out of it. So how come you found us here?

BRIGHELLA.   Used my brains. How else? I brought along the grand vizier, Togrul. Also Tartaglia. And his stutter. Next to me, those two are the prince's most loyal advisers. You see, the king died.

TRUFFALDINO.   No!

BRIGHELLA.   I'm telling you.

TRUFFALDINO.   Poor old Atalmuc.

BRIGHELLA.   After eight years, he thought his son must be dead.

TRUFFALDINO.   So Farruscad is now king?

BRIGHELLA.   Yes, but from here on in, the story gets complicated. (*Rapidly*) Morgone, that ugly giant who's king of the Moors, demanded to marry the Princess Canzade, Farruscad's sister and daughter of his late majesty, and when she said no he attacked the kingdom and be-sieged the city, so her fiance Togrul, the grand vizier, rushed off to the cave of Geonca the magician to ask whether Farruscad was still alive and, if so, where, and Geonca told him to climb Mount Olympus and he'd find the prince there in a cavern—

TRUFFALDINO.   On Mount Olympus? A tavern?

BRIGHELLA.   A cavern, you nit. He also gave Togrul a fistful of weird spells and some belly patches.

TRUFFALDINO.   Poor Togrul. He had a cut, a boil, a boo-boo?

BRIGHELLA.   These are magic belly patches. The nourishment kind. You put one over your belly button, and you don't get hungry or thirsty for two months. So I brought Togrul and Tartaglia to Mount Olympus. The trip took us almost two months and our belly patches just about wore out. We entered the cavern, lit our torches and went in and down forty million, seven thousand, two hundred and four steps. And that's how we reached this desert.

TRUFFALDINO.  I don't believe it.

BRIGHELLA.  Ask Togrul and Tartaglia.

TRUFFALDINO.  Where are they?

BRIGHELLA.  Resting under a tree. Just around the corner there. What happened to the prince and Pantalone?

TRUFFALDINO.  They're searching the desert for Her Daintiness his wife. The prince is going off his chump trying to find her. But the two of 'em'll be back here by nightfall to eat and sleep.

BRIGHELLA.  Eat? What do you eat? I don't see a thing here except rocks and thorn bushes. They don't look very tasty.

TRUFFALDINO.  This is a funny place. It's like a restaurant, only better meals, and free. When you ask for food, it appears, just like that, cooked to a turn.

BRIGHELLA.  And you sleep on the sand?

TRUFFALDINO.  In tents. When the palace vanished, the tents appeared.

BRIGHELLA.  I don't believe it. How soon do the meals show up? After two months my belly patch is losing its strength.

TRUFFALDINO.  Come, I'll take you to the tents.

BRIGHELLA.  And Togrul? And Tartaglia? They'd like to eat too.

TRUFFALDINO.  Why not? We'll take 'em along. Later, I'll tell you about all the other wonders we've been through in the desert. A miracle . . . (*He continues his narration as they leave.*)

## SCENE 3

FARRUSCAD *and* PANTALONE

FARRUSCAD (*Entering, agitated*).  My search has failed, old friend. Will I never see my dearest Cherestanì again?[6]

PANTALONE. My brain is boiling, my head's frying. Your Highness, my boy, if we stay out in the sun all day we'll catch some horrible disease—inflammation of the kidneys, spotted fever, who knows? There aren't any doctors here, no surgeons, no apothecaries. We could die like animals. Dear boy, try to forget this enchantress.

FARRUSCAD. How could I? Forget so much love, tenderness, passion? My faithful old servant, I've lost everything—everything.

PANTALONE. Sure, tenderness, love, passion—but for what? What was she, anyway?

FARRUSCAD. The most noble, generous, lovable princess since the sun began to shine.

PANTALONE. A damned witch, you mean, who takes whatever form she wants. She must have five hundred years riding on her backside. I wish I had Angelica's magic ring—the one that showed Ruggiero how ugly the witch Alcina really was.[7] Then I could cure this poor boy and prove to him that his Cherestanì is really an old hag.

FARRUSCAD (*Dreamily, aside*). Beautiful silken hair, where are you now? Lost forever.

PANTALONE (*Parodying* FARRUSCAD *in an aside*). Mangy bald squash with four white hairs on your skin, show yourself in your true colors!

FARRUSCAD (*As above*). Brilliant eyes, stars! alas, where are you?

PANTALONE (*As above*). Sunken, bleary peepers, like a pooped-out nag's, let's get a look at you.

FARRUSCAD. Ruby lips, teeth like pearls, will I never see you again? Who took you from me?

PANTALONE. Purple gums, rotten with sores; fat lips, mouth brimming with black spit, damn you! Show up!

FARRUSCAD. Oh, cheeks like roses and lilies, who stole you from me?

PANTALONE. Floppy cheeks the color of dead fish, let him see what you really are! Cure this poor boy of his damnable fixation.

FARRUSCAD.   Beautiful breasts, bulging with her milk, where are you hidden?

PANTALONE.   Hairy bags of leather, dangling down to the waist, show your true selves and give this poor boy a knock on the noggin to wake him up. Your Highness, my lad, don't you remember that trick the witch Dilnovaz played on the king of Tibet?

FARRUSCAD.   What trick was that? What do you mean?

PANTALONE.   The witch was three hundred years old thanks to a magic ring she wore on her pinky. She made herself look like the wife of the king of Tibet, a beautiful little jewel only twenty years old. Then she had the queen exiled as an imposter. So, what happened? That witch was a first-class slut. One day the king caught her doing . . . well, you know, something he didn't like with a stranger. He couldn't help himself, he took a swipe at her with his sword, and by chance cut off her little finger, with the magic ring on it. On my word as a faithful servant, he saw her turn back into an old hag without a tooth in her mouth and with so many hairs on her chin, and so many wrinkles on her face she looked like a dead lump of beef. The king was lucky enough to find his wife again. The poor girl was going around begging for charity and singing those famous lines, "I'm a king's daughter, and yet I'm not. A princess, I am, but I'm not what I seem." I'll bet that Cherestanì is another witch, like Dilnovaz. If I'd only found her magic wand, I'd have . . .

FARRUSCAD.   Enough! I don't believe a word. How could Cherestanì be old if she bore me two babies? Oh, my lost children! (*He weeps.*)

PANTALONE   (*Sniffling*). They stole my heart, too, they did, the little darlings. Bedredino was some lively little boy; you could have high hopes for him. And my lovely, sweet Rezia . . . I can almost see them now, pulling away at my beard and calling me gramps. I shouldn't think about it—it makes my heart break. But Your Highness, we must face life bravely. After all, they were the children of a witch. Be strong. Forget you ever loved them.

FARRUSCAD.   I betrayed myself, Pantalone! I disobeyed my wife. "You may not know my name," she said, "until the proper time." I tried to, and she punished me. Curse my curiosity!

PANTALONE.   Some crime that is! Don't you have the right to know your wife's name? That rule, let me tell you, turned my stomach, and so did your marriage. Just think! Marrying a deer! How do you know she won't turn you into a stag? I still worry that you'll sprout horns one morning. You know what *I* think? We should thank heaven for getting rid of that witch. Now let's go. There must be some way out of this inferno and back to your father. Poor Atalmuc! Who knows how many tears he's shed for you? Who knows if he's alive, after all this time? Who knows if there's even a kingdom to go back to? His enemy, that barbarous Moor, King Morgone, wanted to marry your sister Canzade. You could end up a king without a kingdom, a wandering beggar for the rest of your life, the husband of a hag, of a witch, of a devil, may lightning blast her!

FARRUSCAD.    Silence, Pantalone! I swear I will die before I ever leave this place. I dreamed I saw my love here. I can almost see her standing before me. I beg my father's pardon, if he is alive. If he is dead, I still ask it—but I will comb this desert forever for my dearest Cherestanì. Rezia! Bedredino! my children, my wife! (*Exit distracted.*)

PANTALONE.    Poor old Pantalone! Let him go. I haven't enough breath left to follow.

## SCENE 4

*Enter* TOGRUL, TARTAGLIA, *and* PANTALONE.

TARTAGLIA    (*Enters upstage, sees* PANTALONE, *and is overcome with joy*). S-s-sir! T-t-togrul, Your Excellency!

TOGRUL    (*Entering*). What is it, Tartaglia?

TARTAGLIA.    Look, sir, Pantalone! See?

TOGRUL.    Is it possible? Heaven, I thank you! Tartaglia, we've found Farruscad.

PANTALONE    (*Seeing them from a distance*). Togrul . . . Tarta . . . It's getting worse . . . this heat is making me see things.

TARTAGLIA.    My dear Pantalone!

TOGRUL    (*Embracing* PANTALONE).    My old friend, I am so relieved to find you!

PANTALONE. Pardon me . . . sir . . . Excuse me, Tartaglia . . . I'm choked up . . . (*He faints;* TARTAGLIA *holds him up.*)

TARTAGLIA. Togrul, sir, the old fellow's dying but we still have no idea where the prince is. Pantalone, tell us where to find the prince. Then you can die in peace.

TOGRUL. Pantalone, my friend.

PANTALONE. (*Regaining consciousness*). Your honor, what brings you to this bleak place?

TOGRUL. That is a long story. First, where is Farruscad, my king? There's no time to waste.

PANTALONE. He's here, alive and well—but up to his eyes in trouble. Awful, just awful! I'll tell you about it. But I'm dying to hear how you reached this god-forsaken spot.

TOGRUL. I came with the help of Geonca, the wizard, together with Tartaglia and my servant Brighella. Geonca taught me many powerful spells to rescue my king from this nameless wasteland. And now— where is he?

PANTALONE. Geonca may have taught you a trick or two, the kind that are good for making your corns disappear. But none of them'll cure the prince's misery. It'll take more than that. Not like falling off a log, I promise you. If you think—

TARTAGLIA. Come on, old fellow, just say where he is. Don't give us a hard time.

TOGRUL. Pantalone, any delay could have the most fearsome consequences.

PANTALONE. He must be nearby. He goes out searching, then heads back here. But all your pleas won't get him to leave. If you know these powerful spells, like you say, we ought to hide so he doesn't see us. This'll take a lot of planning. I can't speak out in the open. I have deep secrets to tell you. But don't you need something to eat and drink?

TARTAGLIA. We sure do! My belly patch is losing its power, and I feel weak . . . famished.

PANTALONE. What belly patch?

TOGRUL. Let's go, Pantalone.

PANTALONE. Hide behind that bank, I'll be right with you. Tartaglia, didn't you say Brighella was with you too? Where is he?

TARTAGLIA. Somewhere around here.

PANTALONE. Oh, balls! If the prince sees him . . . But what are these spells the grand vizier mentioned?

TARTAGLIA. Astonishing! Listen to this. (*He whispers into Pantalone's ear.*)

PANTALONE. Holy cow! Maybe we do have some hope. Here, you take cover. If you see the prince, don't let him see you. The same with Brighella: give him a signal to hide and keep quiet. Then you come join us behind the bank. Let's pray the prince hasn't already seen him, so we can drag him away from this nonsense. (*Exit.*)

TARTAGLIA. Hey, Pantalone! What about some food? They leave me here with this belly patch pinning my gut together. It was only good for two months. If I don't get something to eat after fasting for fifty-nine days and five hours, I'll be the skinniest body ever buried. Still, this patch is great. Think how many poor people could use it! Father comes home with a pocketful of patches; the family's crying from hunger, and zap! One patch on everybody's belly button. That's the way to take care of their poverty. And how many actors, how many poets would go for it! How many con men with their phony remedies for loss of appetite! They could turn honest. Now I'd better hide, but I'm hungry enough to eat an ox raw! (*He hides.*)

### SCENE 5

FARRUSCAD; TARTAGLIA, *in hiding; a* WOMAN'S VOICE *offstage*

FARRUSCAD (*Enters, wildly*). I can't find her! Will I ever come to the end of my search through this grim desert? Cherestanì, don't be cruel. Don't spurn my sorrow. I disobeyed you, but now I beg your forgiveness. My adored wife, let me see you again if only for one moment. Let me kiss my children once more, then let me expire, that is all I ask.

TARTAGLIA   (*Behind* FARRUSCAD, *aside*).   Prince Farruscad! . . .
Yes, without a doubt. I'm so happy I can hardly restrain myself . . . I
want to hug him. (*He takes a few steps, then stops.*) Tartaglia, what are
you up to? Die of joy if you want, but don't forget your orders.

(*He hides again. A little table appears, set with food.*)

FARRUSCAD   (*Seeing the table*). No, I'll take no food. I want to perish
of hunger and sadness. What tyranny this is, to make me stay alive, but
in anguish. Every moment I die a thousand deaths.

TARTAGLIA   (*Upstage, behind him*). That table wasn't there before.
Who brought it in? I'm dying of hunger. Could I sneak off with a
mouthful of that food? (*He creeps toward the table.*)

OFFSTAGE VOICE.   Eat, Farruscad. Take your nourishment.

TARTAGLIA   (*Frightened*). A voice? What have those guys pushed me
into? (*He hides at the other side of the stage.*)

FARRUSCAD.   You are not my wife's voice, but a cruel stranger's. I
have resolved to die if I do not see my family again.

VOICE.   You will not die. You will learn the price of your disobedience.

TARTAGLIA   (*Again approaches the table to steal some food. The table slides
away from him and offstage. He runs to hide at the opposite side of the stage*).

FARRUSCAD.   Voice, how can I appease Cherestanì after I offended her
so deeply? I will do anything. (*He pauses to listen. No reply. He continues.*)
Answer! At least tell me if I will ever see her again, or my children? (*He
pauses again.*) Voice! It no longer answers me. I am unworthy, abandoned, alone. My counselors must now be gorging themselves on wine
and food. Only Farruscad is left in anguish. No, it is unfair to complain
about those who feel no passion. I must die alone. I cannot eat. Let
these stones be the final bed for my collapsing limbs. (*He sits on a stone,
puts his head on one arm, and sleeps.*)

TARTAGLIA   (*Reappears, upstage*). My head is spinning like a pinwheel,
blazing like a fireball. The marvels I've seen and heard! Aha! Looks as if
the prince is sleeping.

## SCENE 6

*Enter* TRUFFALDINO *and* BRIGHELLA, *carrying food.* TARTAGLIA *is in hiding.*

TRUFFALDINO   (*Shouting as he appears*). Brighella, where did you say they are? Yes, Togrul and Tartaglia. I don't see 'em.

(TARTAGLIA *lifts his head and makes wild arm signals for them to be quiet.*)

BRIGHELLA.   There he is! Hi, Tartaglia!

TARTAGLIA   (*Gesturing frantically, in a whisper*). Will you two stop yelling!

TRUFFALDINO   (*More noisily than before*). What's the matter, Tartaglia? Dropped your tongue down your throat?

TARTAGLIA   (*Whispering, gesturing*). For God's sake, keep your voices down!

TRUFFALDINO   (*Loudly*). Look at all this chow!

BRIGHELLA   (*Guffawing raucously*). Maybe he lost his appetite.

TARTAGLIA   (*Hoarsely*). Don't you see the prince?

TRUFFALDINO.   The what?

TARTAGLIA.   Prince.

BRIGHELLA.   Where?

TARTAGLIA.   There.

TRUFFALDINO.   Not dead?

TARTAGLIA.   Asleep.

BRIGHELLA.   Oh.

TRUFFALDINO.   Oh.

(*They tiptoe in a line around the prince, almost tripping over him, and circle the stage, still carrying the food, before they go off to eat.*)

## SCENE 7

PANTALONE *enters without his usual mask but disguised under huge mustaches and a flowing white beard that hides his normally scraggly one. He is wearing a gigantic miter, under which his usual mask is hidden, so that it can fall down onto his face when the miter is removed. He is wearing outlandish priestly vestments, under which is his normal costume. This should all be arranged to permit his transformation from priest to* PANTALONE. *When he is dressed as a priest, nothing about* PANTALONE *allows the audience to recognize him. Until his transformation back into* PANTALONE, *he mimes gestures to an* OFFSTAGE VOICE. *These gestures should be grave and dignified, appropriate to the behavior of an elderly priest.*

PANTALONE (*Enters upstage, miming gestures to an* OFFSTAGE VOICE). Farruscad! Awaken!

FARRUSCAD. My God! Whose voice is this?

PANTALONE. The voice of Checsaia, the hermit priest. Divine grace has given me the power to see all, and to assist those who obey heaven and scorn hell.

FARRUSCAD. Blessed Checsaia, heaven has surely sent you to help me. You can see all things, priest. Take pity on me—tell me where to find my children and Cherestanì.

PANTALONE. Hush! Never name that filthy witch, abhorred by heaven! I have come to free you; yes, drag you from the coils of that Circe, that barbarous, sinful temptress. Foolish boy! You became her prey, and now you must suffer to expiate the sin of having married her!

FARRUSCAD. Checsaia . . . Are you telling me? . . . No, impossible!

PANTALONE. Silence! Are you a man or a brute? I say disaster hangs over you. The animals, the trees, even the stones that you see here in this deserted valley, were once men. Every time the infamous, lascivious witch had sated her lust, she turned her lover into a beast, or a plant, or a rock . . . And they moan in unheard despair.[8]

FARRUSCAD (*Frightened*). My God! Can it be true?

PANTALONE.  Fool! Free yourself from your futile dreams, or you will be changed into a dragon with fire pouring out of your eyes, and poisonous slime dripping from your fangs. Filthy and deformed, you will drag your scaled belly through this desert, withering the grass as you mourn your misfortune.

FARRUSCAD  (*Still more frightened*). Save me, Checsaia! What must I do?

PANTALONE.  Follow me.

FARRUSCAD.  And abandon my children? I haven't the heart to.

PANTALONE.  Shame on you! Follow me. Banish the memory of such children, born of a filthy love, children of the darkness. Give me your hand.

FARRUSCAD.  I will follow you, holy one, but my heart stays here . . . I give myself into your hands.

(*He reaches toward the priest, who is suddenly transformed back into* PAN-TALONE. *Without realizing that the change has taken place,* PANTA-LONE *continues in his own voice.*)

PANTALONE.  You do well. Obey, Farruscad. My wise counsels and magic potions will help you to forget Cherestanì and your children, the abominable fruits of your marriage.

FARRUSCAD  (*Surprised at Pantalone's transformation*). What's this? Is Checsaia really Pantalone?

PANTALONE  (*Still not realizing that a change has occurred*). What! Madman, do you already go back on your resolution?

FARRUSCAD.  You insolent wretch! How dare you deceive and affront your king? Out of my sight!

PANTALONE  (*Looking around him*). Confound it, I *told* 'em their precious spells wouldn't work against that slut of a witch! (*Exit, running.*)

FARRUSCAD  (*Dreamily*). Cherestanì, you love me still, and want me to wait here for you . . . But now . . . this miracle?

## SCENE 8

TOGRUL *enters transformed into an old king, richly dressed—Atalmuc, Far-ruscad's father. An* OFFSTAGE VOICE *speaks for* TOGRUL, *who mimes appropriate gestures until transformed back into himself. This follows the pattern of the preceding scene.* TOGRUL *enters from the side of the stage opposite Pantalone's exit.*

TOGRUL.    It is indeed a miracle that the vile witch has power enough to subvert an act of charity and make a priest appear as your old tutor. I saw what happened.

(FARRUSCAD, *seeing his father, is shocked into immobility.* TOGRUL *advances, and continues.*)

Nothing is hidden from me. Listen, my son. He whom you saw as Pantalone is in truth Checsaia, the priest. Do not be misled by his change or his flight, for those are also the work of the witch.

FARRUSCAD    (*Confused*). Father! You here! In this desert? My dearest father! (*He runs to embrace him.*)

TOGRUL.    No closer. I was your father, now I am his implacable spirit. (*In a tearful voice*) I was destroyed by losing my son. For eight years I grieved. Finally my body yielded to my anguish and lay silent, cold ashes in a shallow grave. That was your doing.

FARRUSCAD.    My dear father! I caused your death? And now I behold you, in this form? The most beautiful woman ever seen held me here: my wife, who bore me two children. Three days ago, father, she disappeared, and . . .

TOGRUL.    No more! I should despise you. Cherestanì, the disgusting witch, held you in her thrall! She appeared to you as a doe and you, madman . . . I will not say how much more I know . . . I am horrified. If there is still a flicker of respect and love in your heart for your father, follow his ghost. My son, tear yourself away from this refuge for every filthy vice.

FARRUSCAD.    My father—I cannot explain the pain I feel at having lost you. Let this be the proof of my respect: I will follow where my father commands, tormented by remorse, confusion, and pain. Farewell, Cherestanì! You know the effort I must expend to leave.

TOGRUL. My son, I praise you. Follow me. (*He is about to set out, when he is transformed from Atalmuc back into* TOGRUL.)

FARRUSCAD (*Astonished*). Togrul, the grand vizier!

TOGRUL (*Proudly, in his own voice*). Your Highness, this witch's power is stronger than my magic. My faithful attempts to save you are useless, and I am bitterly dismayed.

FARRUSCAD. Arrogance! Insanity!

TOGRUL (*Grandly*). The madness is not mine, Your Highness. Your friend Geonca helped me here, although he said I might never drag you from your folly. But if the wizard's spells had no effect, at least be moved by the truth. Your father is dead, his realm attacked, destroyed by the Moorish king, Morgone. Our fields, our homes, our holy temples were sacked and scoured by steel and fire. Rape, ruin, and the blood of your subjects—these are the rewards of a blind prince who lives in sloth, far from his land, caught in the toils of a contemptible witch, and scorned by the gods.

FARRUSCAD. No more, Togrul, enough!

TOGRUL (*Boldly*). What do I have to fear? A lazy coward who abandons his subjects, his dear ones, to barbarism and torture? Your kingdom's capital, Tiflis, is by now probably destroyed. The brave Princess Canzade, your sister and my beloved, may be Morgone's captive, and vilely shamed. I alone had the courage to believe the faithful Geonca when he promised that if our Farruscad again appeared, a miracle would save the kingdom. I alone could leave my love in danger, leading your country's troops—a few frightened men. For what? To rescue my sovereign and save his realm. But what a kingdom! What a king! One may now be subdued, the other has been enslaved by an abominable woman. You forget your dead father, sister, your tortured subjects and defeated realm. You wallow here in your own harm. Farruscad, I know the path back from this place. If your kingdom's miseries or your own state cannot move you to act as you should, beware the wrath of heaven. And if my words cannot convince you, grant me this: pardon for a faithful counselor, who out of zeal has spoken far too frankly. (*He kneels.*)

FARRUSCAD. Togrul, say no more. It is late. Rest in one of these tents. Leave me on my own for a few moments, to contemplate my fate and my misfortunes. I promise that at dawn I'll go with you.

TOGRUL.   My lord, we should waste no time.

FARRUSCAD.   Go and rest for a few hours. I'll follow you.

TOGRUL.   Your Highness. (*Exit.*)

<br>

## SCENE 9

FARRUSCAD   (*Alone*). Oh, these thoughts . . . in turmoil . . . must I
go, leaving my children and my wife behind? But what kind of wife,
what kind of children are they, in truth? I would do better to depart
with no further thinking. Suspicions assail me, anxieties, passionate
yearnings. You were here, Cherestanì. Here I disobeyed you and you
took yourself and our children away—and the joyful palace, our home.
Joys? Or diabolical illusions? My father, my kingdom and my subjects,
my sweet sister, I must go to you and tear myself away from this sterile
land. (*Preparing to go*) I cannot stay, and yet . . . I wish . . . I can't . . .
(*He sits on a stone.*) This unexpected . . . strange sleepiness . . . must
mean . . . something . . . (*He falls asleep.*)

<br>

## SCENE 10

FARRUSCAD, CHERESTANÌ, *retinue of* LADIES-IN-WAITING.
*While* FARRUSCAD *sleeps, the desert is transformed into a garden. The
background changes from a desert, cliffs, and boulders to a magnificent, shining palace. Meanwhile, sweet orchestral music is playing. The music ends with
a loud, boisterous allegro vivace.* FARRUSCAD *is awakened by the noise,
and looks around in amazement.*

FARRUSCAD.   What! Where am I? What beautiful music is this? (*He
sees the palace and jumps to his feet.*) My wife's palace. Oh, what a sweet
dream! If so, may it never end!

(*He runs to the palace, from which* CHERESTANÌ *emerges richly dressed and
majestic. She is followed by a retinue of* LADIES-IN-WAITING. *Overjoyed,* FARRUSCAD *continues.*)

Cherestanì . . . Cherestanì . . .

CHERESTANÌ   (*With noble sadness*). Cruel husband! You wanted to
leave and forget your wife.

FARRUSCAD.   My counselors . . .

CHERESTANÌ.   Yes, they came to take you away from me with their magical arts, but my power made them fail.

FARRUSCAD.   But my father . . .

CHERESTANÌ.   Yes, he died of sorrow after losing you.

FARRUSCAD.   My kingdom . . .

CHERESTANÌ.   Flows with rivers of blood. It has been sacked and put to the torch. Your sister is in danger. But Farruscad, you loved me, as I loved you, as I love you still. I cannot tell you how stricken I feel to have caused so many horrors. But I am controlled by the stars. My fate and my love for you force me to seem ruthless toward you. I am condemned to make you suspect that I am a witch, ugly and deformed—all because of my fervent love for you. (*She weeps.*)

FARRUSCAD.   Please don't cry, my love. If you cared for me, why did you abandon me?

CHERESTANÌ.   You disobeyed me. You sought to know my name.

FARRUSCAD.   You love me? Then can't you tell me who you are, your father and your country?

CHERESTANÌ.   I cannot say. Oh, how much your curiosity afflicts me! Your love is not yet sure. You still mistrust me because you do not know my identity. Don't you see how your doubts insult my love? You are ruled by your curiosity. Tomorrow, alas, it will be satisfied. I must pay the penalty for my love. I know your heart is not faithful enough to withstand all you will see tomorrow, and so your Cherestanì will die. The sun will rise bloodred tomorrow through dark air, the earth will tremble, and Farruscad will no longer find refuge in this land, for at last he will know who I am. Then he will repent and weep in vain for the misery of his wife, who will suffer the punishment alone. (*She weeps.*)

FARRUSCAD.   No, my love, don't cry. If only my counselors could behold such beauty in such pain, they would appreciate my passion. Cherestanì, what destiny? . . . what stars? . . . Oh, you heavens . . . Why am I—why are we both—so afflicted? For pity's sake, let me know more!

CHERESTANÌ.   I cannot tell you more. My love makes me torment both you and myself. Tomorrow is the fatal day for me. Farruscad, I beg you—calmly endure what you will witness. Do not seek an explanation. There is a reason for everything. Above all, never curse Cherestanì. Although I know you will.

FARRUSCAD   (*Agitated*). You frighten me with these secrets. I can't understand . . . I'm baffled . . . desperate . . .

CHERESTANÌ   (*Tenderly taking him by the hand*). Farruscad, will you endure it?

FARRUSCAD.   If it costs my life.

CHERESTANÌ.   I wish I could believe that. Tell me again . . . you won't curse me?

FARRUSCAD.   I would stab myself first in the heart.

CHERESTANÌ.   Swear it . . . No, I don't mean that! Don't swear, my love. You would only break your word, and my life depends on your vow.

FARRUSCAD.   By the most sacred gods of heaven, I swear it.

CHERESTANÌ   (*Flinging away from him*). And *I* was the one to drag that fatal promise from you! Now I cannot escape the sentence. Farruscad, my life depends on your courage and faithfulness. But no, I am lost. Your love can never reinstate me. (*Again taking his hand*) Dearest husband, I must go now.

FARRUSCAD.   No, no . . . Why? Our children, where are they?

CHERESTANÌ.   You will see them tomorrow. If only you were blind, and could not!

FARRUSCAD.   Blind? What do you mean?

SCENE 11

*Enter* FARZANA, *followed by* LADIES-IN-WAITING.

FARZANA.   Cherestanì . . .

CHERESTANÌ.   Yes, my father is dead, and now my woes begin. Poor Father! (*She weeps.*)

FARZANA.   From every mountain and shore your name echoes. Crowds of your subjects clamor for Cherestanì; they want their queen. Your kingdom and crown await you. Do not delay.

CHERESTANÌ.   Farruscad, I must leave you. You have heard in part who I am, but you do not know all. My kingdom is hidden from the world, but it is many times larger than Tiflis. Rest if you can until the new day, and then be faithful and firm of heart. May your anguish not exceed the misfortunes of your wife. (*She goes into the palace with the retinue of* LADIES-IN-WAITING *and* FARZANA.)

FARRUSCAD   (*Following her*). Let me follow . . . Let me come with you and die beside you.

(*When he tries to enter the palace, thunder rolls, lightning flashes, and the ground shakes. The palace and garden vanish, and the stage is again the desert—in darkness.* FARRUSCAD, *in a frenzy, groping with his hands in front of him, continues.*)

Oh, counselors and you gods! Cherestanì is a queen, the daughter of a mortal. Listen to these marvels, listen! (*Exit.*)

## Act Two

*The same desert*

### SCENE 1

*Enter* TRUFFALDINO *and* BRIGHELLA.

TRUFFALDINO.   Brighella, what was that din last night?

BRIGHELLA.   Din?

TRUFFALDINO.   Noise, uproar! Didn't you hear it?

BRIGHELLA.   Not a peep. That scrumptious grub, that glorious wine . . . I slept like a corpse. Thank you, God, for sending me here. Truffaldino, this is what I call easy living. Even if that meal came from Satan himself, I don't give a damn, it was so great.

TRUFFALDINO.   True enough. We're much better off in this desert than we ever were in the city. Back there in the palace you cook and carry the food; you don't get to taste it.

BRIGHELLA.   Except maybe scraps. And the wine left in the glasses. When nobody's looking.

TRUFFALDINO.   You stand and watch those courtiers pretending not to lick their delicate fingers.

BRIGHELLA.   And your tongue's hanging out. Once I almost bit mine off.

TRUFFALDINO.   Who'd want to be a servant? They keep you on your feet all day and wake you up in the middle of the night. Yes, master. No, ma'am. They remember every stupid little job they asked you to do like taking out the chamber pots and scraping out the stables and burying the garbage.

BRIGHELLA.   They have such good memories. How come they always forget payday?

TRUFFALDINO.   You take those servants in the comedies. They don't get beaten as much as we do. That's what I like about 'em. Smarter than their masters, too, every time. When the master falls for a beautiful girl, who wins her for him?

BRIGHELLA.   The servant.

TRUFFALDINO.   And three months later, when she finds she's pregnant . . . ?

BRIGHELLA.   The servant.

TRUFFALDINO.   Right. Now Arlecchino—he could pull the wool over any master's eyes. That's why the upper crust don't laugh at him the way I do. He makes fools of them. They say his pratfalls and horsing around are dumb. I don't. He kills me, that Arlecchino. Gets away with murder. You'd have to stick a pin up your ass to stop laughing at the stunts he pulls.[9]

BRIGHELLA.   I know. These days when I go to the theatre and look around at all the hoity-toity types, I have to laugh under my coat.

TRUFFALDINO.   Sometimes, though, he's so funny you'll see the gentry laugh out loud, real belly laughs. Can't stop themselves, the lousy fakes. Me, I couldn't be happier about escaping from that world, all those people who struggle so goddam hard to be serious and all the time they look ridiculous. I enjoy this desert. You're alone. You're your own boss. The air is clean—

BRIGHELLA.   Fresh enough to give you an appetite.

TRUFFALDINO.   Sure is.

BRIGHELLA.   For breakfast!

TRUFFALDINO.   God almighty, I almost forgot about breakfast. What the devil are we going to ask for?

BRIGHELLA.   Tell him I want something first class, something with a fancy sauce for starters.

TRUFFALDINO.   None of that fancy crap for me. All I ask is a meal fit for a gourmet from Venice. Like . . . stewed eels.

BRIGHELLA.   Too squirmy.

TRUFFALDINO.   And broiled larks . . .

BRIGHELLA.   Too many bones.

TRUFFALDINO.   An ocean of rice . . .

BRIGHELLA.   I'd rather have ravioli.

TRUFFALDINO.   A mountain of polenta . . .

BRIGHELLA.   No good, Truffaldino. Too fattening.

TRUFFALDINO.   Brighella! Since when are you on a diet?

(*They go out, arguing fiercely.*)

SCENE 2

*As* TRUFFALDINO *and* BRIGHELLA *depart, enter, from the opposite side,* PANTALONE *and* TARTAGLIA, *trembling and looking over their shoulders.*

PANTALONE.   I thought it would never stop.

TARTAGLIA.   The noise?

PANTALONE.   All night. Did you sleep, Tartaglia?

TARTAGLIA.   Not a wink. I heard this dripping sound and stuck my hand out of the tent. What do you think? Black rain. Look at these spots.

PANTALONE   (*Examining Tartaglia's hand*). Horrible. It never rains that sort of filth in Venice.

TARTAGLIA.   And the owl hooting.

PANTALONE.   The dogs howling.

TARTAGLIA *and* PANTALONE   (*Together*). All night, nonstop!

TARTAGLIA.   Thank goodness for one thing. The prince'll be ready to leave at dawn. Or so Togrul told me.

PANTALONE.   That's good. But look.

TARTAGLIA.   Where?

PANTALONE.   There. The sun. It's coming up red as blood.

TARTAGLIA   (*Quaking*). Oh, my God, I see trees that have dried out, and mountains that have shifted from where they were yesterday, streams of purple-black water, terrifying clouds—Help! Pantalone, they're coming down at us!

PANTALONE.   Signs. Signs of an evil day.

TARTAGLIA.   Let's run, before they fall on us.

PANTALONE.   No, Tartaglia. We mustn't abandon the prince.

TARTAGLIA.   Let's save him. But where is he?

## Scene 3

*Enter* FARRUSCAD *and* TOGRUL.

TOGRUL.   Your Highness, nothing you have told me must weaken your resolve—your fears are all the more reason for us to hurry away.

FARRUSCAD.   I am troubled, Togrul. I lack the strength to leave. Ill luck hangs over me, ready to fall. I must stay and endure it. "The sun will rise bloodred tomorrow." That is what she said—and there it hangs. "The earth will tremble, the air will be dark"—all true, every word. "And Farruscad will no longer find refuge in this land"—yes, I know that I must follow you. And then these ghastly words that tear my heart: "At last he will know who I am. Then he will repent and weep in vain for the misery of his wife, who will suffer the punishment alone."

TOGRUL.   These are infernal arts, cruel snares. You must escape them at once. You swore to come with us—remember? This enchantress is an ally of your enemy Morgone. She is seeking to destroy your realm, and you yourself, in some mysterious fashion.

PANTALONE   (*To* TARTAGLIA). I choke up, watching this poor boy change into an idiot. You go help him out; I'm too upset. I can't do anything but drop tears.

TARTAGLIA   (*To* PANTALONE). There are three of us here—Truffaldino and Brighella must be close by. Between the five of us we can tie him up and carry him off.

FARRUSCAD   (*Aside*). "Farruscad, I beg you—calmly endure what you will witness. Do not seek an explanation. There is a reason for everything. Tomorrow you will see your children. If only you were blind, and could not!" (*To the others*) My friends . . . Oh, God! Who knows what I will have to suffer!

SCENE 4

*After a flash of lightning and a long roll of thunder enter* BEDREDINO *and* REZIA.

PANTALONE   (*Overjoyed*). What do you mean, suffer? It's my little bunnies, my sweetykins! (*He runs to hug them.*) My little honeys, my chickabiddies—nobody's going to take you away again from your grandpa Pantalone, you beautiful little poopers.

FARRUSCAD.   My precious Rezia and Bedredino! Your mother told me I would see you again. (BEDREDINO *and* REZIA *kiss Farruscad's hand.*)

TOGRUL.   Beautiful children! What a miracle! I can hardly believe it.

TARTAGLIA.   I'm flabbergasted! How did those two cute little pissers get here?

FARRUSCAD.   Rezia, my dear daughter, where is your mother?

REZIA.   Father, she . . . Bedredino, do you know where she is?

BEDREDINO.   She was in a lovely, shining palace, Father, and musical instruments were playing and crowds of happy people were all shouting—it gave me a headache. They crowned her queen . . . But I don't know the name of the city.

REZIA.   Bedredino and I were in a pretty room, Father, with hundreds of servants . . . Oh, if only you could have seen it!

FARRUSCAD.   How did you get here?

BEDREDINO.   I don't know, do you Rezia?

REZIA.   I know just what you know. I think a big wind brought us here in a flash.

PANTALONE.   Listen to that. A wind, she says . . . a wind!

FARRUSCAD.   What did your mother say before you were sent here?

REZIA.   She came to our room. She looked hard at us. She sighed. She sat down. Then she started to cry. We ran over to her, and took her hands, and kissed them. But she cried harder. She put one arm around Bedredino and the other around me, then she kissed us both over and over. She couldn't stop crying. I started to cry too. So did Bedredino, didn't you? We were all crying. We didn't know why.

FARRUSCAD.   What can this mean? What did she say?

BEDREDINO.   She scared me. "Go to your father," she said. "Poor children, if only I'd never given birth to you! Now you'll have to suffer. Now your mother must be cruel. And cruel to herself! Go ahead of me to your father; I will join you shortly. Tell him how much I have wept for you." As soon as she said that, an unknown force swept us into the air. It brought us here. I'm frightened! (*He cries.*)

REZIA. Bedredino, you're crying again. You're making me cry too. Please, Father, save us from the bad things that are going to happen! (*She cries.*)

TOGRUL. Farruscad, why delay? Save your children from this inferno.

FARRUSCAD. No, I must face my ordeal here. I will not disobey my wife.

PANTALONE (*Determined*). Tartaglia, take the boy's hand; I'll take care of my girl. Oh, you poor little beggars. Gone to sleep, have we? (*He goes to pick up* REZIA.)

TARTAGLIA. I'm ready for anything, Pantalone, if you are.

(*He goes to pick up* BEDREDINO. *Thunder and special effects.* CHERE-STANÌ *appears wearing a crown and followed by a retinue of* LADIES-IN-WAITING *and* SOLDIERS. *Everyone cowers.*)

SCENE 5

*Enter* CHERESTANÌ *and her retinue.*

PANTALONE. Here she is! Look! The witch! No time to get away. (*He runs back to his former place.*)

TARTAGLIA. Wait for me! I'm not ready for this! (*He runs back to his former place.*)

CHERESTANÌ. Don't take another step. You cannot rescue those children from the fate they were born for.

TOGRUL. Such majesty! Such beauty! At last I understand my prince's behavior.

CHERESTANÌ. My children, my dear babies.

REZIA (*Taking her hand*). What's the matter, Mother? Why are you crying?

CHERESTANÌ. (*Still crying*). My little ones . . . I want what I do not want. I must do what I cannot do . . . I weep for you and for me and for your father. (*She embraces them, weeping.*)

FARRUSCAD.   Cherestanì, must you still make me suffer? What are your tears for? What is this fate in store for my children? Kill me, if you must, with a single blow, but don't prolong my torment.

TARTAGLIA   (*Softly*). What are these mysteries, Pantalone?

PANTALONE.   So mysterious that if I don't burst today, I'll live forever.

CHERESTANÌ.   Farruscad, your vow! You have begun to waver. Never ask the reason for what you see. Keep silent. Whatever befalls, do not curse me! Before the day is over, if you are faithful and brave, you shall be the happiest man alive. All that you will see proceeds from my love for you. I can tell you nothing more. Be silent. You must endure everything you see. Believe me, I am being harsher on myself than on you. From now on our unmerciful trial has started. (*Weeping*) Alas for my children! (*A chasm appears upstage: flames roar out of it.*) Soldiers, take these children and throw them into the flames. (*She covers her face.*)

REZIA.   Father! Help!

BEDREDINO.   Father, father! Oh, gods!

(*The two children race offstage, pursued by two* SOLDIERS.)

TOGRUL.   Stop this! (*He draws his sword and immediately freezes into immobility.*)

PANTALONE.   "All that you will see proceeds from my love for you." Ha! Hold it there! Cut it out, you scum! (*He draws his sword and freezes.*)

TARTAGLIA.   Leave this to me, Pantalone!

(*He freezes like the others. The two* SOLDIERS *reenter, carrying dolls that are close likenesses of the children, which they throw into the flaming chasm. The children's screams are heard. The chasm closes.*)

PANTALONE   (*To* CHERESTANÌ). Demon! Harpy! Oh, this mother! My poor bunnies! (*He weeps.*)

TARTAGLIA.   May lightning sizzle this woman to ashes!

TOGRUL.   I cannot contain myself. For pity's sake, let us escape.

FARRUSCAD.   You cruel—

CHERESTANÌ.   Silence, Farruscad! Remember your vow! I beg your forgiveness. Your wife has not yet come to the cruelest point of her trial. Farruscad, leave. There is no refuge for you here. Go back to your kingdom. Disaster has overtaken it. You are needed there. Run to that hill, you and your followers. A supernatural force will sweep you up. Before long you will know much more suffering, but less than mine. We may meet once again, but through your own barbaric fault it will be the last time you see me in a pleasing form. You will betray my love and break your promise. Because of your cowardice, I will wear a hideous shape for centuries.

(*With crashing thunder and great bolts of lightning,* CHERESTANÌ *and her retinue disappear. The others remain, frightened and astonished.*)

PANTALONE.   What more do you want? Waiting to have your butt fried?

TARTAGLIA.   You couldn't get me to stay here if you cut off my legs!

TOGRUL.   My prince, come out of your stupor.

FARRUSCAD.   This hellish desert—and my lost children! Why can I not die of sorrow? My friends—we must run to the hill! I will curse myself, not my wife. To the hill, all of you! (*Exit with* TOGRUL.)

TARTAGLIA.   To the hill! Run, Pantalone! The witch! (*Exit.*)

PANTALONE.   She won't scorch *my* rear end. (*He runs off.*)

SCENE 6

*Enter* TRUFFALDINO, *shaking his head and blinking, and* BRIGHELLA, *wiping his tongue as if dashing something obnoxious from it onto the ground.*

TRUFFALDINO.   What a breakfast, Brighella! What a letdown! All those mouth-watering dishes . . .

BRIGHELLA.   And suddenly, on the way into our mouths . . .

TRUFFALDINO.   They turn into slimy toads.

BRIGHELLA.   And giant scorpions.

TRUFFALDINO.   And spitting snakes.

BRIGHELLA.   Truffaldino, this desert is not what it was.

TRUFFALDINO.   Not by a long shot. It's a chamber of horrors.

BRIGHELLA.   A grisly prison.

TRUFFALDINO.   A death trap.

BRIGHELLA.   That meal put me off food forever. At least till lunch.

TRUFFALDINO.   Let's get away before something terrible happens to us.

BRIGHELLA.   Where are the others?

TRUFFALDINO   (*Scanning, with his hand over his brow like an eyeshade*). Aha, I see them. Over there.

BRIGHELLA.   They're moving away. Quick, after them! (*They run out, yelling, "Hi! Stop! Wait up!"*)

SCENE 7

*A room of the palace in Tiflis.* SMERALDINA *and* CANZADE, *armed and dressed as Amazons*

SMERALDINA   (*Carrying a scimitar*). My heart is racing, as if those devils were close behind me. I must have chopped down five hundred, but there is an ocean of them left. And I don't see my mistress anywhere. Canzade, beloved princess! She's so reckless, always taking terrible risks. Just imagine, we attacked the enemy camp with only a thousand men, against more than a hundred thousand merciless Moors. Who knows what they've done to her? If Morgone has taken her prisoner, it's good-by Canzade! That giant could smash a wall flat with his head. Poor Canzade . . .

SCENE 8

*Enter* CANZADE.

CANZADE   (*Carrying a drawn scimitar*). Smeraldina! We have lost.

SMERALDINA.   Oh, my dear princess! Heaven be praised. How did you escape, my lady? What happened?

CANZADE.   Fury and despair drove me. I spurred my horse deep into the enemy's troops, clearing the way with my sword, and left a trail of dead horses and dying soldiers. In my rage, I called out to challenge the barbarous Morgone. I was ready to die if I could slice off his evil head. I showered him with sword thrusts, slashing right and left. Desperately, he tried to strike back with his iron mace, but my horse jumped to one side and his blow went wide. He howled like a raging lion as blood spouted from the wounds I gave him. A crowd of soldiers rushed at me. The air was thick with arrows. I thought my time had come. But Morgone, in love with me still, despite his wounds, swore to kill the soldiers if they hurt me, and ordered them to take me alive. I saw how foolish I had been to get cut off from my own troops. I spurred my horse through the surrounding soldiers, striking again and again as my sword whistled through the air. Finally I reached the bridge. The horde of enemies behind me hamstrung my horse, cut him from under me. In desperation, I turned my sword against the bridge, and struck—once! twice! against a supporting beam. It groaned under the weight of that crowd of armored men, and the floor of the bridge gave way. Horses, knights, beams, and boards crashed down into the river. I seized a chain dangling from a standing pillar, and hung on for dear life until our troops helped me to safety.

SMERALDINA.   I'm shivering just listening to you. I was quicker to save my skin, and was here alone, crying over your death. The gods be praised you're alive.

CANZADE.   Perhaps not for long. Morgone is enraged. He is preparing to assault the city. We're too weak to defend ourselves. My beloved Togrul is gone, my brother probably dead—that Moor will soon be here, but before he takes me I will plunge a knife into my breast.

SMERALDINA   (*Looking off into the wings*). My lady . . . Look! Your brother! And the grand vizier! Hurray! Hurray!

## SCENE 9

*Enter* FARRUSCAD *and* TOGRUL.

CANZADE.   Farruscad, Togrul, what heavenly power has brought you back? If only you had not come too late. (*She weeps.*)

TOGRUL.   Take heart, my lady.

FARRUSCAD.   Sister, your tears fill me with remorse. This familiar place—it reminds me of my father. His death was my fault, and I seem to hear him rebuke me. I wish I could die! (*He weeps.*)

SMERALDINA.   Togrul, sir, where's Tartaglia, where's Brighella? Are old Pantalone and Truffaldino . . . dead?

TOGRUL.   No, they're alive, in another room, telling the king's counselors their adventures.

SMERALDINA.   Adventures? I want to hear them, too! Truffaldino, alive . . . I'm so happy! (*Exit.*)

### Scene 10

FARRUSCAD, CANZADE, *and* TOGRUL

TOGRUL.   My prince and princess, we must not waste time weeping for what can't be changed. Think instead of how we can save the city.

FARRUSCAD   (*To* CANZADE). Canzade, dearest sister, tell me—how does my kingdom fare?

CANZADE.   Tiflis is defeated. The brutal Morgone is preparing his final assault. Our resistance has collapsed. Nearly all the soldiers are dead. Since the start of the siege half the civilians have perished of hunger. When our supplies ran out we ate horses, dogs, other pets. And worse! I cannot speak of it without shuddering. Living men fed on the dead, fathers on their sons, sons on their fathers; the bodies of husbands became meals for their famished wives. Sobs and screams echoed through the city. The people heaped curses on your head. You and I remain alive, with a few faithful servants, but the rest is gone.

TOGRUL.   What did I tell you, Farruscad?

FARRUSCAD.   Don't load me down with more pain—I'm sick enough with anguish. Oh, Father! You and my dead subjects need not ask the heavens for revenge. I have been punished already.

CANZADE.   Brother, your desperation does not move me. We have only one hope left. Your counselor Badur went, by secret paths, to seek provisions. Perhaps he will find them. Then, with your strength, we may defeat the Moors. Badur must be on his way back, not far off now. Heaven keep him safe, and help him to relieve us.

TOGRUL. I will not give up yet. The wizard Geonca promised that when Farruscad returned the kingdom would be saved in some mysterious fashion. This is possibly what he meant.

FARRUSCAD (*Looking off into the wings*). Is that not Badur? I recognize him. Badur, tell us swiftly—do you bring us life or death?

SCENE II

BADUR *enters with two* SOLDIERS, *who carry baskets filled with bottles of liqueurs.*

BADUR. You, here, my lord!

FARRUSCAD. Yes, but did you find food to relieve the siege? Or must I kill myself in despair? Tell me at once.

BADUR. I bring only news of death and misfortune.

CANZADE. Could you find no provisions?

BADUR. Yes, and I had them with me, but . . . God! What happened seems impossible.

TOGRUL. Why do you keep the news from us?

FARRUSCAD. Quickly! I want to know, even if your words shatter our last hope.

BADUR. On the way back to Tiflis with our wagonloads of meat and drink, wine and fodder, we were attacked on the banks of the river Cur. Not by Morgone, but by a huge troop of ferocious soldiers, unlike any I had ever seen, dressed in golden robes and jewels. A queen led them, more beautiful than any living woman. She cried out to her soldiers, "Destroy these provisions and anyone who defends them!" The soldiers overwhelmed us in just a few moments. We could put up no defense. That heartless woman threw the food we had hauled such a distance into the river. Afterward, she came to me and said proudly, "Tell Farruscad, my husband, what I have done here." Then she disappeared in a flash of lightning. I had taken a hundred men with me. Ninety-eight were killed in her attack. Only these two remain alive, and these few bottles of liqueur are all the provisions that we have left. (*He shows the bottles.*) Can they restore your strength a little?

TOGRUL.  Unnatural enchantress! She has blasted your last hopes of saving your life and kingdom. Did I not tell you she must be Morgone's ally, using her magic to snatch your dear ones from you: your father, kingdom, subjects, and now your life.

CANZADE.  Your own wife! So cruel? Now, Farruscad, we are finished.

FARRUSCAD.  Enough! At last I understand. But it's too late; there is no escape. That pitiless woman sent me here to see this final massacre, to realize my misery, and then to die in despair. I'm blind with fury. My father lost . . . and my children killed in such a gruesome way . . . My kingdom in shreds, and my life. All my own fault! So many innocent people have perished. Oh, gods! How can you allow such evil deeds? "Withstand it all?" "Do not curse me?" What is left for me to do but curse you, vicious creature, hell's own witch? I curse the moment when I first saw you, I damn you as a demon from hell. But curses cannot lighten my sorrow.

## Scene 12

*The ground shakes, lightning flashes, and there are several thunderclaps. Enter* CHERESTANÌ.

CHERESTANÌ.  Treachery! Now I am lost forever. (*She weeps.*)

CANZADE.  She is . . . ?

TOGRUL.  Yes, the evil monstrosity your brother married, the cause of our plight.

BADUR.  My prince, this is the woman who attacked us.

FARRUSCAD.  Give me back my father, my kingdom, give me back my children! Take away the misery you have created! Your spells have emptied my life, and soon they will remove that.

CHERESTANÌ.  You have betrayed my love. Only one more test, and the ordeal was over. You would have been happy. God, give me the strength to make him repent . . . Give me one more minute so that I may tell him what I was forced to keep a secret . . . One more moment to prove my innocence and my love for him. After that I will yield to my cruel fate.

FARRUSCAD.   The same mysteries. You still have something to say to me? Speak.

CHERESTANÌ.   Then listen. My father was mortal, my mother an immortal of the fairy kingdom. Like her, I was born to live forever in Eldorado, a realm unknown to you of earth. I did not want to continue in that life. I could not bear the fate that makes us change our shape from time to time, living for a span in the form of wild beasts, suffering misfortunes at the hands of men and infinite tortures at the end of time. I fell in love with you . . . A fatal moment! I took you for my husband. More and more, I wished to become mortal, to unite with you during life, to die with you, and accompany you still after death. I asked our king to grant my wish. He raged and threatened. Finally he agreed, but on these conditions: "Go," he said, "you may give up your immortality, if for eight years and one day your husband does not curse you. But I command that on the last day you must commit so many apparently atrocious acts that Farruscad will be sorely provoked. And if he curses you, then a slimy garment of scales will enclose you. Your fair shape will turn into a monster's. You will be a serpent for two hundred years. . ." You cursed me, and now the change is coming over me. We will not see each other again.

FARRUSCAD.   *Apparently* atrocious acts? I have lost my kingdom. I am near death. You have destroyed our last hope of aid—all this is only *apparent*?

CHERESTANÌ.   You need not fear for your life or your kingdom. I had reasons for everything I did, as I assured you. (*Pointing at* BADUR) This man is a traitor. His provisions were poisoned. He is in league with your enemy Morgone. Now you know why I waylaid him.

BADUR   (*Frightened, aside*). My God! I'm done for. (*To* CHERESTANÌ) You wicked enchantress! (*To* FARRUSCAD) My lord, she is lying.

CHERESTANÌ.   Be silent, traitor! Drink some of these liqueurs that you saved from the provisions. Prove who is telling the truth.

BADUR   (*Desperate*). My lord . . . I regret it's true . . . I have betrayed you . . . These are poison. But I will evade the shame of a felon's death by taking my life with my own hand . . . (*He draws a dagger, stabs himself, and staggers into the wings.*)

CANZADE.   This is all unbelievable. Togrul, tell me . . .

TOGRUL.   I am too bewildered. Let us see what happens.

FARRUSCAD.   But I don't . . . Togrul . . . Canzade . . . I'm trembling . . . Cherestanì: did you only *seem* to burn my children?

CHERESTANÌ.   The magic flames did not kill them, only purged them of their immortality. (*She looks off.*) Here they are, mortal now, like their father. Faithless man! I must now abandon you, change my shape to that of a foul and solitary serpent, lost to my children and to you. (*She weeps.*)

## SCENE 13

*Enter* BEDREDINO *and* REZIA, *escorted by two* SOLDIERS.

FARRUSCAD.   Children . . . My children . . . But may the rest of what you say not come true . . . Cherestanì, I could not live with the misery and remorse.

CANZADE   (*To* TOGRUL). This poor soul . . .

TOGRUL.   Say nothing!

CHERESTANÌ   (*Very agitated*). I feel . . . I feel . . . cold down to my bones . . . Oh, God, I am changing . . . The horror! The revulsion . . . The pain . . . Farruscad, I leave you. You could still free me. No, I cannot hope for that! It would take too much strength. Do not risk your life; your life is precious to me even when I cannot be near you. I have few powers left, but let me do what little I can for you and your kingdom, as the last proof of my love. Vizier . . . Canzade . . . my children . . . hide your faces . . . Do not watch your mother's agony! Go! I am ashamed to have you see. Farruscad, you alone shall watch. You, who brought this base transformation upon me. May you find satisfaction in what you have done! (*From the neck down, she is transformed into a long, writhing serpent, then falls to the ground.*)

BEDREDINO.   Mother! Mother!

REZIA.   My mother . . .

FARRUSCAD. Cherestanì! Forgive me . . . My wife . . . (*He runs to embrace her.*)

CHERESTANÌ. I am no longer yours. You broke your promise. Away from me! (*She slithers down through a trapdoor in the stage.*)

CANZADE. Brother!

TOGRUL. Prince . . .

BEDREDINO. Father . . .

REZIA. My dear father . . .

FARRUSCAD (*In a frenzy*). Away from me, all of you. Earth, you have taken my beloved. Now you must welcome me as well. (*Exit, possessed.*)

CANZADE (*Taking the children by the hand*). Togrul, children, quickly— after your father. (*Exeunt.*)

## Act Three

*The scene remains the same.*

### Scene 1

FARRUSCAD *and* PANTALONE. FARRUSCAD *enters, fleeing everyone who would like to console him.*

FARRUSCAD. Away from me, all of you! You are the cause. You made me so suspicious and enraged that I cursed my wife and brought about her ruin and mine. Out of my sight! Leave me to die! That is all I want, death.

PANTALONE. Your Majesty, God knows I'm sorry. My heart aches for you. Yes, you're right, you're right. But what can we do now? At least you have your children. King Morgone is attacking the city. You must try and save it for them, if not for yourself. The grand vizier and your sister, poor beleaguered things, are readying our defense, but they're discouraged because you aren't there. Cheer up, boy, snap out of it! Show yourself at the walls. See how your faithful subjects take heart as soon as you appear. Each one will fight as hard as a hundred men, and we'll run those stinking Moors right off our land. We'll whip their asses till they scatter like flapping partridges.

## SCENE 2

*Enter* TARTAGLIA.

TARTAGLIA.   Your Majesty! Your Majesty! A miracle! All of a sudden, nobody knows how, the stores, the restaurants, the butcher shops filled up with meat and bread, wine, oil, soup, cheese and butter, all kinds of fruit, and even larks and songbirds.

PANTALONE.   Tartaglia, you're joking.

TARTAGLIA.   Would I play a trick on His Majesty?

FARRUSCAD.   Another sorrow, new grief heaped on my breaking heart. This is what she promised with her last words: "I have few powers left, but let me do what little I can for you and your kingdom, as the last proof of my love." This stinging memory! . . . Go! I cannot bear the sight of you, but even more, I hate myself.

TARTAGLIA   (*Softly,* to PANTALONE). Pantalone, give him time. He'll calm down if we leave him alone. We mustn't abandon the princess and Togrul, who're setting up our defenses.

PANTALONE.   You're right. It's pointless to dawdle here while every other citizen is sharpening his sword—that's not the way a good Venetian acts. We'll send some servants here to keep track of him and make sure he doesn't harm himself. Now let's cut off a few dozen goddam Moorish heads. There aren't many of us left, though?

TARTAGLIA.   Ten against ten thousand, maybe. Do I care? Why count? It's better to die from battle wounds than starvation. (*Exeunt.*)

## SCENE 3

*Enter* FARRUSCAD, *followed by* FARZANA.

FARRUSCAD.   Her final words! She said this, too: "You could still free me. No, I cannot hope for that! It would take too much strength. Do not risk your life for me; your life is precious to me even when I cannot be near you." Sweet words—they tear my heart! Cherestanì, Cherestanì, how can I save you? My life doesn't matter—death would come as a blessing. If you can, if you don't detest me, give me a sign. How can I help you, or die in the attempt? (*He weeps.*)

FARZANA  (*Aside*). I must lead him to his death. He must not free Cherestanì and take her from us. While the others have gone to fight, he will vanish with me—and die. (*She approaches him.*) You? Free your wife? You lack the spirit. You're a coward.

FARRUSCAD.  Lovely fairy . . . Sprite . . . I recognize you! My wife's companion. Where is she? What can I do to regain her?

FARZANA.  You free her, you timid waverer? Why, you're more like a weak woman than a man! After losing her through your cowardice, where will you find the courage? It would take a stronger arm and stouter heart than yours to save her now!

FARRUSCAD.  No insults. Put me to the test. I am happy to die for her. Why the delay?

FARZANA.  Give me your hand.

FARRUSCAD.  Here. Take me where you will.

(*He stretches out his hand to* FARZANA. *A gigantic flash. They disappear.*)

SCENE 4

*Enter* PANTALONE *and* TARTAGLIA *in a hurry.*

PANTALONE.  Your Majesty . . . Your Majesty . . . A miracle! I'm de-lighted!—Tartaglia, where did he go?

TARTAGLIA.  He should be here . . . He was in one of these rooms hardly a minute ago.

PANTALONE.  I told you we never should have left him alone. I thought we were in luck at last, but what do you bet, Tartaglia? There's been some catastrophe. He was out of his mind with worry for his wife, the serpent. He's killed himself for sure.

TARTAGLIA.  Who could blame him? My wife's a snake too. I can hardly stand her any more!

PANTALONE.  Come on, this is no time for jokes.

TARTAGLIA.  Let's look for him, Pantalone. This palace is too damn large. He probably went into one of the rooms that face south. (*Exit.*)

PANTALONE.   Good. We'll scour the south rooms; but I'm afraid he's already thrown himself from one of the west windows. (*Exit.*)

## SCENE 5

TRUFFALDINO, *later* BRIGHELLA. TRUFFALDINO *wears a short ragged cloak and worn-out hat. He carries a bugle and an awkward arm-load of pamphlets. Over his shoulders and cloak he has what looks suspiciously like a sandwich board. He puts down the pamphlets, sounds a couple of blasts on the bugle, and waves one pamphlet at the audience.*

TRUFFALDINO.   Hear ye, hear ye! Read all about it. First account. The whole gory story. Hot off the presses. Get your copy now. Most thrilling battle ever fought under the walls of Tiflis! The giant Morgone attacks with two million Moors! Tiflis defended by only four hundred soldiers, most of them old, lame, or asleep. Moors flattened, wiped out. The river Cur rises and floods the battlefield, drowning the enemy . . . Two or three copies left. Get yours now! Only a copper. A copper and a half for the deluxe illustrated edition with genuine bloodstains on the cover.

(*Enter* BRIGHELLA.)

Read all about it!

BRIGHELLA.   Hey, Truff, what's all this yelling outside the palace?

TRUFFALDINO.   Didn't you hear? We won the battle. It just ended. Here: the whole gory story.

BRIGHELLA.   Just ended is right. How can you put out the whole gory story in about three minutes?

TRUFFALDINO.   When it comes to making a bit of coin our people are fast as lightning.

BRIGHELLA.   You won't sell many of those copies in Tiflis. All the folk who're still here know about the battle. They fought it, for God's sake. Truffaldino, take your copies to Venice. Blast the people there with your shouting. They'll buy you out to get shut of you.

TRUFFALDINO.   To sell in Venice, the story would have to be thirty times as complicated, full of politics, scandalmongering, and lies. You know what? There's an idea. I could dress it up a little . . .

BRIGHELLA.   You . . . you *entrepreneur!* Have you seen the prince?

## SCENE 6

*Enter* TARTAGLIA *and* PANTALONE, *looking frantic.*

TARTAGLIA.   Have you seen the p-p-p . . . pr . . . pr . . .

PANTALONE.   The prince?

BRIGHELLA.   Not a sign of him.

TRUFFALDINO   (*Deafeningly*). Hear ye, hear ye! The whole gory story. Five hundred million Moors . . . defeated by two infants and a nursemaid . . . Prince Farruscad vanishes. Missing in action. May be dead. Or taking a siesta.

TARTAGLIA.   Shut him up!

PANTALONE.   Grab his pamphlets!

(*The three of them try to pursue* TRUFFALDINO *offstage, but he keeps circling and yelling about the whole gory story. They seize his pile of pamphlets and toss them offstage. Noise, confusion, antics, ad lib.*)

## SCENE 7

*Enter* CANZADE, TOGRUL, *and* SMERALDINA.

CANZADE.   Where is my brother?

TARTAGLIA.   My lady, something terrible. He was in this room. We left for the battle. When we came back, he was gone. We looked in the south rooms, but couldn't find him.

PANTALONE.   That's right. Out of his mind with grief, he was. Crazy men play wicked tricks on themselves.

CANZADE.   Are you saying . . . No! What can we do?

TOGRUL.   What awful news!

(*They are all stricken with grief.*)

SMERALDINA.   Ye gods!

## SCENE 8

GEONCA'S *voice*

VOICE. Wretches! No more wasting time! Obey the voice of Geonca. An evil sprite has lured your prince to the mountain behind the city. She will have him killed. Bring his children to him. Move him to pity. Convince him to draw back. In his state of grief, he has ventured into the utmost danger. In case you reach him too late, I shall warn him before you arrive.

CANZADE. Togrul, you heard that?

TOGRUL. We must obey that friendly voice. Now! (*Exit* TOGRUL *with* CANZADE.)

SMERALDINA. I'll run and get his children. We'll be back in a moment. (*Exit.*)

PANTALONE. My poor boy! Help him! Some marriage he walked into! Follow me, men. Tartaglia, bring up the rear. (*Exit.*)

TARTAGLIA. Ha! I'll be way ahead of you. I don't have rickety old bones like yours, you wreck. (*Exit.*)

BRIGHELLA. Put off the celebrations. Who knows how this catastrophe will end? (*Exit.*)

TRUFFALDINO.

> "He who goes far from his homeland sees
> Things far different from what he believed." [10]

Hear ye, hear ye! Read all about it! Gory beyond belief . . .

## SCENE 9

*The setting changes to a wild outdoor scene. In the background, below a mountain, is a tomb, and off to one side a column, from which hangs a gong, kettledrum, or similar instrument that makes a booming noise when struck. Next to it hangs a hammer. Enter* FARRUSCAD *and* FARZANA. FARRUSCAD *is wearing light armor, and carries a shield and sword.*

FARZANA. This is where we'll see whether your heart is as bold as your tongue.

FARRUSCAD.   Why do you excruciate me in my despair? I wish I had a thousand lives. I'd sacrifice them all for my wife. What must I do? I see only a tomb. Do I fight with the dead? How must I die, Farzana? Lift this hellish uncertainty.

FARZANA   (*Aside*). Now to hurry him to his destruction. (*To FAR-RUSCAD*) You're anxious to die? Strike the gong with that hammer. Its sound will echo through the hills, and you'll know your task. Your life is worth little, but if you win, she will turn mortal, and be yours. (*Exit.*)

FARRUSCAD.   Strike the gong? Good. No more waiting. Let me strike it. Let death come!

(*He strikes the gong with the hammer. The sound is accompanied by claps of thunder and flashes of lightning. The stage grows darker. FARRUSCAD continues.*)

Tremble, earth! Sun, turn dark! Lightning bolts, fall by the hundreds— I defy you!

### SCENE 10

*A ferocious* BULL *enters, spitting fire from its mouth, horns, and tail, and attacks* FARRUSCAD. FARRUSCAD, *then* GEONCA'S *voice*

FARRUSCAD.   Do you think you frighten me? Never!

(*The stage grows lighter. A fierce combat ensues. The* BULL *drives* FAR-RUSCAD *back with its flames.*)

No, the beast is undefeatable.

VOICE.   Farruscad, take heart. You fight in vain unless you cut off his right horn.

FARRUSCAD.   I thank you, friendly voice. I heed your words.

(*He fights the* BULL *and cuts off his right horn; the* BULL *collapses, bellowing, and disappears.*)

Who are you, voice? What do I fight next in order to free my sweet Cherestanì?

VOICE.   I am Geonca. So far you have done little. Keep resisting. Be brave. Defend your life.

SCENE 11

*Enter* FARZANA.

FARZANA.   What has happened here? Who has helped him?

FARRUSCAD.   Farzana, tell me what I must do to see my dear wife again as her true self, and take her once more in my arms?

FARZANA.   Hopeless! You have done nothing yet. Strike the gong again, and conquer what comes out of the tomb. But even if you succeed, you will have accomplished little compared to the trial that remains. Poor boy, you will never have the nerve to win through to the end. (*Exit.*)

FARRUSCAD.   If courage is all I need, she is wrong. Let every devil in hell issue from this tomb! (*He runs and strikes the gong again. The scene grows dark, thunder is heard.*) Tremble, earth! Sky, crack open! I will never retreat! (*The stage grows light again.*)

SCENE 12

*Enter a* GIANT *with a monstrous sword in his hand.*

GIANT.   No, you'll never retreat. You'll leave your head here next to your dead body, food for crows and wild beasts. (*He attacks* FARRUSCAD.)

FARRUSCAD.   Perhaps you have predicted your own fate. The crows will make an even bigger feast of you, deformed ogre. Heaven assist me!

(*They fight: after several blows,* FARRUSCAD *cuts off the giant's arm, which falls to earth together with the sword it holds.*)

Fight back now, if you can. Run, giant, save your life; I do not need to kill you.

(*The* GIANT *kneels, picks up his arm, puts it back in its place, and takes up a fighting stance again.*)

GIANT.   No need to kill me? You'd better try. You can't escape otherwise. (*He renews his attacks.*)

FARRUSCAD. Uncanny! But I will not lose heart.

(*The duel continues. After several blows,* FARRUSCAD *cuts the giant's leg off.*)

GIANT. Bad luck! You've won . . . I'm dying.

FARRUSCAD. Yes. Die quickly, monster—bleed to death.

(*The* GIANT *picks up his leg and puts it back in place.*)

GIANT. Fool! You had your illusion of victory, your childish dreaming. Now you will die. (*He challenges* FARRUSCAD *again.*)

FARRUSCAD. Astounding! Unbelievable! Geonca, how can I resist him? Please! No answer! Breathe deeply, don't give way yet.

(*A new, fierce duel.* FARRUSCAD *cuts the giant's head off.*)

There. Now die, you infernal monster! Back to your abyss.

(*Groping, the* GIANT *recovers his head, and puts it back on.*)

GIANT (*Laughing*). Ha ha ha ha, lunatic! Now I have you.

FARRUSCAD. How can I finish him off? Geonca, my friend, I'm out of breath and drained. (*They prepare to fight again.*)

VOICE. Chop off his head, then cut off his left ear.

GIANT (*Attacking* FARRUSCAD). Rash fool, your time has come.

FARRUSCAD. One more push, the last . . . Geonca's advice . . . I must fight back.

(*He throws down his shield and fights desperately with his sword, using both hands. Again he cuts off the giant's head, then picks it up. While the* GIANT *fumbles for his head,* FARRUSCAD *cuts off the left ear. The giant's body falls and sinks out of sight.*)

FARRUSCAD (*Throwing the head into the wings*). Put it back on now, if you can, and come back to life. Geonca, I would surely have died, if you had not come to my aid. How will I ever repay you?

[*In the third act, all these scenes of fantastic illusions so pleasing to the lower classes were executed to perfection by the theatrical company of Antonio Sacchi.*]

## SCENE 13

*Enter* FARZANA.

FARZANA   (*Aside*). Still alive! And the giant is destroyed! Who can be helping him? Geonca must be nearby. I should have taken account of him: Zemina was right. Our own Cherestanì, we are losing you! Farruscad is releasing you from your enchantment. How shall I frighten him away?

FARRUSCAD.   Come, Farzana, where is Cherestanì? Must I do still more?

FARZANA.   Brave warrior, I feel pity for you. Give up, Farruscad. What you have done is nearly nothing compared to what you must still do. Listen to what I say. Leave. Save your life.

FARRUSCAD.   Leave? When I have vowed to die if I do not free my wife? Keep your promise. Give me death, or give me back Cherestanì. What is left for me to do?

FARZANA.   One trial is left, too difficult for you. You have done enough. Leave now.

FARRUSCAD.   Farzana, you are wasting your breath. I will complete the trial or die.

FARZANA.   Very well, fool. You will not need your sword for this last trial, but we shall see if you can come out victorious. Put your hand on that tomb (*Pointing to the tomb upstage*). Swear by your prophet to kiss the mouth of whatever you see when the crypt opens.

FARRUSCAD   (*Running to the tomb, and with noble unconstraint, placing his hand on the stone*). My hand! In Mohammed's name I swear to kiss the mouth of whatever I see within this tomb.

FARZANA.   Madman! Take the hammer, and strike the gong once more.

FARRUSCAD.   Is that all? Here, then, I'll strike it.

(*He strikes the gong with the hammer; the stage grows dark, and there is thunder as before, then the stage grows lighter again.*)

FARZANA.   Approach the tomb. Kiss the mouth.

FARRUSCAD.   What can this be? A disgusting, cold cadaver? It will take worse than that to frighten a desperate lover. This is an easy trial. I will prove it.

(*He runs to the tomb, bringing his face next to it. A SERPENT with a repellent head emerges halfway from the tomb, opens its mouth bristling with long, sharp teeth close to Farruscad's face. He jumps back, frightened, putting his hand to his sword.*)

My God, what's this? Evil fairy! You have betrayed me.

(*He tries to strike the SERPENT with his sword, but it glides back into the tomb.*)

FARZANA.   Heathen! What are you doing? You had to win your opening trials with your sword. This last trial you can win only with a kiss. But you lack the stomach. Didn't I warn you that this was the hardest test of all? Keep your vow, or give way to your terror. (*Aside*) May fear wipe out his courage!

FARRUSCAD.   Yes, I have the heart for it. I will conquer my loathing.

(*Again he resolutely approaches the tomb, and brings his face near the entrance to it; the SERPENT emerges, and comes close to him, opening its hideous mouth. FARRUSCAD retreats. He tries again to force himself to kiss the SERPENT, which keeps gnashing its teeth.*)

What holds me back? What a hellish trial this is. And yet—wasn't my wife turned into a serpent? Couldn't that vile creature be Cherestanì? Coward! What prevents you from kissing her? (*He approaches the tomb again, then stops.*) But perhaps his sprite is tricking me. She wants me to give up my defenses, to risk my head inside the foul jaws, which can crush me. (*He is lost in thought.*)

FARZANA   (*aside*). Oppress him, fear! Make him flee and end the trial.

FARRUSCAD   (*Resolutely*). Then let me die. If a kiss inspires such horror, it may dissolve the enchantment.

(*He approaches the tomb; the* SERPENT *snarls even more violently.* FAR-RUSCAD *retreats, and the* SERPENT *again sinks back into the tomb.*)

Bitter fortune, you could not put me through a more terrifying trial. Geonca, where is your voice? Speak! Advise me in this extremity! No? Then with this sword, which defeated my other adversaries, I will destroy this tomb and kill the serpent. (*He is about to strike the stones of the tomb.*)

VOICE.   Stay your rash arm or you will be sorry for the rest of your life! Farzana, you have lost all hope of recovering Cherestanì. Return to your assembled sisters. Tell them she is now human. She can remain the wife of Farruscad. My son, fear nothing. Kiss the serpent. She is your wife. She will not bite you, for her serpentine form is an enchantment. Your trial is at an end. Remember me.

FARZANA.   Cruel fate and cursed voice! My sisters, we have lost Cherestanì!

(*She vanishes, weeping. The cries and lamentation of many women are heard.*)

FARRUSCAD.   I will shut my eyes and fight down my revulsion. Sweet Cherestanì, you no longer frighten me.

(*Impetuously, he approaches the tomb. The* SERPENT *emerges, as before. After quelling his disgust,* FARRUSCAD *kisses the* SERPENT. *The stage grows dark. Lightning and thunder. The tomb is transformed to a magnificent triumphal carriage. On it stands* CHERESTANÌ, *richly dressed as a queen. The stage lightens again.*)

### SCENE 14

CHERESTANÌ *and* FARRUSCAD

CHERESTANÌ   (*Embracing* FARRUSCAD). Farruscad, my love, my happiness! I owe you everything.

FARRUSCAD.   My love, you are finally mine forever. I have paid the penalty for my errors.

### SCENE 15

*Enter* CANZADE, REZIA, BEDREDINO, TOGRUL, PANTALONE, TARTAGLIA, BRIGHELLA, TRUFFALDINO, *and* SMERAL-DINA.

CANZADE.   We are here, Brother, to defend you. Is this . . . ?

FARRUSCAD.   My beloved wife. Canzade, embrace her. My children . . . My children . . . I am overjoyed! I long for all of you to be as happy as I am.

(*In glad amazement, they all embrace.*)

TOGRUL.   My lord, tell me . . .

FARRUSCAD.   There is no time now for that. Later, I will tell you everything that happened. Cherestanì, I am too happy to speak. Will you make certain that everyone receives a reward?

CHERESTANÌ.

> I will arrange it all. Now I am free,
> You and the children shall return with me
> To dwell in Eldorado where I reign,
> That spacious realm, which soon will entertain
> You as its king. And we four will play host
> To Pantalone and Tartaglia, most
> Devoted of your followers. Togrul can wed
> Canzade, ruling Tiflis in your stead.
> Now Truffaldino, Smeraldina's only
> Waiting to be your wife. And as for lonely
> Brighella, there's a bride in store for you
> At last—and wealthy presents, too.
> But tell me, someone, how will I be able
> To beg these gracious folk who watched our fable
> So patiently to pardon all our flaws?
> (*To the audience*)
> Please show us your forgiveness with applause!


The end of
## *The Serpent Woman*

## Notes

1. By the time of this *Tale's* performance in October 1762, Goldoni had in fact left Venice for Paris, where he became the director of the Théâtre Italien. His departure was due at least in part to the successful competition of Gozzi's plays in a tight theatrical market, though other factors also contributed: salary disputes with his employers, conflicts with actors, and the large size of the San Luca Theatre, unsuited to intimate, realistic comedies.

2. For "marvelous" Gozzi uses the term *il mirabile*, which along with its near-synonym *il meraviglioso* was a keystone of literary theory in the preceding century, when the primary purpose of art was thought to be that of astounding the reader or spectator. Gozzi means to say that his plays rely on surprising theatrical inventions and effects, unlike the more realistic plays of his rivals, for whom *il mirabile* was a term of scorn—hence Gozzi's ironic self-denigration.

3. Probably a reference to Pietro Chiari, director of the *Gazzetta Veneta* during this period.

4. There were two sorts of newspaper in Venice at this time: those with a literary-cultural focus (such as *La Gazzetta Veneta*) and those with a newsier quality. The latter, however, were far from resembling the modern newspaper and usually no larger than a pamphlet or a broadside. Most of their "news" was fictional, more remarkable for its entertainment value than for its informational content. They were often the butt of theatrical satire: see, for example, Goldoni's comedy *La finta ammalata* or his opera libretto *Lo speziale*.

5. Horace's dictum that art should mix the useful with the pleasurable is a commonplace of eighteenth-century theatrical theory. It is worth noting that while Gozzi claims elsewhere that his *Tales* have a moral or critical value, his concept of usefulness is limited, in this passage, to the financial rewards and acclaim the play might reap for a theatrical company.

6. Oddly, Farruscad knows his wife's name, though Gozzi will continue to stress the fact that he was forbidden to ask it. We may perhaps presume that he discovered it while searching her desk (see the previous scene), but the contradiction is never explicitly resolved in the text.

7. A literary reference to Ludovico Ariosto's *Orlando furioso,* canto 7. The poem was so popular in Venice, in both written and oral forms, that even illiterate members of Gozzi's audience could be expected to understand such allusions.

8. Cherestani's supposed behavior resembles that of Circe in Homer's *Odyssey.*

9. The commedia dell'arte masks Arlecchino (Harlequin) and Truffaldino were virtually identical. Consequently, Truffaldino is here praising his own character, in effect exploding the fiction of Gozzi's plot, and emphasizing, through a sort of alienation effect, the *Tale's* essential theatricality.

10. A quotation from Ariosto's *Orlando furioso,* canto 7, lines 1–2: "Chi va lontan dalla sua patria, vede / cose, da quel, che si credea, lontane." In Gozzi's Venice, such quotations had the force and flavor of proverbs.

# The Green Bird

## A Philosophical Tale for the
## Theatre in Five Acts

### Preface

The *Tale of the Green Bird* is the most daring play that ever issued from my inkwell.

I had decided to use every effort of my imagination to conclude the series of my theatrical works with a tremendous popular success.[1] I had not wanted any financial return from my plays, but neither did I want to continue the effort they had begun to cost me, especially since I thought I had reached the goal I had set for myself as a purely whimsical, literary point of honor.

I made this *Tale*'s plot a continuation of *The Love of Three Oranges,* but underneath its substance was very different.

I doubt that any eccentric writer has ever done what I did in this *Tale,* hiding under a childish title and a very broad style of comedy an insidious, facetious, moral treatment of serious matters.[2]

Renzo and Barbarina, the two protagonists of the play, are modern philosophers steeped in the pernicious maxims of Messrs. Helvétius, Rousseau, and Voltaire. They mock humanity by putting into practice a philosophical system of self-love. When they are poor, they are happy to accept and praise the generosity of charitable men, but when they become rich, they go mad and desire the impossible. Truffaldino is a miniature Machiavelli. The statue Calmon is a moralist. Smeraldina is a good, pious woman who, when the two young philosophers ridicule her actions, believes that she is no longer obliged to love her neighbor, as can be seen explicitly in the fourth scene of act one. Tartagliona is a vain, malicious old woman, while Brighella, the poet and fortune-teller, is interested only in her will. Tartaglia is a comical king, but his facetious character is a critical mirror for some great fools and boorish people. These ingredients of my *Tale,* developed in accordance with the requirements of the genre, had the effect that I desired on every sort of spectator—save for my critics, whom I will not offend by including them in the infinite number of people who were kind enough to attend and applaud this piece of foolery.

The serious, moral points I made in this daring theatrical spectacle were hotly debated all over the city, and some of those discussions were of such an unusual sort that many monks of the severest orders took off their habits, put on masks, and went to listen with the greatest attention to *The Green Bird*.

Such an event should not confound those who call my plays "insulting burlesques" and who have educated our populace by producing *Jeneval and His Noble Passions* in our theatres.[3]

In addition to the serious element of this *Tale,* I spared no effort to make it amusing to the common people. To excite their interest, I even thought of bringing on stage several huge, well-known statues found in various neighborhoods of the city. I did this solely to attract the lower-class people of those neighborhoods and make them curious to see if their statues, moving and speaking on stage, resembled the originals. When they found that they did, they returned to the theatre again and again.

This scenic monster of mine appeared at Venice's Sant'Angelo Theatre, played by Sacchi's company, as usual, on 19 January 1765. It was performed nineteen times, and closed the spring season with houses so full that often people were turned away from the doors.

If such a play has no literary merit, it at least had the concrete merit of being useful to the company that performed it, and which continues to perform it every year.

# The Green Bird

TARTAGLIA, king of Monterotondo
TARTAGLIONA (TARR-tahl-YOH-nah), his mother, the old queen
NINETTA (nee-NET-ah), wife of Tartaglia and mother of
RENZO (RAYN-tzoh) and
BARBARINA (barr-barr-EE-nah), who are twins
POMPEA (pom-PAY-ah), a statue loved by Renzo
CALMON (kahl-MOHN), king of the statues, a very elderly moralist
BRIGHELLA, poet and fortune-teller, pretended lover of Tartagliona
TRUFFALDINO, sausage seller
SMERALDINA, his wife
PANTALONE, prime minister
GREEN BIRD, king of Terradombra, in love with Barbarina
APPLES, which sing
GOLDEN WATERS, which play music and can dance
STATUE, the Treviso fountain
RIOBA (ree-OH-bah) and his four BROTHERS, statues of Campo dei Mori in Venice
SERPENTINA (SAYR-pen-TEE-nah), a fairy
CAPPELLO (kahp-ELL-oh) and CIGOLOTTI, public storytellers, statues
SERVANTS, GUARDS, and various ANIMALS

*The settings are the imaginary city of Monterotondo, Serpentina's garden, the ogre's mountain lair, and other suitably fabulous places.*

## Act One

*A street in the city of Monterotondo*

### SCENE I

BRIGHELLA, *as a caricature of a soothsayer, and* PANTALONE, *as commentator, off to one side*

BRIGHELLA    (*As if entranced*).
O sun, which always glows
On the patterns of life,
Reveal to those whom heaven knows
The future and its strife!

PANTALONE    (*Aside*). I'm crazy about this poet. He says things you have to remember, lines you could publish to celebrate a wedding.[4]

BRIGHELLA    (*As before*).
O Tartagliona, queen of misery!
O Tartaglia, king of bliss!
O Renzo, o Barbarina, by wizardry
Born the fruit of a curdled kiss
To a family of state
Singled out by fate.

PANTALONE    (*Aside*). Aha, he's referring now to the royal family of Monterotondo. So the queen of the Tarots is miserable? Yes, sir: misery is what she deserves. The old hag has been nothing but a tyrant since her son, King Tartaglia, went away. But how does he deserve to be the king of bliss after he left the government in the hands of that witch for eighteen years? If only the infection she had in her legs when her son got married had killed her off! The rest of it I don't follow. Renzo? Barbarina? The fruit of a curdled kiss? Singled out by fate?

BRIGHELLA  (*As before*).
O noble spirit, king of hearts,
Now passed to the beyond—Oh
How many marvels and foolish starts
Will spread the name and fame of Monterotondo?

PANTALONE  (*Aside*). Even more famous? Wasn't it enough to see oranges turn into women, women into doves, and a dove become our dear, late Queen Ninetta?[5]

BRIGHELLA.
Tartaglia, I perceive you
Return with mighty stride,
Ninetta, I believe you
Have never really died.
Our royal house revives
And will renew our lives.

PANTALONE  (*Aside*). What can you do but stand with your mouth open, listening to him like a booby, as you try to take it all in? And yet this soothsayer is six times more accurate than an almanac. "Tartaglia, I perceive you / Return . . ." That must mean that the king, who went to war against the rebels eighteen years ago, will be back tonight. That must be what he means. "Ninetta, I believe you / Have never really died." I don't get that. I saw what happened. Queen Ninetta was buried alive, eighteen years ago, under the drains of the palace kitchen. All because of the persecution by that hag of a queen mother. By now Ninetta's turned to mud—or dust. "Our royal house revives / And will renew our lives." Fine, but how can that come true? I remember shortly before they lowered poor Ninetta into that foul pit, she'd given birth to twins, a buttercup of a golden cherub and rose-pink little angel. The old harpy handed her own grandchildren to me, ordered me to cut their throats and not say a word to a soul, or she'd have me done away with, too. She tossed two flat-snouted puppies into the cradle, the offspring of the king's pet bitch, Mascherina. Then she sent reports off to the king. The accusations! The lies! They led to orders so tragic that people will tell them around the fire, like fairy tales. Me, I didn't have the heart to slay those little ones. What I did—and I remember it clearly—was roll them up in twenty-four lengths of the finest oilskin from that place near the Rialto bridge. I made sure the package was waterproof before I dropped the poor little dears in the river. Then I took the hearts of two young goats back to the grandmother, as loyal ministers do in such cases. No, after eighteen years they must have died, either from hunger or because there was no way they could grow bigger: I tied the bundle tight with stout cords. So please, my dear fortune-teller, be a good poet, not an imitator, write fine Venetian, not false Tuscan. Give us solid stuff, not just words.[6] Heaven has blessed some people with a gift, but even gifted people sometimes say such idiotic things you could laugh in their faces. There's no way out of it . . . The royal line is definitely extinct.

BRIGHELLA    (*Still standing entranced, his hands to his brow*). Tartagliona, o my mistress, a prophecy from your apologetic astrologer . . .

> If you cannot be saved
> By the apples that sing
> And the waters that dance
> And the bird who's a king . . .
> If my acids and alkalis,
> Solid or wet,
> Don't help to preserve you
> You'd better forget
> That you now are a woman
> And be ready to switch
> Into a turtle
> Down in the ditch.

(*He emerges from the trance.*)

Ah, well, too bad. My divine inspiration's over. I'm an insignificant clod again, like everyone else. I'm weak, lungs worn out, about to collapse. What's that doorway there? A sausage seller's? Let's squander a couple of coins on their stew to cure the exhaustion caused by my Apollonian trance and poetic fury. (*Exit.*)

PANTALONE.    O my Venetian blood, what a slab of poetry that was! I couldn't follow one goddam word. Could anything be more divine? Apples that sing? Waters that dance? Acids and alkalis, solid or wet? Say what you like, something great is about to take place in this court. I've seen the impossible happen so often I've become a real old skeptic. What's left to see after all those furious transformations? Smeraldina, a black woman, and Brighella, servant of the jack of hearts, were burned at the stake. Smeraldina is reborn white, like an old pipe tossed into the fire. She marries Truffaldino, and they set up a sausage shop. And Brighella, who was burned like . . . I don't know, like a sonnet written for somebody's graduation . . . he rises from the ashes as an fortune-teller and a respected poet! Nothing can shock me any more. Anything, everything is possible. (*Exit.*)

SCENE 2

TRUFFALDINO, *dressed as a butcher, and* SMERALDINA

TRUFFALDINO. Smeraldina, I happen to hate your guts. In the old days, before they burned you alive, you were smart but wicked—a useful broad. Then, as soon as you came back to life, you grew honest and silly and a pain in the ass. I liked you a lot more as a heap of charcoal. I curse the day I married you. You're driving me into my grave.

SMERALDINA. It's true—I'd have been much better off as a pile of charcoal than tying myself to a thieving swine of a sausage seller. You guzzle the sausages and stews—all our stock—and leave us penniless.

TRUFFALDINO. Who built up that stock in the first place? I was the one who earned all the capital by sweating my guts out as the court cook and once in a while stealing a few odds and ends the way cooks do. It would have made more sense to toss it all in the river than open this shop, where you let every fast-talking glutton in town load up on my tripe and sliced salami at cut prices. You give open credit to rundown porters and hackdrivers and even—no one would believe it in times like these—to the lowest of the low: poets.

SMERALDINA. All right, I'm a little too easygoing, but I swear to God I have a good head for the business, even if I have a soft heart, even if I do go easy on the credit. But you, you hog, I watch you eat nonstop through the day and then tuck a hunk of fried liver under your pillow for an overnight snack. You take up with tarts and pay them with sausages. They pay you back with diseases. Medical bills! Drugs! Doctors! Surgeons! No cash? Settle with prosciutto, our best lean bacon, and pig's trotters. That's where our capital went.

TRUFFALDINO. You! You're right every time, must get in the last word, when all we have left in stock is four shriveled sausages and a couple of fried eels. Your big heart—it's driven me bankrupt. Why did you have to go find two children after the one we had died as a baby? Yes, you hauled 'em out of the water in their twenty-four oilskin wrappings, gave 'em the titty, and fussed over 'em till you lost so much flesh I didn't fancy you any more. Truth is: you disgusted me, you bony wreck. That's why I took my favors to other women. After eighteen years of doting on that girl and boy, your good heart has destroyed our marriage. And our income.

SMERALDINA.  If you ever—but I mean *ever*—do or say one nasty thing to Renzo or Barbarina, all hell will break loose.

TRUFFALDINO.  Not one more word. I want them out of the house now.

SMERALDINA.  Never. These are wonderful youngsters. They're gentle and considerate; they never grumble; they eat our leftovers; they're good students; and they help out. Renzo catches rabbits and birds. Barbarina chops wood, sweeps up, washes the clothes, and—

TRUFFALDINO.  I don't like 'em! Renzo's more of a philosopher than I am. Barbarina's too damn modest. Will she go out and make money like some girls do? Not a hope! And the two of 'em together drain us dry.

## SCENE 3

*Enter* RENZO, *carrying a musket and a book, and* BARBARINA, *with a bundle of wood and a book. They are both dressed in rags. They remain at first in the background.*

BARBARINA.  Renzo, Mother and Father are fighting.

RENZO.  So they are. Let's listen.

SMERALDINA.  You better not say one wrong word to either of those children—or else . . .

TRUFFALDINO.  I can't wait to throw them out.

SMERALDINA.  Oh, Truffaldino, no! You can't do that.

TRUFFALDINO.  I have no children and I refuse to keep someone else's bastards.

RENZO  (*To* BARBARINA). Bastards? Not us?

BARBARINA.  Is that what he meant?

SMERALDINA.  Truffaldino, never let me hear you use that word again.

TRUFFALDINO. I've tried to choke it down for too long. Let it come out. I'll be able to breathe again. The second they walk in I'll spit it in their teeth. Bastards, a thousand times bastards!

SMERALDINA. Their parents might be a lord and lady. You can see what beautiful manners they have, what noble features. You can hear how polite they talk.

TRUFFALDINO. You don't fish up the children of a lord and lady wrapped in oilskins. I'll say it again: I've spent enough on those bastards.

RENZO (*To* BARBARINA). Barbarina, it seems we are. I'll ask him right out. (*Coming forward*) Is it true, Father? We're bastards?

BARBARINA (*To* SMERALDINA). And not your children?

(*Unable to answer,* SMERALDINA *weeps.*)

TRUFFALDINO. I don't know a thing about tears or tender, heroic scenes. Those I can't afford. My shop's empty. So's my wallet. I've kept the two of you in luxury all these years. For all I know, yes, you're bastards. We fished you out of the river and, apart from the wrappings that kept you dry, the only things you had on were your birthday suits. Don't blame me if you're still alive. As God is my judge, I told Smeraldina to keep the oilskins and throw you back in. To spare you the misery of living. But this soft and loony wife of mine wouldn't hear of it. Nobody can say I didn't give you all the education you need. You know how to eat, drink, and relieve yourselves. Now you have to learn how to earn your way. Your way is out there. And don't come back. (*Exit.*)

## SCENE 4

RENZO. Glad tidings, Barbarina! Strange but wonderful. I thank heaven I'm so strong-minded.

BARBARINA. I confess I'd have felt a touch of anguish if it wasn't for our readings in philosophy and our discussions of human nature and reason.

SMERALDINA. My dears, take no notice of that jackass.

RENZO. But are we your children? Or not?

SMERALDINA.  You're not. You heard how we found you. But who cares? I nursed you and raised you as if you were mine. You *are* mine. You must stay with me.

BARBARINA.  No, Smeraldina. All your kindness will be rewarded if we make our fortunes. We're not your blood, and it wouldn't be fair for us to stay and make you even poorer, especially since your husband resents us. I imagine you're upset over our leaving. Perfectly natural. You're used to us, and you think it would displease us to be thrown out into the street. But your concern for us is mere self-love.

SMERALDINA.  Self-love? Where did you pick up that expression?

BARBARINA.  You feel hurt that we have to go. Ergo, you find reasons for us to remain and relieve your sorrow. Ergo, you seek a strictly personal good. There's no denying it. When Renzo and I stroll through the woods, we plumb the latest books of enlightened philosophy, the ones Truffaldino buys as scrap and tears pages out of for wrapping sausages. We understand the innermost motives of human action: nothing surprises us. We are not in the least responsible for this discomfort of yours, since it is born of self-love. Discipline yourself with the aid of reason. We will go out into the world with our usual imperturbability. If we ever make our fortunes, we will repay you, as I said, for all you have done for us, but in consonance with the laws of society, not because we have any personal obligation. Good-by.

RENZO.  Well said. You're a true philosopher, Barbarina. You distinguish clearly between subjective beliefs and the objective values of communal laws. Smeraldina dear, may you enjoy health. Go back into the house with the husband society has given you. Attempt to free your reason from its emotional bonds, if you can, and employ it to curb the self-love that causes you so much vexation. Good-by.

SMERALDINA.  Why, you silly little sprouts! What are you babbling about? Self-love? Human action? Reason? Society? Who taught you to think and talk like this, you demented children?

BARBARINA  (*Laughing*). Renzo, do you detect a certain heat in those remarks? What a sad fate it is not to be an objective philosopher!

RENZO.  Beware of self-love, Smeraldina. It inflames you. Go back in the house. You'll make a fool of yourself if a cultured person, lacking your old-fashioned prejudices, should pass by and hear you.

SMERALDINA.   I swear to God, if I knew I was going to raise two ungrateful brats, I'd have left you to drown. So I took you home out of self-love, did I?

BARBARINA.   There's no question here. Your decision made you feel better. Ergo, you carried it into action.

SMERALDINA.   I fed you on my milk and grew thin. I went without clothes to dress you. I took bread from my mouth to put into yours. I've deprived myself of a thousand things, I've suffered a thousand worries for you. And I did all this out of self-love?

RENZO.   I can't help laughing. Certainly—from pure selfishness. You were carried away by the pleasure of being altruistic. Yet every act you supposedly performed on our behalf asserted your power over us. Of course you were prompted by self-love.

SMERALDINA.   Almighty God! Then you don't appreciate my sacrifices?

BARBARINA.   Not so noisy, Smeraldina, please! You cannot expect to benefit from the intrinsic value of your actions. If fortune smiles upon us, we will act as society prescribes and compensate you for the sacrifices you made out of self-love.

SMERALDINA   (*Enraged*). I curse my self-love for making me suffer so for the sake of these thoughtless, thankless things. And now they walk out on me with their noses in the air. If I ever again rescue anyone who's drowning, or put warm clothes on anyone who shivers, or hand the smallest coin to anyone dying of fever or hunger or thirst, may I be pinched, punched, twisted, mangled, strangled, cut up, and for the second time burned alive! (*Exit.*)

SCENE 5

RENZO.   She's angry, the poor, ignorant woman.

BARBARINA.   Yes, but doesn't it bother you, Renzo, that here we are, in rags, about to set off on our unknown wanderings, and we don't know whose children we are?

RENZO.   Not at all. My reasoning brings me to this conclusion: if we have no father or mother, we need not submit to such external pressures as obedience and subjection. Furthermore, we do not wish our parents to die in order to inherit their property and so attempt to satisfy insatiable human passions. This is one advantage of our disadvantaged situation. To proceed: are you in love with anyone?

BARBARINA.   Certainly not.

RENZO.   Nor am I. Love is the wellspring of warped desires. It breeds a mania for dressing in elaborate clothes and for playing at gallantry, for wooing and giving presents. It makes lovers look foolish and merchants sweat with worry if they've extended credit to anyone in love. We are not, and so our good fortune outweighs our poverty. We must never allow our natural selves to grow used to anything that is considered convenient or comfortable. We must never fall in love, never contract friendships. Every man and woman, remember, is actuated by self-love. Let us hold to the conclusion that men and women in general are proud, greedy, vain, vindictive, and antisocial. Let us root out every trace of self-love, and we will be happy. Come.

BARBARINA.   Ah, Renzo, as I said, I'm not in love and I will hew to the life of a philosopher. But I confess I do like a certain green bird, which seems to like me. Now and then he flutters around me.

RENZO.   I will cure you of that love with an explanation. By instinct, birds flutter around flirtatious women.[7] This bird thinks you are a flirt. Hence the fluttering around. We had better hurry away from this city's temptations. (*Exit.*)

BARBARINA.   Oh, what a sad world if even love proves false and I cannot trust the friendship of a green bird! (*Exit.*)

### SCENE 6

*In the drains below the palace kitchen. Here* NINETTA, *dressed in dreary clothes, has been imprisoned for eighteen years.*

NINETTA.   Am I still alive? After all these years in this stinking pit, where so much filth keeps pouring down? What a fate for Concul's daughter, poor Ninetta! Wasn't I less miserable when I was trapped inside that fatal orange, a prisoner of the giantess Creonta? I committed no crime, yet as soon as I'd given birth, they buried me alive in this fetid hole. Here comes the only being who pities me, the green bird. He flies down the shaft from the world above to bring me food. Green bird, it would be better if you'd let me die! Then my inhuman husband and his hateful mother would be satisfied. (*She weeps.*)

## SCENE 7

*The* GREEN BIRD *has entered, and gives her a flask and a loaf.*

GREEN BIRD.   You don't need to weep any more, Ninetta; perhaps this imprisonment is almost at an end.

NINETTA.   A miracle! The green bird can speak!

GREEN BIRD.   My words strike you as miraculous, Ninetta, after I've kept eighteen years of silence. But remember your own miracle—how Tartaglia peeled away the orange and found you inside. You know such transformations are possible. I am a king's son. In my youth an ogre put a spell on me and changed me into a green bird. My future and yours are in the hands of your daughter Barbarina, whom I love. Destiny's brutal decrees lie heavy on us both.

NINETTA.   I must know more. What did I do to deserve this punishment? How is my husband? How are my precious children?

GREEN BIRD.   Your only crime was to incur the hatred of Tartagliona. After your husband left, she wrote to him and accused you of adultery, saying you had given birth to two puppies. He thought you were guilty and sent her back instructions to take whatever action she pleased. The cruel old woman ordered you to be imprisoned and your children put to death. Don't be distressed. They are not dead, thanks to that good old man Pantalone. Their names are Renzo and Barbarina. They believe their parents are unknown, and they are homeless wanderers. But you still have cause to hope, Ninetta. And to pray. For if they escape the dangers that lie ahead of them, you will return to the throne; Tartagliona will perish; and I will slough off this plumage and take Barbarina for my queen, so long as she proves worthy. I can tell you no more. I must turn tail and fly. (*He takes off and disappears.*)

NINETTA.   Astounding! I can hardly believe it. Yes—I'll eat and pray to survive. If I escape from this living death, no story ever told will be more astonishing than my eighteen years of endurance.

## SCENE 8

*A street in the city.* BRIGHELLA, *alone*

BRIGHELLA.   I feel spiritually refreshed. After putting away a ton of sheep's liver and a mile of bologna, I've got astrology, poetry, and prognostication all gurgling away in my gut. Any minute now they'll burst out in a blast of inspiration. Some great event bears down on us. What can it be? Queen Tartagliona, you'll need my help, you magnificent old wreck. I still respond to your wrinkled allure. You're an old bag, but still a queen. Besides, there is no accounting for taste. Poets have inclinations that set them apart from the masses. I'll woo you with tiny attentions, dainty compliments, and irresistible rhymes . . .

Your silvery hairs like dainty lace
Tumble around your golden face.[8] (*Exit.*)

## SCENE 9

BARBARINA *and* RENZO *on an open beach*

BARBARINA.  Renzo, it's nearly dark. There's nothing here but a deserted beach. I'm cold. The sea air is freezing my tears, making my hands shake and my teeth chatter. I'm afraid of being overcome by self-love.

RENZO.  Suppress it, Barbarina. Be strong. I'm so hungry I can hardly stand up. But this empty, sterile beach puts us at a healthy distance from treacherous people who act only out of self-love. It renews my spirit.

BARBARINA.  But if, by chance, some person came along and took us to an inn with a blazing fire, a hearty meal, and a good bed, be honest— would you turn them down?

RENZO.  I would probably enjoy the meal, the fire, and the bed. But as for the giver—I'm convinced he would be helping us only out of self-indulgence, and I would be suspicious of taking his gifts.

BARBARINA.  But I'm so hungry, cold, and weary I believe that darling person would be showing love for us, not for himself.

RENZO.  Exactly. Love. That person might be a woman, doing it to seduce me, because I'm a man, or might be a man doing it to seduce you, because you're a woman. Either way, don't you see, the act has an ulterior motive. At the very least, it's performed for reasons of fanaticism or love of glory, so that people will say the giver is noble, heroic, hospitable, loving, or generous. Such acts are always drenched in self-love. Always, always, always!

BARBARINA.  Renzo, the hunger, cold, and exhaustion are beginning to overwhelm me and make me think you are a maniac, more drenched in self-love than anyone else.

RENZO.  How so?

BARBARINA.  All the rage and disdain you direct against others has its source in your own self-love. Rather than soften, you'd freeze and starve to death. Doesn't that look to you like fanaticism?

RENZO  (*Pensively*).  Wait a moment. I wonder if you're right. I can't deny that if you are, I'd regret it.

## Scene 10

*The earth shakes, strange sounds and colors, then darkness. Out of it appears* CALMON, *the ancient statue.*

CALMON.  Barbarina *is* right. Open your eyes, Renzo.

BARBARINA.  Oh, God, a statue that moves! And talks!

RENZO.  This is the sort of phenomenon that philosophers do not allow themselves to believe in. And yet it's real. What are you?

CALMON.  What was I? A shabby philosopher, like you, who thought he could unmask the souls of others and detected self-love behind all their actions. I saw, or in my ravings I imagined I saw, reason enslaved by the senses. I thought I saw the bold intelligence of humanity becoming miserly, ungrateful, self-seeking. I could discern no generosity in others. I viewed the human species and its most beautiful and illustrious Maker with superb contempt. If only my tongue had been torn out before it belittled generous behavior by one man toward his fellows, ascribing it to fanaticism and folly, the consequences of self-love and extreme, complacent stupidity. With the aid of such preachings I probably put a stop to I don't know how many kind actions. What good, Renzo, what earthly good can come out of suspecting and ridiculing everything, and employing my eloquence to persuade others that man is always wicked and selfish, that reason is a slave to the senses? You do nothing but provoke hatred and make men suspicious of one another. Renzo, you are a man like all the rest. If anyone told you that he could judge your soul, as you claim to judge others, you would be ashamed. Driven by your self-love, you would do anything to convince people that you are loyal, kind, sympathetic, humane. That is how you want to be. That is how people *should* be. Reason is not the slave of your senses; it allows you to distinguish good from bad. So love yourself in moderation by loving others. Follow your reason. It is a gift from heaven; it does not serve the senses but controls them. Learn to love yourself and you will become the man you wish to be.

BARBARINA.   Renzo, that doesn't sound like bad philosophy.

RENZO.   But what is he, after all? A statue, a musty, decrepit moralizer. And he still hasn't disproved that self-love is the underlying motive of all action.

CALMON.   My boy, I once thought and spoke the same cynicism. Four hundred years ago! I too despised others. I wanted to suppress my feelings and conquer all traces of self-love. But as my heart hardened, so did my body. I turned into marble and fell. I lay for many years on the ground, half-buried in filth, a stony shape on which passers-by answered the calls of nature. The same would happen to any person who wished to act against self-love, the basis of every action.

RENZO.   How does this tedious recital of yours apply to me, Signor Statue? You're agreeing with me that everything is self-love—everything, everything!

CALMON.   Foolish sophist! You reason like those heathens who seek to excuse their faults by mocking the exquisite workmanship of our eternal Maker. Where you find self-love, there you also find compassion, pity for the unfortunate, the longing for virtue, the fear of death and everlasting punishment. Do not distort the truth. Man is only a part of God, and in loving himself, man loves his Creator. Self-love proceeds from heaven, and no one feels it more keenly than the person who acts with compassion, virtue, and pity, assuring himself of an eternal life by loving his divine essence. Such a man loves honor, which your false teachers call fanaticism to excuse their own defects. But a judgment day will come at last, when everyone will turn from you in disgust. Your only consolation then will be that, while you lived, you sought an earthly, a mundane greatness. Do not follow the lead of those devilish philosophers who reject a supernal and immortal shelter. Raise your vision, lowly creature, from the earth to the empyrean and the stars, and do not restrict it to the emptiness of our earthbound senses.

BARBARINA.   He does seem to know what he's talking about.

RENZO.   Perhaps. But he cannot stop me from remaining a philosopher.

CALMON.   I will not stop you, but you will never be one. Men are too weak, as you, my callow friend, will soon see. Philosophy exists, maybe, but not philosophers.

RENZO.   Enough of that. Who are you? Where are you from?

CALMON.   My name is Calmon. Once I was a king. Now I am the king of statues. My subjects are superior to you mortals with your corrupt and vicious philosophers. Your ancestors dragged me out of the mud and stood me in a garden not far from the city you came from. To repay their good deed, my dear children, I have tracked you down.

BARBARINA.   Then you knew our ancestors, our parents? Please, Calmon, tell us—who are they? You must remember.

CALMON.   I do, but I cannot say. I can tell you only that momentous events are still to come and that how they are resolved and how you are identified depend on the green bird that flutters around Barbarina.

RENZO.   I'm beginning to think I'm a sheer fool. Obscure predictions . . . There's a green bird . . . Our fate depends on it . . . A man of marble can talk . . . My head's in a whirl.

CALMON.   Don't be surprised, Renzo. Plenty of human beings are more like statues than I am. You will learn how powerful a statue can be and how like a statue a man can easily become. That pebble at your feet—pick it up. Go back to the city. Stand in front of the palace and throw the pebble at it. You will instantly become rich. If you find yourself in danger, call my name. Calmon will be your friend.

(*The earth shakes. Prodigious happenings.* CALMON *is gone.*)

RENZO.   Very helpful. Here we are, orphans, starving, freezing, frightened, and holding a pebble. Now what?

BARBARINA   (*Who has picked up the pebble*). Do as he said. Go back to the city. Throw this pebble and wait for the miracles he promised. Perhaps our run of bad luck is coming to an end. But even if it doesn't, we'll be happy as long as our audiences like us.

## Act Two

*A hall in the palace. Loud music: a marching band*

### SCENE I

*King* TARTAGLIA, GUARDS, *and* PANTALONE, *who fidgets in the background*

TARTAGLIA.   Yes, I'm sad. And irritable. All that brass! (*Shouting*) Cut it short! You're splitting my head open. (*To the* GUARDS) And you— out! You give me the jitters, standing there like corpses.

PANTALONE   (*Aside*). Poor king, what the devil's wrong with him? I wanted to congratulate him, as soon as he returned, for putting down the rebellion, but he's in an ugly mood, as skittish as a colt.

TARTAGLIA   (*Aside*). This is where my Ninetta used to walk. There's the kitchen where she made the cook burn the roast beef. That was while she was still a dove, before she changed back into a woman. And there's the scullery, where the old king of hearts had us hide, before he condemned Smeraldina and proclaimed our marriage. All those memories![9] How sweet she was, how gentle! (*He turns away, so as not to be seen weeping, then hurriedly wipes his eyes and regains his composure.*)

PANTALONE   (*Aside*). I think I saw tears. For his queen, I'll bet, imprisoned eighteen years ago in that disgusting vault. I'll cheer him up, welcome him home, remind him of his victories, tell him the future looks rosy.

TARTAGLIA   (*Aside*). I'll never be happy without her. Oh, Ninetta! (*He again turns away, weeping, then recovers as before, putting on a stern front.*)

PANTALONE.   Your Majesty, I hope you feel on top of the world. Your eyes look red. When you weep, you make the whole court sad. We were so anxious to see you again, and now you're back we're overjoyed to—

TARTAGLIA.   Who says I'm weeping? How dare you, a mere minister, speak to me as if you were my equal—and about personal matters! Get out of my sight this instant or I'll put you in the pillories.

PANTALONE   (*Aside, leaving*). Argue with a king! I wanted to bring him up to date about Brighella's predictions and what the queen mother did to Ninetta and the children and how I tried to save them even though she threatened to cut out my tongue. We could have had a friendly chat. Too bad. When you've grabbed a dog by the tail, you have to know how to let go of it. (*He bows his way out.*)

## Scene 2

TARTAGLIA.   Rally yourself, Tartaglia! A king must act like a king, or seem to, and suppress his weaknesses, or seem to. Otherwise, how can his people respect him? But oh, I feel so miserable. Not one friend to share my grief. It was different when my cook Truffaldino was here. I looked on him as a companion, better than a brother. But he betrayed me. After all the favors I lavished on him, he made his little pile, married Smeraldina, then walked out on me and into the sausage business. The proverb is right. It's as easy to make a true friend as to wipe your ass on a rose. So I am alone. And with no one watching, I'll throw off all restraint and enjoy my sorrow to the full. (*Howling*) Oh, my little Ninetta! Come back. Comfort me. Look at this waterfall gushing out of my poor red eyes! Stop the flow. Where's your handkerchief? You've come! Hold still. (*He stalks an imaginary Ninetta, but cannot catch her.*) Gone! She escaped. (*He brays like an ass.*)

## SCENE 3

*Enter* TRUFFALDINO.

TRUFFALDINO. I thought I heard the king braying something. Yes! Your Majesty, greetings!

TARTAGLIA (*Aside*). Truffaldino! Did he hear me? Will he talk about what he heard? Will he make a fool of me? He certainly will. He's no longer my friend.

TRUFFALDINO. Don't you recognize your old pal? Truffaldino. Somebody just told me you'd got back. I rushed over to give you a hug, clap you on the back, tell you hello. When I remember the great times we had . . . the laughs . . . the kicks . . . Crawling across the desert, sand flies biting us almost to death, running away from the ogre—didn't we do everything together? And then back in the palace when the queen put me to sleep in the kitchen and burned the roast beef to cinders? Old times, great times . . .

TARTAGLIA (*Aside*). My pal, is he? I wonder . . . It would do me good to have a friend again, but can I trust him? Last time, he left me for a sausage shop. I'll see if I can test his true feelings. (*Gravely, aloud*) How are you, Truffaldino? You've put on weight. You look well.

TRUFFALDINO. Thanks. You know, six square meals a day, couple more at night. My piss is clear as lemonade. Beautiful bowel movement, perfect color and shape, smooth passage, reasonable smell, every morning, ten-thirty on the dot—I set my watch by it. At your service. Any other questions?

TARTAGLIA. You love your wife?

TRUFFALDINO. Yes. I did. Insanely. For two weeks it was bliss, heaven, exhaustion. We tried everything. After that she started to turn my stomach. I speak from the heart. We can't find one topic we agree on. She doesn't know enough to put up a decent argument a man can quarrel with. I speak from the heart. She's one of those old-fashioned women who's so soft she'll do anything for other men. Or other men's children. Imagine, she finds two orphans drowning, so she brings 'em home and brings 'em up. Imagine, for eighteen years she snatches the bread out of her mouth to feed 'em. Imagine, she has no mind worth mentioning, only prejudices, complaints, objections, and other weaknesses. No decent philosophy at all. Not like me. I speak from the heart. Imagine, not only is she stupid, but she's also repulsive. She starves herself; I watched her getting thinner day by day. Finally, I was driven by natural pressures to look for something more attractive in certain premises in a certain district your majesty probably doesn't remember any more. I speak from the heart.

TARTAGLIA  (*Aside*). It sounds as if he didn't come here out of friendship. (*Aloud*) How is your shop doing?

TRUFFALDINO. We're almost bankrupt. I speak from the heart. Not my fault. My wife handed out credit, free meals, even hard cash to every shabby ruffian that walked by. You know me, I'm thrifty. I never went near a bar, hardly ever, twice a day at the most, and then only to make friends, cultivate new customers, enjoy some philosophical ruminations. It's true, I did visit a few ladies, as I said, to refresh my eyes after looking at Smeraldina all day. But always at a discount, because I'd pick a chippy with sores all over her legs or no nose.[10] It's also true that I sat down to a game of cards now and then. But only to make up for my wife's private charity. Not that I ever won. Somebody kept dealing me queens. I'd take one look at the queen of spades with those sucked-in cheeks and think of Smeraldina and honestly, I'd feel ill and lose my concentration—and the hand. I speak from the heart.

TARTAGLIA  (*Aside*). He's a sex fiend, a cuckold, and a bankrupt—a genuine modern philosopher. He was always greedy. I remember how he wanted to eat those two oranges with the princesses in them. The cannibal! Did he come here out of affection? More likely, self-love. Out of friendship? More likely, hardship. (*Aloud*) The truth now, Truffaldino. Not your truth, the true truth. If you were not starving; if you didn't loathe the sight of your wife; if your business were flourishing, would you have come to the palace to make friends again?

TRUFFALDINO. I'll have to think that one over.

TARTAGLIA.   No thinking. I want a straight, quick answer. If I don't get it, I'll cut out that heart you keep speaking from.

TRUFFALDINO.   Let's see now. If I had plenty to eat and a wife I loved and a shop full of customers and money in my pocket, why, no, I would never have thought of you as a friend or anything else. This time I really do speak from the heart.

TARTAGLIA.   Out, you swindling, parasitic hedonist! (*Kicking his behind*) Out!

TRUFFALDINO   (*Aside, leaving*). He got so mad. And all I did was speak from the he—(*Exit.*)

TARTAGLIA.   Now what? I'm lonelier than ever, a joyless, unloved king . . .

(*He walks around raging, but pulls himself together when* TARTAGLIONA *enters.*)


SCENE 4

TARTAGLIONA.   My son, why do you ill-treat me so? For eighteen years you stay away from my loving embrace. Then, when I think I have you back, you become involved with ruling the country and with other frivolities, instead of rushing into my arms with a royal kiss.

TARTAGLIA.   My revered royal mother, do me one kindness. Retire to your royal chambers and leave me to my royal rage.

TARTAGLIONA.   Insolent boy! You don't act like the son of Tartagliona. I can read into the depths of your shallow soul. I see you remembering Ninetta. The horns she planted on your brow are more precious to you than the crowning glory of your mother's love. What else could I have done with a worthless, faithless woman who, instead of royal children, gave birth to puppies? Your letters left her punishment up to me. Now, as my reward, you neglect me. Show some respect! Remember: I am the queen of Tarots.

TARTAGLIA.   Mother darling, an old wreck like you should not heat up a son whose blood is at boiling point. When I wrote to you, your letters had already inflamed me. If I'd only stopped to—no, it's too late. I know you hated my poor Ninetta. We'll say no more about that. Only, please, royal mother mine, I ask you with all due respect to get out of my sight and stop being a pain in the royal ass.

TARTAGLIONA.   I can't believe what I heard. I, an old wreck? God in heaven, what an affront! Are you saying I did wrong? Should I have let everyone discover the disgrace that young gutter slut brought on you?

TARTAGLIA.   My father managed to bear the disgrace you brought on him. It didn't lead him to bury you alive. If I have anything to be ashamed of, it's your doing, not mine.

TARTAGLIONA.   My only disgrace lies in having borne an ape like you.

TARTAGLIA.   If you didn't want to bring an ape like me into the world, you should have died at childbirth.

TARTAGLIONA.   Ingrate! Is this my reward for carrying you for nine cruel moons?

TARTAGLIA.   A reward? I'll buy you a donkey to haul you around for the same number of moons.

TARTAGLIONA.   Inhuman son! When you were tiny, I never used wet nurses. You took milk from my breasts. And this is how you repay me!

TARTAGLIA.   No, *this* is how: When the milkmaids come by, I'll give you back twenty crates of sour milk. But you, you can never give me back my Ninetta, my princess, my queen. What's left for me? After eighteen years of fighting my own people, I'm worn out. I want peace in the kingdom again and a wife's lovely bosom to rest my head on. But you buried her alive under the drains of the palace kitchen, and now I have no peace, no wife, no friends. (*He weeps.*)

TARTAGLIONA.   My poor baby, I forgive you, but you get depressed too easily. Let me cheer you up. We'll play our little games every day, Postman's Knock, Chase the Pussy, and Under the Stairs. I'll send Big Babetta and Isabella the Hot to your room at bedtime.[11] They'll lift your morale. And Mommy will find you a delicious new queen.

TARTAGLIA.   Was that one of your games, Mother, banishing Ninetta? Find me the most seductive nymphs in the woods and the most dazzling goddesses in heaven. They won't get under my skin. Once and for all—go!

TARTAGLIONA.  Your own mother! You dismiss your own royal mother? Heaven, strike him down with a thunderbolt!

TARTAGLIA.  If you won't go, I won't stay. Your catarrh is choking you. I won't embarrass you by watching while you cough it up. I'm going to bed. (*Exit.*)

## SCENE 5

TARTAGLIONA  (*Coughing*). Oh this rage, this catarrah, this rage! I can't get it out of my throat. It's killing me. This is my punishment from heaven. Extraordinary that one can't put an innocent person to death, even with the best of intentions. The day of reckoning always comes. Ah, my astrologer, my poet—just in time. (*This last remark follows the arrival of* BRIGHELLA.)

## SCENE 6

BRIGHELLA.
  Greedy flames
  Of the torch
  In my mind,
  Do not scorch.
  In ignorance
  I felt content.
  Our perseverance,
  Is it spent?

TARTAGLIONA.  What was that again?

BRIGHELLA.
  The twins come closer,
  The walls grow higher,
  The night looks murkier.
  Take off your dress
  And shake out the fleas.
  It's time to sleep.
  As your guardian owl
  I'll spy into your future
  And do all I can
  To keep you from your fate.
  I'll try, I'll try,
  But time rushes by.

TARTAGLIONA.   He makes my brain ache and my buttocks shake.

O wicked prophet,
I hereby command:
Speak only poetry
Queens understand.

BRIGHELLA.
Dear lady, my sighs—
I'm sorry, excuse me—
Your gummy old eyes—
My queen, don't abuse me
But your great hanging tits,
Which make my blood curdle
And shake up my guts—
No, now you're a turtle!

(*Aside*) What inspiration! That ought to do it. I bowled her over, I hope. If she falls for my compliments, the poetic quintessence of my mental perspiration, she'll maybe put me in her will. (*Exit.*)

### Scene 7

TARTAGLIONA.   He agitates me with his dark remarks. At least, he seems to be fond of me. That's something. I'll take his advice and rest these limbs worshiped by the most renowned poet of the century. I am not without allure, and can surely keep him at my feet forever. But I hope my favoritism toward him will not arouse the jealousy of my other admirers. Unlucky stars! My very beauty is my enemy.

### Scene 8

RENZO *and* BARBARINA *are looking at one facade of the palace.*

BARBARINA.   Here's the palace, Renzo, and I still have the pebble Calmon told us to throw. Shall we do it?

RENZO.   He said we'll be rich. Yes. Throw it.

BARBARINA.   So you do want to be rich. I see your philosophical detachment draining away.

RENZO.   You keep saying that to me, Barbarina. Your taunts almost make me forget I'm hungry and cold. And this illustrates once again that when a powerful enough passion takes over a man's mind, it becomes dangerous in enabling him to neglect the demands of nature. But I love philosophy still and am not ashamed of doing so.

BARBARINA.   Can't we nourish ourselves on philosophy, then? Forget the stone. Becoming rich in an instant will make us suddenly feel all sorts of ridiculous and extravagant yearnings. You'll want all the women, all the delights you dream of at night. I'll become vain: I'll want suitors, lovers, ornaments, fashions. We'll go mad, tormented by possibilities. We'll despise the poor and the miserable who live like us now. No, I will not throw the pebble.

RENZO.   Enough of these doubts. Philosophy can survive among the rich. This hunger and this cold I feel convince me that once we are rich we will still know how to defend ourselves from foolish thoughts, and that, with our books to guide us, we will remain philosophers.

BARBARINA.   So hunger and cold do make you think? I'm afraid that all philosophers are people in want, compelled to think by hunger, cold, and the demands of nature. How marvelous it must be to rule the weak minds of philosophical followers, and develop a theory to make oneself the ruler of those fools who are impressed by charlatans! So . . . I will throw this and make a wish that, if I become rich, I never forget that I owe everything to a dirty little pebble.

(*She throws it. A stately mansion rises opposite the palace. The rags worn by* RENZO *and* BARBARINA *are transformed into sumptuous clothes. From the mansion come two* SERVANTS, *with lighted torches, who escort them respectfully to the front entrance.*)

RENZO.   Barbarina, look at this! I'm overwhelmed.

BARBARINA.   You see? We can believe what Calmon predicted. We mustn't let this palace fool us into thinking we will grow happy. There will be misfortunes and tears.

## Act Three

*A room in the palace*

### SCENE I

BRIGHELLA *and* TARTAGLIONA

BRIGHELLA.   I turn pale as I gaze upon that wrinkled brow, against which the darts of love and death grow blunted.[12]

TARTAGLIONA.   Poet, enlighten me about the imposing structure there. It outshines my own palace in splendor and majesty. How could it rear up during a single night?

BRIGHELLA.   Dear queen of my heart, a higher power constrains my tongue. Destiny!

TARTAGLIONA.   If my charms have any power over you, tell me who lives there.

BRIGHELLA.   Eyes of pearl, crossed orbs! My ravishing one, I know everything, but I may not speak. I will merely state that those who dwell in that mansion have arrived to undo these milky lips, these snowy lashes, and these dehydrated breasts.

TARTAGLIONA.   Will you cease these recondite ravings? Take what you want from me, only tell me in straightforward words how to undo these people who mean to undo me. You are my only hope.

BRIGHELLA.   Majesty, joy of my poetic fecundity, before you do a thing, think of the future. Make out your will. Don't overlook the one who loves you to the point of folly and will immortalize your name with a poem, which will resist the rotting teeth of time and that offspring of envy, criticism.

TARTAGLIONA.   Don't say anything more about death. Immortalize me while I'm still alive and youthful.

BRIGHELLA   (*Aside*). Oh, the crone! When it comes to the will— tough as tortoiseshell (*Aloud*) You wanted it; you'll get it. I'll speak the plain truth, though a poet shouldn't. Doom hangs over your head. So listen with ears aflame. In that mansion are a boy and girl, brother and sister. Before they got rich they were paupers. They lived off talk, air, philosophy. Overnight they found themselves rolling in gold, so they kissed philosophy good-by. They're spoiled by greed now, like a washerwoman who married a count or a customs man on the take. They won't accept anyone else's advice, but anything else that anyone else has—they must have. And the more they have, the more they want. And that is how we'll tempt them to destruction.

TARTAGLIONA.   I'm still listening. I will do whatever you suggest.

BRIGHELLA.   Fatal fascinatress, you've heard of the forbidden apple that sings and the musical waters that dance. These wonders are to be found far from this city, guarded by Serpentina the fairy.

TARTAGLIONA.   Yes, it's a dismal, dangerous spot. Go on.

BRIGHELLA.   We must arrange for you to see the girl who lives in the mansion. She's lost touch with her philosophy and has become philosophy personified. Here's what you do. Spit out these magic words to her:

> You are lovely, but you'd be the loveliest thing
> In the world if you owned the apple that can sing.

(TARTAGLIONA *repeats the lines.*)

BRIGHELLA.   Excellent! Next, you toss out this second little ditty:

> You are lovely, but you would enhance
> Your beauty with the waters that dance.

(TARTAGLIONA *repeats the lines.*)

BRIGHELLA.   Flawless! Those words will work a miracle. You have to study the human heart under all conditions. And just in case these two spells don't do the trick, I have something better up my sleeve.

TARTAGLIONA.   I'll memorize them. "You are lovely, but . . ." (*Exit, rehearsing.*)

BRIGHELLA.   We'll do what we can to add a few years to this luscious antique. But if I can't wear her down and get her to slip me into her will, what good does it do me to wear the laurels of Apollo and read the future and wallow in poetic frenzies? As Petrarch says in his sonnet,

> "My hopes slip through my fingers now, alas,
> No more the diamonds that they seemed, but glass . . ."[13]

(*Exit.*)

## SCENE 2

*The twins' mansion, a magnificent hall.* BARBARINA *primps before a mirror.*

BARBARINA.   Tomorrow I hope to make a dramatic impact in my scarlet robe with gold embroidery.

## SCENE 3

SMERALDINA *is pushing her way in past the servants.*

SMERALDINA.   Will you let me in? I'm sick of this! Calling cards, appointments, delays—how many times am I supposed to come back later?

BARBARINA.   Who's that shouting?

SMERALDINA.   It's me, dammit.

BARBARINA   (*To* SMERALDINA). Outrageous! How dare you! (*To the* SERVANTS) Where did you pick up your training? You have the audacity to admit beggars to my dressing rooms?

SMERALDINA.   Hey, snotnose, is this how I brought you up? Is this how you welcome people into your place? Not long ago you were as poor and shabby as me.

BARBARINA.   Insolent woman, moderate your tongue! Have you no respect for my position? Not one step closer! Yes, I recognize you, worst luck, and I'll gladly pay you to get out of this house, and this town. You revive too many bad memories. Lackeys, give this creature money and show her out.

SMERALDINA.   Why, you green sprout, you upstart, you high-stepping clotheshorse, you want to make me feel out of place here? I fed you my milk. I spanked you a thousand times. And now you think you can scare me away? I'm not here for your money. I came out of love. Even after you walked out on me so roughly I couldn't stop crying. And then when I heard you were back here, and rich, I ran all the way to congratulate you on your good luck. May lightning strike me dead if it was self-love. No, it was because . . . because . . . I do love you, and . . . to hell with self-love! I'm trying to say I came to kiss you, not curse you. You look so pretty, so sweet, dressed up like that, bless your little heart. I will kiss you, I must. I could eat you up. (*She tries to embrace her.*)

BARBARINA.   Intimacy, too? This is intolerable. (*To a* SERVANT) Hurry! Give this woman some gold and get rid of her. (*The* SERVANT *bows and leaves.*)

SMERALDINA.   Barbarina, the truth now: you're not serious? You wouldn't do this to me, turn me away? You've known me so long, so well, you couldn't really believe I came to beg or sponge. You know I came here out of love for two people who're like my flesh and blood, kids I took care of like a mother.

(*The* SERVANT *returns with a purse of gold coins.*)

BARBARINA   (*Ironically*). Take this gold. It'll repay your love and any good deeds you've ever done. Then go. I don't wish to see you again. I find you nauseating.

SMERALDINA   (*Aside*). She's tormenting me. And yet I can't give her up. (*Aloud*) Barbarina, you're wrong. I still hope you won't put me out of your home after I kept you for eighteen years in mine—out of pure love, too, not for gold. I couldn't help it when you were kicked out. I told you: I've been in tears ever since. (*She weeps.*)

BARBARINA   (*Aside*). She's making me feel sorry for her. But I don't have to put up with this any longer. (*Aloud*) Take the gold, Smeraldina, and go. I can't stand the sight of you or the way you try to ingratiate yourself. (*To a* SERVANT) Get this woman out of here. Walk her back to her hovel and carry her gold and leave her there.

(*The* SERVANT *takes* SMERALDINA *by the arm.*)

SMERALDINA.   Don't! Have pity on me! Daughter, maybe I did act too familiar. I'm honestly sorry. I'll never take liberties like that again, as if I was as good as you. I'll treat you like a real lady, with respect. I can't face it, being separated from you. Let me stay. I'll be the lowest of your servants. I can eat throwaway food, other people's leavings. Barbarina, please! I got used to being with you. I'm so fond of you and Renzo. I'll be the most faithful and devoted servant in your home. But if you've made up your mind to put me out, at least let me leave as poor as I came. Keep your gold. Motherly love brought me here, love for two ungrateful children, not for riches, not for gold. (*She weeps.*)

BARBARINA   (*Aside*). Why do her naive words have such a strong effect on me? The more she talks, the more reluctant I feel to discard her. I can't be altogether heartless. (*Aloud*) You may stay, Smeraldina, but only if you never again mention the past. Those memories you dredge up are like reproaches. They incense me. Treat me according to the position I have now, not like the beggar I was once. Now follow me. Say no more. (*Exit.*)

SMERALDINA.   So this is the philosopher! Yesterday she went out to get firewood. And today . . . Amazing! I'd like to stay because I love her. That's settled. I'll stay. And I'll try to keep quiet. I may not succeed. I don't know her any more. She's so haughty. How the devil did she come by all this wealth? I hope that the little flirt didn't . . . with some lord, maybe? I'll soon find out. (*Exit.*)

<h2 align="center">SCENE 4</h2>

*Enter* RENZO *in a yearning mood.*

RENZO.   Never have I seen a woman of greater beauty than the statue in my garden. I gaze at her and can't look away. Some madness has taken hold of me. How can I, who always scorned women, have fallen in love with a woman carved out of stone? Yes, Calmon, you spoke of it—the frailty of the human heart. You knew I'd suddenly learn the power exerted by a statue. Now let me take advantage of my riches. I'll summon magicians from all over to bring her to life. Gold makes everything possible. I can still hope.

<h2 align="center">SCENE 5</h2>

TRUFFALDINO   (*From offstage*). Anybody home? I've been yelling my guts out. He wasn't upstairs or outside. Renzo, jackass, wooden-head, where are you, you dope?

RENZO.   That sounded like Truffaldino, but I can't believe he'd ever have the nerve to face me again after what he did to us.

TRUFFALDINO   (*Entering*). There you are, Son. Great to see you again. What the hell are you up to? Hiding from me? Why didn't you answer? (*He takes off his butcher's apron and brushes off his clothes.*) When do we eat?

RENZO.   Who do you think you are, barging in here? What do you want?

TRUFFALDINO.   Dinner. Mug of beer. And then, I think, a snooze.

RENZO.   Perhaps you don't recall how you behaved toward us yesterday?

TRUFFALDINO.   Course I do. For a philosopher, you sure ask dumb questions.

RENZO.   What's dumb about that question? Why did you throw us out?

TRUFFALDINO.   It's obvious. You were orphans and broke. You didn't bring home a scrap of food.

RENZO.   And you have the impudence after that to trespass on my property?

TRUFFALDINO.   What a crass thing to ask! Not a trace of philosophy in it.

RENZO.   Why, you squirt . . . How dare you?

TRUFFALDINO.   Easy. I heard you got rich. I figured you could support me: feed me, pay off my gambling debts, rent a few girls for me. Why are you shocked? You look like something out of the dark ages, no philosophy visible.

RENZO.   (*In a fury*). I'll philosophy you, up the rear end.

TRUFFALDINO.   The boy's raving. I'm trying to give you sensible answers to stupid questions. Any enlightened man will tell you the same thing . . . The poor go to the houses and homes of the rich to eat them out of house and home. That's how the world turns. Ask any beggar. I speak from the heart.

RENZO.   (*Starting to laugh*). I never heard a more candid philosopher. I'm almost tempted to let you stay, because I don't dislike your frankness. But you're such an evil character that, unless you go voluntarily, I think I'll have you whipped off the premises.

TRUFFALDINO.   Let me think. (*Aside*) I don't like the choice. I made the same mistake with the king. Sincerity doesn't pay. I'll try something different. Insincerity. It might be worth a decent meal. (*Aloud*) May I have one more word with you?

RENZO.   You may not. What is it?

TRUFFALDINO   (*He goes out, then reenters, cap in hand*). My lord, may I be so bold as to inconvenience your lordship with a petty request? Perhaps you will be magnanimous enough to extend your aristocratic pardon to me for having expelled you and a certain other person from my habitat. Inexcusable! However, I have several excuses. I am a poor and uneducated man. I didn't know any better. I should have, but I didn't. Also I was drunk. The poor, my lord, drink to console themselves for not being able to afford more to drink. Now I bitterly repent for not showing you the respect you deserve and, yes, demand. I fall at your feet to worship the most worthy, the most excellent, the most generous of high-minded, noble, sagacious masters ever to forgive his excessively humble and contrite servant. For that is the honor I seek—to serve you until the day one of us is reduced to dust. Or both of us. Was that better?

RENZO.  Now I'm beginning to wonder. Are you slow-witted or a little too fast for me? A fool or a fake? You're a fool, a clown! And that's what you will be from now on, my clown. I'll keep you for entertainment.

TRUFFALDINO.  I'm sorry if I made such clumsy fun of you. In future I'll do it with more grace, more art, more finesse, and the most up-to-date tricks, lies, and cunning.

RENZO  (*Smiling*). If you make me smile you'll help take my mind off my overpowering passion. Besides, a rich man needs a clown to ratify his social standing. Come. (*Exit.*)

TRUFFALDINO  (*After extravagant bows and ceremony—aside*). What a pity. It's impossible to be honest and speak from the heart to the rich. (*He improvises some exaggeratedly servile behavior. Exit.*)

## SCENE 6

*A balcony of the palace facing the balcony of the twins' mansion.* PANTALONE *and* TARTAGLIA *in nightcaps and with a telescope*

TARTAGLIA.  I don't understand this, Pantalone. It's as if I'm asleep and dreaming or taking part in a play with transformations. I never imagined a mansion could spring up overnight like a mushroom.

PANTALONE.  But it did, Your Majesty, and what a fancy fungus it is! Last night I was hurrying back here in the dark across the square, which I thought was empty, when I walked right into that wall. Poor old me. Almost cracked my skull. Luckily, my belly got in the way. It took me half an hour to find a way around it and get back to the palace.

TARTAGLIA  (*Looking through the telescope*). A big and beautiful structure. Big and beautiful columns. Big and beautiful design. There's more architecture there than in the whole Coliseum.

PANTALONE.  Wait till you see the owners, Your Majesty. Marvels!

TARTAGLIA.   You've seen them? What are they: gods or devils?

PANTALONE.   A boy like an apricot and a girl like a dab of butter. One look at her, I swear, and you'll come clean out of the dumps.

TARTAGLIA.   Don't remind me of how unhappy I am. My darling Ninetta, I'll never stop grieving for her. (*He weeps.*)

PANTALONE.   Hush, they're coming out. There she is! Please! Will you look at that glorious creature?

## SCENE 7

BARBARINA *and* SMERALDINA *come out onto the balcony of the mansion.*

SMERALDINA.   The king's on his balcony, Barbarina. Let's go back inside.

BARBARINA.   So that's the king? What do I care? I'll pretend I can't see him. Anyway, kings are only men.

TARTAGLIA   (*Looking through the telescope*). Pantalone, Pantalone, what a face! What hands! My heart's pounding. My sadness has flown away.

PANTALONE.   Of course it has. One glance at a face like that and anybody'd be happy, even if he was up to his eyebrows in debt.

SMERALDINA.   Barbarina, see that? He's staring at us through the telescope. When it comes to kings you have to be cautious.

BARBARINA.   Stop pestering me. What's wrong with my looks? Are they displeasing? Let him stare all he wants. We'll retire in good time, and by then he'll have caught fire, you'll see, and won't know what's taken hold of him.

TARTAGLIA.   Pantalone, Pantalone, what lips! What a bosom! My memories of the late Ninetta are fading.

PANTALONE   (*Aside*). She's taken him by storm. But what if the poet's vision comes true? Leave well enough alone. Let him feel better. The king's minister shouldn't oppose his passions but encourage them. Your Majesty, how do you like her hairdo and that tasteful dress?

SMERALDINA.  Please, Barbarina, come. The way he's eyeing you, if he does catch fire, watch out. Rulers have long arms; they take whatever they want. Shame on you, come away.

BARBARINA.  I hope he does fall in love. He's a widower, isn't he?

SMERALDINA.  Now listen, that's too much. You and a king!

BARBARINA.  Quiet, presumptuous woman! He's not good enough for me.

TARTAGLIA.  The coiffure must be by Carletto and the gown is probably a creation of Canziani. Pantalone, I'm mad about her. I can't stand it. Look at my eyes; they must be on fire. What beauty, what a creature! I want to greet her, say something, anything, to her. But I feel bashful. What if she doesn't respond? The monarch in me has dissolved. I've turned into a helpless boy.

PANTALONE.  Now, now, Your Majesty. Don't let it get you down. You mustn't demean yourself for her. She's honored when you so much as look at her. A king throws a kiss and three thousand girls jump off a balcony.

TARTAGLIA.  I'll try it, Pantalone, I'll try it!

PANTALONE.  With regal dignity, Your Majesty.

(TARTAGLIA *throws a kiss with exaggerated regal dignity.*)

SMERALDINA.  Now we're coming to the dirty stuff. A kiss on the wind.

BARBARINA.  Watch this. I can't be bothered to look back at him. (*She turns away.*)

TARTAGLIA.  That was like punching water. Pantalone, I'm desperate.

PANTALONE.  She has some gall, this chit.

TARTAGLIA.  My head's spinning. Teach me a couple of words in your winning Venetian dialect. Help me out: be my pimp.

PANTALONE.   Thanks for the honor, Your Majesty. In Venice, though, we make love in French or English, and I wouldn't know how to go about it.

TARTAGLIA.   Wait, I've got it. I'll get acquainted by throwing off some brisk and witty observations. (*Calling out*) Hello, beautiful young lady. Can you feel this scirocco wind? (*Quietly*) How was that, Pantalone?

PANTALONE.   Ideal. I've often heard that line used, and it always made a powerful impression.

BARBARINA   (*Calling back*). The scirocco feels warm, signor, but your words leave me cold.

SMERALDINA.   What a cheeky reply to a king!

TARTAGLIA.   She answered me, Pantalone! She answered with a delicious insult. Wonderful! Now I must follow up with something clever and enticing, which alludes to her beauty. (*Calling out*) This morning the sun rose very bright.

PANTALONE.   Better still! You don't need a prompter, Your Majesty. You're a whiz at this.

BARBARINA.   A bright sunrise, sire, is brighter for some people than for others.

PANTALONE   (*Aside*). She got him good that time, the little flirt. She knows the territory.

TARTAGLIA.   She's so vivacious, the little devil. I'm hot. I can't resist her, and I need a wife again. I feel much better now. Ninetta's dead and luckily there are no other obstacles. I forgive my mother completely. And here she is! Mother, Mother! Cupid has converted me. I love you again. I love everybody, especially . . . But come here and see this monstrously beautiful maiden.

PANTALONE   (*To himself*). Oh, God, now the fat's in the fire.

BARBARINA.   Well, Smeraldina, can a king resist a woman like me?

SMERALDINA.   Well, Barbarina, you have the looks, the style, and the wealth. But don't be so proud of yourself. Maybe there's something else missing.

BARBARINA.  Don't answer me back. There is nothing missing.


SCENE 8

BRIGHELLA *and* TARTAGLIONA *appear on the king's balcony.*

BRIGHELLA  (*To* TARTAGLIONA). Now, lips that lock my heart, remember the magic lines.

TARTAGLIONA  (*To* BRIGHELLA). Rely on me. (*To* TARTAGLIA) So, my son, where is this divine object that has captivated you?

TARTAGLIA.
There, on that rich verandah, is the one—
Aurora, who outshines the noonday sun.

PANTALONE  (*Aside*). Infatuated isn't the word. He's sinking into verse.

TARTAGLIONA.  Yes, quite fetching. (*To* BRIGHELLA) Now I'll put your spell on her. (*To* BARBARINA)

You are lovely, but you'd be the loveliest thing
In the world if you owned the apple that can sing.

TARTAGLIA.  Mother, you're senile. What the devil was that about?

PANTALONE  (*Aside*). Whoo! That's what I call being picky.

BARBARINA.  Smeraldina, did you hear that? An apple that sings. And I don't have it. I want it!

SMERALDINA.  I told you there's something you're missing.

TARTAGLIONA  (*To* BRIGHELLA). Listen to this. I'll finish her off. (*To* BARBARINA)

You are lovely, but you would enhance
Your beauty with the waters that dance.

TARTAGLIA.  Mother, stop interfering! What's the matter with you?

PANTALONE  (*Aside*). Apples that sing? Waters that dance? This sounds like one of Cappello's weird fairy tales.[14]

BARBARINA  (*Furiously*). Does she dare find fault with me? If they cost the earth, I'll have the apple that can sing and the waters that dance. (*Exit.*)

SMERALDINA.   And the stars in gravy, and the sun fried. (*Exit.*)

BRIGHELLA   (*Aside*). Vanity can conquer the heart and poetry take possession of the soul. (*Exit.*)

PANTALONE   (*Aside*). The royal boy looks pale; the old witch looks jubilant. This is my cue to take off. I have no desire to be a balcony spectator at a bloody tragedy between a mother and a son. (*Exit.*)

TARTAGLIA.   You tyrannical mother. You won't be happy till you've killed off your children.

TARTAGLIONA.   What exactly have I done to you, insolent boy?

TARTAGLIA.   If you were not my mother . . . God almighty!

TARTAGLIONA.   Silence, wretch! What are you accusing me of?

TARTAGLIA.   You've sent the woman I love to her death. You must have heard how dangerous it is to try to steal the apple that sings and the golden waters that dance! You wicked crone, you're so envious of beauty in others! Your eyes are all rheumy and you've lost your teeth, and still you try to persecute your son beyond endurance. What do you want? That I never remarry? Or marry my mother? Would you like to roast and devour my heart? I curse the moment when I came out of your adulterated womb to inherit this scepter, this throne, and this kingdom. (*Exit.*)

TARTAGLIONA.
So long as I avoid the fate Brighella could foresee,
Go grind your teeth, my saucy son—it's all the same to me. (*Exit.*)

### SCENE 9

*A room in the mansion.* RENZO, *holding a sheathed dagger, and* TRUFFALDINO

RENZO.   Truffaldino, did you ever come across anything more beautiful than the statue in my garden? Be honest. Don't flatter.

TRUFFALDINO.  More beautiful? Never. (Aside) And I never came across anything more cracked than falling for a statue.

RENZO.  And anybody looking at her would appreciate my loving a statue?

TRUFFALDINO.  Naturally. That's the finest kind of love. One-sided. Unselfish. Platonic. It makes nonsense of the old song. (*Singing*)

> Is there any record of
> A man and woman in platonic love?
> A devil might insist we could achieve it—
> But me? No hope! I simply don't believe it.

(*Aside*) I could never go for a statue like her. Unless she had softer lips.

RENZO.  While I was kneeling and entreating her to come to life, did you hear what the green bird said to me?

TRUFFALDINO.  No, I didn't hear a thing. And I never saw any green bird.

RENZO.  The green bird that's in love with Barbarina.

TRUFFALDINO  (*Aside*). This is like the one about the pink elephant getting a ride on the back of a flea. (*Aloud*) Green bird, hey? That's a wonder. But no, I don't know anything about it.

RENZO.  You don't keep your eyes and ears open. Didn't you even see this dagger which landed at my feet?

TRUFFALDINO.  A bird *and* a dagger out there! Who'd have thought it! (*Aside*) He's beyond help.

RENZO  (*To himself*). The green bird said he couldn't reveal the names of my parents, but he filled my mind with mysterious questions. I must not turn away from danger. Why? And if I survive the greatest danger of all, I will bring my statue to life. How? And what use do I make of this dagger?

(*During this speech* TRUFFALDINO *mimics Renzo's gestures and expressions, enjoying the insanity of it all.*)

## SCENE 10

*Enter* BARBARINA *and* SMERALDINA, *who tries to restrain her.*

BARBARINA.   Smeraldina, stop dragging at me. I was sure I had everything. A woman of my station may not tolerate nonownership of the
miraculous apple and waters.

SMERALDINA.   You can't do a thing about it, child. Everybody in the
past who went after them died horribly. It's hopeless.

BARBARINA.   I must have them—waters that dance! an apple that
sings!—and I don't care if they're easy to get at or not, or if the whole
world dies.

RENZO.   Truffaldino, look at my sister. What put her into this wild
state? Do you know anything about this?

TRUFFALDINO.   She's in love with the green bird. (*Aside*) Or a stone
statue.

BARBARINA.   Renzo, I'm so miserable. Everybody scoffs at me. I'm
a joke.

RENZO.   Miserable? Why? People scoffing? It doesn't sound likely.

BARBARINA.   It's worse than likely. This mansion and its gold and jewels and lavish trappings and servants, as well as my own beauty, have all
become worthless. I've been jeered at for not possessing the apple that
can sing and the waters that dance. I'm no better off than any other
woman. Don't you understand the humiliation? Renzo, darling, do you
value your sister's life? I can't go on without those two treasures.

TRUFFALDINO.   I have to agree with her. An apple that sings and
waters that dance—she needs them more than her daily bread. (*Aside*)
She's further gone than he is. Since they got rich, nothing's too much
for this pair of bastards.

RENZO.   Barbarina, calm down. Those treasures are simply not obtain-
able. Don't you realize what's involved? Do you expect me to risk my
life for your vanity? To gratify a whim?

BARBARINA.   Barbarian brother! I knew it. You never really loved me.
(*To* SMERALDINA) Servant, hold me up. My heart's going so fast . . .

I'm giddy . . . Convulsions . . . A mist over my eyes . . . Oh, Renzo, Renzo, remember that your sister adored you and you killed her by refusing her an apple and some water. (*She swoons.*)

SMERALDINA.   Lousy rotten wealth: it eats away at the brain like a disease. Barbarina, my precious, be strong, be yourself again! People are laughing to see you die yearning for water and an apple.

(TRUFFALDINO *stops laughing helplessly, pulls himself together, gets busy.*)

TRUFFALDINO.   Stand away there! Give her room! Let her breathe! Get a stretcher!

RENZO.   At last I understand. Everything's falling into place. These are the dangers I must not avoid, according to the green bird. And I see the purpose of the dagger. I must undertake this mission to bring my statue to life. My sister's weak—but so am I, as I weep for the love of a statue. Barbarina, I promise you this—you shall have those treasures, and soon, or Renzo will be no more.

BARBARINA.   Thank you, thank you. I can breathe again. You mustn't die, but do bring me the apple and the waters.

RENZO (*Drawing the dagger*).   Keep this dagger while I'm away. As long as the blade remains clear, I will be alive. If it appears bloodstained, you will know I've died. Truffaldino will accompany me on this adventure.

TRUFFALDINO.   Normally I'd be delighted to. I speak from the heart. But right now I have a lot of things to take care of, so if you'll excuse me—

RENZO.   Come, or you're dismissed from my service. (*Exit.*)

TRUFFALDINO.   Who said I wouldn't? (*Aside*) Got to be prudent when you deal with people who are whacked-out. It's even worse when they're rich. But if they go on like this they'll soon be poor. (*He plays a tragic-heroic scene of departure.*) Farewell, fair ladies. Destiny has sounded the call and I must answer—if necessary, with my poor life, which may at last achieve a transcendent end. Unless I fulfill this sacred trust, expect never to see me more . . . (*As himself*) I'd sing an aria to mark my exit, but I forget the words because I have a stuffed nose.[15] (*Exit.*)

BARBARINA.   Smeraldina, I've won! Now I'll say prayers and offer sacrifices to the gods. Surely they will grant my wish, and not let me wear out my remaining days in sorrow. (*Exit.*)

SMERALDINA.   And this is the lady philosopher who made fun of self-love! Now she's rich, she'll let her brother die, so long as she gets what she wants, and she wants even the gods to obey her. The worst of it is—she's not much different from anyone else. (*Exit.*)

## Scene 11

*The underground prison.* NINETTA, *and the* GREEN BIRD, *which has brought her a flask and food*

GREEN BIRD.   Ninetta, Ninetta, fight off your weariness and tedium. Keep hoping, because a perilous quest is now under way and our fate depends on it. Eat your food—perhaps for the last time in this dungeon. The noon hour has struck to herald your freedom—possibly by this afternoon.

NINETTA.   Dear bird, you make my future happiness seem uncertain. What is this quest? Don't leave me in suspense, or these surroundings will make me dream up all kinds of awful possibilities.

GREEN BIRD.   I can tell you only this much. I am a friend to you and your children, and yet I am your enemy. I am even an enemy to myself since the ogre changed me into a bird. I can speak to anyone about anything I wish, anywhere I like—save on the mountain where the ogre lives, and where I must live too. There my words have terrible power. Elsewhere I may not give advice or tell your children who their parents are. Incest is imminent, an abominable marriage, hideous events! I should not have spoken. I must fly back to the mountain immediately and leave you here, but not for long. Be patient and hope. (*Exit.*)

NINETTA.   What do I make of that? Advice from heaven? Isn't it enough that I have been cut off for so long from my husband and dear children? How long must I remain buried in sorrow? (*Exit.*)

## Scene 12

*A wood.* TRUFFALDINO *and* RENZO, *armed*

TRUFFALDINO.   This is a transition scene. I brought a bottle for the water, see? We're lost in a typical wood for getting lost in, on the way to the garden of Serpentina, the fairy. If we stop we'll die of exhaustion. So on, on! And into the next scene . . .

## SCENE 13

*The garden of* SERPENTINA, *the fairy. In the rear, to one side, an apple tree, on the other, a grotto with a huge door that opens and closes with shrieks of protest. Near the entrance to the grotto dead bodies lie on the ground, some rotted away to skeletons, others still whole. A* WOMAN'S VOICE *speaks.*

SERPENTINA.
    You beasts who guard my garden, keep
    My apples safe, and never sleep
    So that my golden waters may
    In musical abandon play.
    New dangers are approaching now.
    I count on you not to allow
    The properties within my portals
    To suffer the touch of invading mortals.
    Whoever does not come too near
    May go his way—but strike with fear
    All trespassers! Defend this site
    From taint and bloated appetite.

## SCENE 14

RENZO *and* TRUFFALDINO *have reached the garden.*

RENZO.   From the descriptions I've heard, this is Serpentina the fairy's garden. That's the grotto where they say she keeps the golden waters that dance and make music; and over there you can see the tree of golden apples that are said to sing. Do you hear anything? Singing? Music? Does anything look dangerous?

TRUFFALDINO.   I don't hear a thing: no music, no voices. And I don't sense any danger. They've spread rumors to frighten boys away from stealing the apples.

RENZO.   Then go on into the grotto and fill that bottle with the water.

(TRUFFALDINO *goes hesitantly toward the grotto, retreats, goes forward again. A wave of music stops him in his tracks. He returns swiftly and gestures to* RENZO *to keep quiet.* RENZO *responds with the same gesture. Orchestral music is heard again and then the singing of the* APPLES.)

APPLE CHORUS.
O greedy people, must you strive
For more, as long as you're alive?
Be satisfied with what you own.
Don't hope to bleed each plant and stone.
Escape! Forsake this fatal zone!

APPLE DUET.
Does it do good to give advice
To human hearts as hard as ice?
To ears that will not heed, and eyes
That see no risk in theft and lies?
Can we make stupid people wise?

APPLE SOLO.
Is reason ever strong enough
To influence two souls in love?
Can mercy and compassion swerve
The love-blind from their tragic curve?
May stars provide
Them with a guide!

APPLE CHORUS.
O greedy people, must you strive
For more, as long as you're alive?
Be satisfied with what you own.
Don't hope to bleed each plant and stone.
Escape! Forsake this fatal zone!

(TRUFFALDINO *and* RENZO *have withdrawn a few paces in fright. They advance again cautiously.*)

RENZO.   Go ahead. Pick an apple.

TRUFFALDINO.   I will, I will. I'll pick the one who likes lovers. I noticed which one it was, and I'll bet you it's a girl apple. There she is: the soloist, the soprano.

(*He creeps toward the tree. From behind a* LION *and a* TIGER *spring out at him, roaring, their fangs bared. He flees. They turn and disappear.*)

RENZO.   Coward! You're afraid of a lion and a tiger?

TRUFFALDINO.   Not afraid. I didn't want to offend them.

RENZO.   Go into the grotto and fill that bottle.

(TRUFFALDINO *enters the grotto and stumbles over a skeleton, looks around, rushes back into Renzo's arms.*)

RENZO.   Now what?

TRUFFALDINO.   The place is alive with ske, with ske, skelly, skeletons and death's heads!

RENZO   (*Drawing his sword and wagging it at* TRUFFALDINO). You'll wear a death's head yourself if you don't get me that water. Meanwhile, I'll attack the animals and go for the apple. The green bird told me not to turn away from danger if I want my statue to come to life.

TRUFFALDINO.   Here I go. I'll work up a little courage first.

(*He performs the* lazzo *of turning into a strong man, then approaches the grotto, pushing the gate open. It swings back fiercely with a shriek, accompanied by a roar of thunder, and strikes him in the chest, sending him reeling and spinning until he falls, senseless. The bottle smashes. The gate snaps closed.* RENZO *has moved stealthily toward the tree. The* LION *and the* TIGER *spring out at him. He flails his sword, but they disarm him. He retreats hastily.*)

RENZO.   We're done for. Truffaldino's dead and I'm disarmed, helpless. Helpless? Didn't Calmon the statue say he'd help me if I called on him when I'm in trouble? Calmon, Calmon! I need your help.

(*Darkness, earth tremors, lightning*)


SCENE 15

CALMON *appears.*

CALMON.   Renzo, Renzo, where is your philosophy now? See what power riches have exerted over two philosophers! One sends her brother to his death out of sheer vanity. The other falls foolishly in love with a woman of stone, cares nothing for his life, and is so proud that he forgets who made him wealthy—his friend.

RENZO.   Forgive me, statue. Please don't reproach me—help me! I know your powers. Bring my poor servant back to life. Show me how to collect the apple and the magic waters. And tell me the names of my parents. Afterward, I implore you to make the statue in the garden you gave us come alive. I won't be able to rest until I hold her, living, in my arms.

CALMON.   Your servant is not dead, only stunned. He's moving. He's standing up.

(TRUFFALDINO *comes to, shakes himself as he performs the* lazzo *of reviving from a swoon, takes one look at the statue, and faints again.*)

As for the apple, you will be able to—

(TRUFFALDINO *repeats the* lazzo, *fainting again when he hears the statue talking.*)

—you will be able to take it. The lion and the tiger are now dying of thirst. As the ruler of all statues, I will call on the fountain statue of Treviso, with the gigantic breasts that shoot out streams of fresh water. Ho there, statue, come do my bidding!

STATUE OF TREVISO   (*Entering*). Here, Your Majesty. My mammaries are at your command.

(*She lets her abundant water flow into a basin at her feet. The* LION *and the* TIGER *appear and lap at the basin greedily.* TRUFFALDINO *revives, sees the drinking spectacle, passes out again.*)

CALMON.   Waste no more time, Renzo. While they drink, pick the apple.

RENZO.   Thank you, Calmon, thank you. I will. (*And he does.*)

CALMON.   Now for the dancing waters. The gate there has magic power, so that when a man pushes it, it flies back at him with tremendous force. He is flung down and killed, like those you see here on the ground. However, I will call upon the five massive statues from the Campo dei Mori in Venice.[16] Together they will push the gate and hold it open. Come, Rioba, with your brothers, and lean on this gate!

(*The statues of the Moorish* BROTHERS *from the Campo dei Mori in Venice enter in single file and approach the gate.* RIOBA *forces it open. The gate shrieks and slams back at them, but the* BROTHERS *stand shoulder to shoulder in front of it and stop it from closing.* TRUFFALDINO *revives, sees the* BROTHERS, *does a double take, keels over again.*)

CALMON.   Send your servant in there for the water. (*To* TRUFFAL-
DINO.) You need not be afraid. You will find bottles there. Take one,
fill it, and hurry out again.

TRUFFALDINO.   The only trouble is, I don't think I can squeeze past
those five giants. I speak from the heart. It's my belly, you understand?
Pork dishes six times a day.

CALMON.   Do you want me to hurl you in?

TRUFFALDINO.   I see what you're getting at. (*He pulls in his stomach
and enters the grotto. To* RIOBA *and his* BROTHERS) Gentlemen, pardon my rear view.

CALMON.   Now, unfortunate boy, you have what you came for. And
yet you have nothing. Your self-love and your sister's vanity have no
limits. You ask for the names of your parents. I cannot give them to
you. You ask me to bring the statue in the garden to life. I cannot do
that, either. For these miracles you will have to appeal to the green bird
who loves Barbarina. The best I can do on my own is confer on your
female statue the ability to speak. Perhaps that will provide some consolation for you. But I should warn you that if she speaks, you may feel
even more tortured.

RENZO.   She'll speak to me? My friend, I will be satisfied and ask nothing more. I want to know everything she thinks and feels and desires.
What raptures we'll exchange, what sweet murmurings as she welcomes
my love and as I listen to her dear, soft voice breathing her thanks and
affection.

CALMON.   Folly! Your longing for her will grow inflamed, will torment
you. You'll be a foolish lover, like all the others. An affectionate word
from beautiful lips incenses love and makes it greedy. The lusts of men
are infinite, insatiable. The happy man is he who desires the good and
spiritual, and looks upward, away from the earth and its filth.

(TRUFFALDINO *reappears with a bottle filled with water.*)

TRUFFALDINO   (*To the bottle*). What are you up to down there? Trying to dance your way out of the bottle? Or smash it? (*To* RENZO *and*
CALMON) Hear that music these waters are playing? Trying to bust
out. Working themselves up to a crescendo, the little bitches, full or-
chestra plus heavy percussion.

CALMON. Renzo, for now you are content with what you have. But I see that your heart is full of foolish thoughts and inflamed with blind passion. You will not be satisfied for long, and your own ingratitude will cause your downfall. Now I must leave. If you find yourself in further trouble, call on me again. I have a modest favor to ask in return. Some centuries ago my nose was chipped by boys who threw stones at me. A mason repaired it, but gave it a different form. It was aquiline before. Have it restored to that original shape. This is little enough to ask. And so, my friend, farewell.

(*Darkness, earth tremors, and so forth.* CALMON *vanishes. The* LION *and the* TIGER *stagger back to the apple tree, bloated with water.*)

STATUE OF TREVISO. My right breast has taken a lot of wear around the nipple. Renzo, don't forget to show your gratitude. (*Exit.*)

RIOBA. One arm broken. (*Exit.*)

A BROTHER. Piece of one ear missing. (*Exit.*)

ANOTHER BROTHER. Chin crumbling away. (*Exit.*)

ANOTHER BROTHER. Legs falling off. (*Exit.*)

ANOTHER BROTHER. Right buttock smashed. Don't forget—be grateful! Get us fixed! (*Exit.*)

TRUFFALDINO. Are you really going to have repairs done on those heels and tits and noses?

RENZO. For now, all I care about is rushing back to hear the voice of my darling statue. Come. (*Exit.*)

TRUFFALDINO. He got what he was after. It's a pain to be indebted to others for their kindness. But it's a pain to pay them back. Gratitude? It doesn't exist. Still, if he does decide to go ahead with the repairs, what with the nose and elbow and holes in the heels and plenty of other bad spots we can find if we search hard enough, I'll be glad to take it over as an assignment, draw up the estimate and contract. And the cost overruns . . . (*Exit.*)

## Act Four

*A room in the mansion. The statue of a woman stands on a stone pedestal in a picturesque pose. A rich gown has been draped over the body, although the head, face, neck, hands, and lower arms, lower legs, and feet are visibly marble.*

### Scene 1

RENZO *is discovered, gazing at the statue, which is named* POMPEA.

RENZO.   I have brought you in here, my dearest, to rescue you from rain and snow storms, the freezing rigors of winter, and the broiling heat of the sun. I've covered your glorious body because I am jealous. I couldn't bear to see others admire you. Listen to my woes. Then speak to me, as Calmon promised you would. I can't wait to hear your voice and feel its echoes in my heart and soul. Will you accept my love?

POMPEA.   Change your tone, young man. You put me in mind of the compliments whispered in the past by perfumed and gilded dandies, corrupt and ignorant youths with nothing in their hearts but lechery. In my present state—

RENZO.   Oh, that mellifluous voice! How soothing it is! So you were not created by a sculptor, but were once a woman? What magic power transmuted you? Who could have deprived this living and unequalled beauty of its flesh and senses, and extinguished the divine light in these eyes, and dimmed the exquisite color of these cheeks?

POMPEA.   Change your tone. Your words are like those of the idle flatterers and chatterers who made me conceited and proud and convinced me that I should be worshiped. If only I had never been ensnared by those fools with their creaking sighs and simpering praises; if I had not turned away from God and laughed at wise men, I would never have known the sudden chill in these veins and nerves that has robbed me of movement, sense, color, breath, and sight. Oh, if only this body, this prison of stone that encloses me, would at least let me vent my grief. (*In a tearful voice*) No matter how hard I try to weep, marble eyes cannot shed tears.

RENZO.   Your grief! What is it compared to mine? These are real tears. Can you see them? We have our pain in common. If only we could shed our tears together and share our griefs. You call me a flatterer. I am not.

I love you. No more harsh words! Please tell me who your parents were, the country you come from, and your name.

POMPEA.    My name is Pompea. I come from a noble family in a part of Italy where lust and vice abounded; where people went to books to learn not knowledge and virtue but depravity; and where they despised the wisdom that comes with age. (*Tearfully*) That is where I was born and where I lived. The life I have now is more like death, like a tomb, a hell on earth.

RENZO    (*Aside*). Calmon was right. I wanted the statue to speak, and its speech only tortures me further. (*Aloud*) But Pompea, if you became human again, could you love me and share a new life with me?

POMPEA    (*Sighing*). Yes, yes, I could love you. (*Sadly*) But now you've given me hope, and when that fails I will feel more wretched than before.

RENZO.    You could love me? When you say that, you quicken my heart and at the same time tear it open. How can I let your beautiful body remain a statue? I can't bear to. I must find the green bird, who knows the magic spell.

POMPEA.    You promised Calmon you'd be satisfied if you heard me speak. You are very generous to try to rescue me from my fate. But I don't want you to risk your life in order to restore mine. Leave me to my punishment.

RENZO.    If I did, I'd be ruthless and contemptible.

### Scene 2

RENZO *is about to leave when* TRUFFALDINO, *all set to travel and carrying a coachman's whip, runs into him.*

TRUFFALDINO.    Quick, quick! All ready to go? No time to waste. Finished making love to your statue? How was she? Nice? You like her voice? Did she chew your ear off? Good. We're leaving.

RENZO.    What's all this about?

TRUFFALDINO.    You haven't heard the big news?

RENZO.    Big news?

TRUFFALDINO.   The king sent Pantalone, the royal pimp, to your sister, to set up the wedding. Know what he's asking by way of a dowry? The apple that sings and the waters that dance. Barbarina couldn't make up her mind if she wanted the green bird or the king. She acted up a big, tragic scene like she was on a stage. Then the royal pimp went to work on her. He asked her why flit off with a bird when she could get on a throne and under a crown? She was tilting toward the throne when the old biddy Tartagliona slammed into the room with her poet in tow. She stuck her hands on her moldy hips and yelled out a rhyme that must have come from her poet:

> "This woman as my daughter-in-law? Absurd!—
> Unless she offers me the green bird."

Then she marched out arm in arm with her poet, while he spouted some garbage-y lines praising big appetites. Barbarina was so mad she pushed Pantalone down the stairs and ran through the house screaming. Got to have that green bird! She fell into an armchair and a fit, making faces, kicking her feet in the air. Talk about a tantrum! It took four women to hold her down. They ripped open her clothes at the boobs. They didn't have any smelling salts, so they burned two books of poetry under her nose. Then they left her to come to, but she didn't. So I sent for the puff-puff devil, you remember him? He pumps his bellows behind you and before you know it, whoosh!—you're miles away.[17] He can puff-puff us all the way to the ogre's mountain, where the green bird is, in no time flat. Everything's ready. We have to cure Barbarina. We don't care about the danger, do we? I speak from the heart. We'll get that bird if it kills us, and it probably will. (*He can hardly hide his laughter.*)

RENZO.   Good, Truffaldino. We'll set out right away.

TRUFFALDINO.   Oh, my God!

RENZO.   Isn't that your wife coming?

## Scene 3

*Enter* SMERALDINA.

SMERALDINA.   Help! Help!

RENZO.   Help yourself, Smeraldina. We're leaving now to capture the green bird from the ogre on the mountain. I must find out who my parents were, and how I can restore my Pompea to life. Remind my sister to watch the dagger I gave her. While it gleams, I'm alive. If it appears bloodstained, I'm dead. Good-by. (*Exit.*)

TRUFFALDINO.   And if I appear bloodstained, I'm dead too. (*He kisses her and runs off, cracking the whip.*)

SMERALDINA.   They're insane! The world's full of nut cases, and this life we love so much is madness—sheer madness.

## Scene 4

*Enter* BARBARINA, *clutching her clothes together at the neck.*

BARBARINA.   Where's my brother?

SMERALDINA.   Cool down, will you? Stay calm, like me. They've gone to flush out the green bird. Renzo says, keep looking at the dagger and if it has blood on it, he's cooked.

BARBARINA.   He's going to get it for me! Thank God.

POMPEA.   Lunatic, hurry! Call him back! You've sent him to die.

SMERALDINA   (*Quaking*). Oh no! Not the statue! Did it speak? A miracle!

BARBARINA.   What miracle! I'm used to this by now. And my brother is dead. (*She examines the dagger, which is still gleaming.*) Who says so? Not until the blood appears.

POMPEA.   You're blinded by pride and vanity. Will you delay until it's too late? He'll be dead by the time you notice the blood.

SMERALDINA.   She's right. You've gone berserk.

BARBARINA.   Will I never know who my parents are? Must I be laughed at by everybody because I can't be queen? No! I will have that green bird!

POMPEA.   Barbarina, nobody wants the green bird more than I do, but the risks are too great. I love your brother. And so do you. I was once as vain as you are. Don't bring the wrath of heaven on yourself, as I did.

Give up this marriage to the king. I can't say more than that. Bring back your brother or you'll be sorry.

BARBARINA. Your words trouble me. Perhaps I have gone too far. I was overwhelmed by these strange desires. Renzo, I'll do what I can to save you. That's what I want most. Come, Smeraldina. To the ogre's mountain!

SMERALDINA. So it is true. When you love somebody you can't let him go off on his own. She's as cracked as an old plate. I'd better go with her. Maybe I'm doing it out of self-love. So what?

SCENE 5

PANTALONE *in one of the palace rooms*

PANTALONE. She did! Pushed me down a flight of stairs, that little tramp. I'll swear this is the first time a royal envoy was treated that way by a penniless no-name just because he asked for a lousy dowry of undrinkable water and an uneatable apple. Down the whole flight! Bouncing like a ball off every step! And then this other stuff—water, apples, green birds. The royal marriage can't go on without them. I don't know. There's something I don't like about this match. I don't know. I have a conscience, after all. Those infants I tossed into the water—what about them? Suddenly we have these twins showing up. And then the poet's words . . . I don't know. That girl, she has a peachy, sort of orange coloring. Reminds me of Ninetta, that's for sure. I can't say a thing if I value my skin. But I feel guilty for keeping quiet. The two of them are said to be the children of Truffaldino and Smeraldina. But that can't be. Why would the parents become the servants of the children? And where did that mansion come from all of a sudden? You don't build a structure like that out of sausages. Blood of Donna Caterina, what is going on? I'd better have a few confidential words with Smeraldina and Truffaldino. If I can worm any information out of them and it turns out to be what I suspect, I'll cough up the whole story, even if it costs me my skin. Because a marriage between a father and a daughter, well, that's a tragedy, positively oedipal, and the only thing left to do is put a noose around your neck and swing. (*Exit.*)

SCENE 6

TARTAGLIA *enters, trying to escape from* TARTAGLIONA.

TARTAGLIONA. What's this? Running away from your mother?

TARTAGLIA.   I loathe you, old woman. I don't want to see you or hear you or hear *from* you. Go bury yourself. It's about time.

TARTAGLIONA.   Son of a witch, felon, cuckold! I won't have you marrying a bastard. She doesn't know who her own mother is. Shame on her! I will not have a bastard for a daughter-in-law and a string of little bastards for grandchildren.

TARTAGLIA.   You don't want grandchildren, bastards or no bastards, period. Blood of Satan, I'm the king. I can marry any woman I please. And you—you can elope with the devil.

TARTAGLIONA.   Vagabond, wastrel! I know how to deal with you. You'll pay back my whole dowry at six percent interest. I'll have the last royal shirt off your back.

TARTAGLIA.   Yes, you've been talking to your impostor of a poet. He's eager to cash in on your property. And you swallow his endearments like nectar. You old dupe! Your threats don't worry me. I'm starting judicial proceedings against you. Twenty-four lawsuits! And prosecutors so explosive they'll blow you and your pet poet sky-high. As for him, I'll boot his ass from one end of the city to the other and into the water so fast he won't know if he's a bird or a boat.

TARTAGLIONA.   Very good. We'll see who comes out on top. Within half an hour, I'll sue you for every stitch of property in the kingdom. You'll have to pawn your teeth. (*Weeping*) Why did I ever marry? Who thought I'd end up with a son like this?

TARTAGLIA.   Go ahead, repossess my whole kingdom if you want to. Bankrupt the king. I don't give a hoot for your crocodile tears.

SCENE 7

*Enter* PANTALONE.

PANTALONE.   Your Majesty, Your Majesty, terrible news! Make it up with your mother. This is no time for family quarrels. We don't have a moment to spare. I've just been to those young people's mansion, and they're gone. The servants are standing around mourning, in black. Ask them a question, they don't answer. The place is like a morgue. They're dead for sure. But don't get upset. We all have to go some time.

TARTAGLIA   (*In desperation, to* TARTAGLIONA). Well, are you satisfied? O Jupiter, O Juno, Mercury, Saturn, and the rest of the hostile heavens! I'm going to put a hot poker through my guts. (*Furious exit.*)

PANTALONE.   A hot poker! Through his guts? Not if Pantalone can help it. (*Exit, running.*)

TARTAGLIONA.   The future has cleared up. Come to me, my supreme poet! I'm safe!

## Scene 8

*Enter* BRIGHELLA.

BRIGHELLA.   They've all left for the ogre's mountain, sweet mistress. They will never return to Monterotondo.

TARTAGLIONA.   It seems so. My son the king has gone to put a hot poker through his guts. And now, poet of poets, I can make my blushing confession. I love you.

BRIGHELLA.   A rare favor, which heaven extends to only a select few of us. And now, Your gracious Majesty, to business. An insignificant act that will not inconvenience you at all. Or hardly at all. Your will.

TARTAGLIONA.   Never let me hear you mention a will. Wills give me goose bumps. Fulfill your duty: the only thing you have to do is write me verses that say, "I love you." (*Exit.*)

BRIGHELLA.   I don't have a prayer if she gets the bumps when she hears the world "will." It's true that the twins have reached the ogre's mountain. The puff-puff devil, who governs the passions of humanity, blew them all the way there. But me, where do I stand? My visions of the future are unclear, and unless things look up a bit, I can see myself hearing the same old refrain till she dies and it's too late.

> "The only thing you have to do
> Is write me verses that say, 'I love you.'"

Poetry is its own reward. But so is money.

## Scene 9

*The ogre's mountain, with a palace in the background. In the foreground the*
GREEN BIRD *over a portal with its feet chained. Statues are scattered*

*about on the mountainside. A scroll lies on the ground. Enter* RENZO *and* TRUFFALDINO, *blown into view by the puff-puff devil.*

RENZO. We certainly got here fast. What velocity!

TRUFFALDINO. Like when I was younger. You always move fast when the devil's behind you.

RENZO. We must have reached the ogre's mountain. See: up there is the green bird on his perch. I don't spot any danger, do you? Look around, Truffaldino, all over. Any lions, tigers, dragons, ogres, or snakes?

TRUFFALDINO. I'm looking, I'm looking. I don't even see an ant. Still, you remember that when we went after the apple and the water, we didn't notice a thing at first? Then suddenly we were up to our ears in doo-doo. Why don't you call in the statue?

RENZO. I don't like to keep summoning him. Why should I cry for help as soon as I get into trouble, like a little boy or a senile old man? I already owe him enough. You know how he asked me to restore his nose. I didn't do it, and I probably never will. Besides, every time I meet him, he delivers a long, marmoreal lecture full of warnings and advice. He'll do you a favor but then you have to listen till your ears go numb. What are you waiting for? Release the green bird and bring it here. Unfasten that little chain on its foot. Should be simple.

TRUFFALDINO. How come you didn't repair his nose? Wasn't much to ask. I say we need his help before we go near the green bird. It doesn't make sense not to call him. Every time we got in trouble before we had to call for help. And he came every time. And now you say you'll probably never pay him back. But if you need help again, you call for it again, doesn't matter how often. And when the help comes with a lecture, why, you suffer through it, and if it's full of warnings and advice, why, you listen with both ears and tears of repentance in your eyes, so that the next time you call, he'll come. You listen, then afterward you forget about him again. I speak from the heart. Look at you. You brag that you studied the latest books of philosophy, but you don't know the first thing about it. Figuring out the world and getting what you want by hook or by crook—*that's* the real modern philosophy.

RENZO. Word spinner! Bring me that bird or I'll . . . (*Swings his foot threateningly.*)

TRUFFALDINO. I have an ornery streak, master. When we come to differences of principle, I can stand any amount of philosophical ass-kicking to avoid taking stupid risks. So either you call the statue, or I stay on this spot and let you bruise your foot.

RENZO. All this delay! I'm boiling with impatience. I'll get it myself and nothing can stop me. (*He rushes toward the* BIRD.)

TRUFFALDINO. Go it, then. You'll see what stops you—the ogre or some other monster, and then we'll be in it again up to the scalp.

(RENZO *has reached the* GREEN BIRD, *and is about to seize it.*)

GREEN BIRD.
What are you doing, idiot? Retract
Your arm, or you'll regret this reckless act!

RENZO. Oh, God, this pain spreading through me! It's unbearable! Help! I apologize. I repent. Forgive me, Calmon. No, I deserve no forgiveness . . . (*He changes into a statue.*)

(TRUFFALDINO, *terrified, runs back and forth. He realizes that nothing endangers him, stops and looks at* RENZO, *who has turned white.*)

TRUFFALDINO. What is it? Lost your color? You've given me your last order, my colorless master. Now I'll tell you something, boy. I'm going to Venice. I'll open a booth at the fair, a sideshow, and make my fortune exhibiting this bird. If I can grab it safely. Caution, caution, all the way.

(*He creeps up on the* GREEN BIRD *and reaches for it.*)

GREEN BIRD.
You overreach yourself! Too late you learn,
O brazen fool, the punishment you'll earn.

TRUFFALDINO. Oh, God, this pain, spreading through me! It's unbearable! Help! I apologize, I repent. Forgive me. I speak from the heart. I'll never do wrong again. I'll never do anything again. (*He changes into a statue.*)

SCENE 10

*Enter* BARBARINA *and* SMERALDINA, *also propelled by the puff-puff devil.*

BARBARINA.  The wind that blew us here so rapidly could be a favorable sign for Renzo.

SMERALDINA.  It would be even more favorable if he didn't drop to the ground on the way and break his neck.

BARBARINA.  But I don't see him anywhere. And this is the mountain. There's the green bird. Oh, Smeraldina, I pray that nothing has happened to Renzo on my account. My heart's beating wildly.

SMERALDINA.  Let's not panic. Perhaps he didn't have as fast a wind behind him as ours.

BARBARINA.  Still, I have a strange sense of misgiving. I should never have asked him to go. I ought to check the dagger to see if there's any blood on the blade, but . . . No, I can't. My hand's shaking. I'm afraid to look.

SMERALDINA.  No more of this weakness. Just before, you were ready to go anywhere and do anything. Now, suddenly, you've lost heart.

BARBARINA.  No, friend, I have a guilty conscience. But you're right. I can't stop now. Whatever the dagger says, I must look. (*She draws it. There is blood on the blade.*) Oh, heaven, he's dead, and I'm to blame! (*She lets the dagger fall and collapses.*)

SMERALDINA  (*Helping her up*). My poor girl! My poor boy! My poor husband! My poor me!

BARBARINA.  Leave me here, Smeraldina. I deserve your hatred, not your help, I've been so unkind to you. You rescued me from drowning. You took care of me. In your unpretentious way, you taught me love and modesty and virtue. In return I ridiculed you. From my foolish studies, I learned nothing more than to overlook reason, with which heaven moderates our passions. Then, when I became rich, I became insatiable, buffeted by a thousand conflicting desires. Now it's too late. I can see my errors. I have enough reason to loathe myself and my vanity. But reason, which can calm others, only torments me. (*She weeps.*)

SMERALDINA  (*Also weeping*). Barbarina dear, I'm so sorry. I feel heartbroken. I'm an ignorant woman, and I wish I could think of something to say that would comfort you, but I can't. Everything is self-love, my daughter, even your tears for the loss of your brother.

BARBARINA.   You're right to throw my own words back at me. (*Taking her hand*) Our old life of poverty seems so precious to me now; so do the rags we wore and our bare feet and tangled hair and the water we drank with you out of the stream, and the meager meals we gleaned from the forest. How wonderful it would be not to have grown rich, and not to hate myself for killing my brother! The gods will never again do anything for so wicked a woman. I'm beyond hope . . .

## SCENE II

*Darkness, lightning flashes, thunderclaps.* CALMON *appears.*

CALMON.   You are not the only one to despair, Barbarina. Every person who follows a false philosophy must despair in the end, for it purports to enlighten you, but only robs you of your hope for a better afterlife.

SMERALDINA.   Oh, Lord, another statue!

BARBARINA.   Calmon, if I am still worthy of pity, if I can do anything to save my brother, please help me.

CALMON.   Your brother is dead, as I predicted. He could be revived, but only at great risk. I advise you to curb your anguish, accept his fate, and leave here. You were not the only cause of his death. His own pride, scorn, and folly were also to blame. At present this advice is all I can give you. But it will be so difficult to follow that you will surely fail— and die.

BARBARINA.   Let these tears convince you! I long to die if I can restore Renzo to the life he lost because of me.

SMERALDINA.   I'll do the same for my husband, even if he was a crook.

CALMON.   Listen carefully. You see the green bird over there. Away from this hill he may be your lover, incapable of harming you. But here he is fatal to human beings. Renzo's life and Truffaldino's depend on the green bird; so do the lives and happiness of many others. He knows the secret of your birth. He could bring you luck—you, the court, and the king—and reveal some wondrous events, and punish the wicked, once you know how to take possession of him. He was born the son of a king and changed into a bird by a spell. Now pay attention to every word I say. Whoever wishes to take him must follow these exact measurements. You need superhuman eyesight. You must stop seven paces, one foot, four inches and a quarter away from him. Don't deviate from this distance by even a hair's breadth. As soon as you stand in the correct place, speak to him before he can speak to you. Recite the ancient lines written on the folio at your feet. (*He points to a scroll on the ground.*) If the bird addresses you first, or if you stand anywhere but on the precise spot, you give up all hope of winning him. Now you understand how difficult a task you face. I cannot help you if you die. It is up to you whether to take the risk or draw back. If you succeed, you must not neglect to repay me, as your faithless brother did. And so, child, I must leave you with your agonizing decision. Only heaven may guide your steps. Farewell.

(*Darkness, lightning, and other accompaniments.* CALMON *disappears.*)

### SCENE 12

SMERALDINA.   What the hell! Some crazy arrangement—seven paces, did he say, one foot, four and a quarter inches, and you mustn't deviate from it by the length of one hair, and then you have to talk first to the bird, or you're done for? Barbarina, we might as well go home and stay widows.

BARBARINA.   This is a test, Smeraldina. I must go through with it. (*She picks up the scroll.*)

SMERALDINA   (*Trying to hold onto her*). Please, Daughter, no!

BARBARINA   (*Freeing herself*). Let me go. I've made up my mind. May heaven guide my feet and clear my vision . . .

(*She goes toward the* GREEN BIRD, *measuring the distance as carefully as she can, and opens the scroll.* SMERALDINA *watches anxiously.*)

SMERALDINA.   My poor darling, do it right. Oh, Lord, I'm sure she's going to die. Not too many paces. Three more. Or is it four? I've lost count. Oh, God, you're going to miss that quarter of an inch, that tiny invisible quarter. Are you sure that's the spot? Absolutely sure? So why aren't you talking first? Quick: out with it! Beat that bird to the punch. This is torture!

BARBARINA   (*Reading*).
Turn to your Barbarina,
Green bird with wings of gold.

I have crossed mountains and valleys
For my treasure of value untold.

GREEN BIRD.
My dearest girl, my wife to be,
I am now yours completely,
Take me and we will both be free
And live together sweetly.

SMERALDINA   (*Clapping*). She did it! It worked! Hooray, brava, brava,
bravissima!

BARBARINA.   Green bird, can you revive my brother?

GREEN BIRD.
From my left wing a single feather take,
Then touch these statues. Renzo will awake.

(BARBARINA *plucks a feather and with it touches the statue of* CIGO-
LOTTI, *which comes to life.*)

CIGOLOTTI.

Leave a familiar spot for some place new?
You'll never guess the grief you may go through.

I thought I'd grab the bird and open a booth at the fair and get rich.
But look what happened to me. From now on I stick to storytelling.
(*Exit, shouting.*) Come one, come all! Only a penny to hear the story of
Charlemagne and his knights . . .

(BARBARINA *touches the statue of* CAPPELLO, *which comes to life.*)

CAPPELLO.   Poor Cappello! If she hadn't set me free I'd never have
eaten another meal. From now on I stick to fish stories. (*Exit, shouting.*)
There was this eel, y'see, and she loved the Moranzani lock on the
Brenta River, y'see, but the lock was jealous over seven pit bulls, y'see,
and . . .

(BARBARINA *touches the statue of* TRUFFALDINO, *which comes to life.*)

TRUFFALDINO   (*Shaking himself*). I'm giving up modern philosophy.
It always kept me poor. I think I'll turn honest for a change. Smeraldina! Come here and give me a big hug, you ugly hugger.

(BARBARINA *touches* RENZO *with the feather. He comes back to life.*)

RENZO.   My dear sister, who brought me back to life?

BARBARINA.   Someone who will be less vain and foolish from now on.

SMERALDINA.   I'm baffled. What next?

GREEN BIRD.
　Dear friends, the best is yet to come. Let's run, for
　The ogre will return, and then we're done for.

(*A burst of wind from the puff-puff devil. They all fly away.*)

[*Author's note: For the characters of Cigolotti and Cappello caricatures of other people known to the audience may be substituted—imitated so that they are easily recognizable.*]

## Act Five

*An exquisite garden. A fountain with a basin on one side; on the other, a pedestal with a flat top. A table, center; around it, chairs bedecked with leaves and flowers*

### Scene 1

TARTAGLIA, BARBARINA, RENZO, POMPEA, TARTAGLIONA, PANTALONE, *and* BRIGHELLA, *all seated.* TRUFFALDINO *and* SMERALDINA, *standing*

TARTAGLIONA   (*To* BRIGHELLA). Poet, I kept silent only because you asked me to.

BRIGHELLA   (*To* TARTAGLIONA). We must make the best of whatever happens. According to my astrological numbering . . .

　　King Tartaglia's doom is sealed
　　If he marries Barbarina.
　　If he doesn't, all is healed—
　　Except that for tomorrow's dinner
　　He'll get some wizards
　　To fry our loving gizzards.

RENZO   (*To* POMPEA). And so, my dearest, we are happy at last. Did we ever dream we'd be revived by a feather from the green bird?

POMPEA.   And by your love! Which I intend to repay for the rest of our lives together.

SMERALDINA   (*To* TRUFFALDINO). The rest of our lives together. Think of it!

TRUFFALDINO.   I am thinking. My nightingale, my rose, my swan, I feel as fond of you as I did the day when you first put the yoke around my neck.

TARTAGLIA.   By the beard of Bacchus, Barbarina, you want me to stay here listening to all this sweetness and joy, while I'm suffering the torments of the inferno. Everyone else is deliriously, drunkenly happy, while the king is parched with longing and frustration. Even my mother's ready to become a grandmother. But you, you abruptly postpone sharing my throne and my bed. I'm as impatient as a horse that's been tied and blindfolded and stung. I want to kick out in every direction.

BARBARINA.   Don't be angry, Your Majesty. I have heard some strange predictions about our marriage. This is the moment when the mysteries will be explained, and I'm extremely eager to see the end of a story that amounts to something like a Greek tragedy. Truffaldino, Smeraldina, bring me the miraculous waters that dance, the green bird that talks, and the apple that sings. I am now ready, if fate wills it, to become yours.

(*Exit* TRUFFALDINO *and* SMERALDINA.)

TARTAGLIA.   That's ludicrous. A royal wedding is delayed for a bottle of water, an apple, and a bird!

PANTALONE   (*Aside*). I'm suffocating. Can't speak. My guts are heaving like the Grand Canal in a thunderstorm.

(SMERALDINA *and* TRUFFALDINO *reenter with the* APPLE, BIRD, *and* WATERS.)

BARBARINA.   The bird here, please, the apple there, and pour the waters into that basin.

(SMERALDINA *places the* BIRD *on the table and the* APPLE *on the pedestal stand.* TRUFFALDINO, *with* lazzo *embellishments, pours the WATERS into the basin. The* WATERS *give off the sounds of a soft melody and begin to dance in the basin. The instruments grow louder and the* WATERS *spring up to form a fountain. The music rises in a full orchestral crescendo.*)

EVERYBODY.   Superb! What harmonies! Ravishing! What talent! Bellissima, bravissimi!

BARBARINA.   Now, waters, soften your sound to accompany the apple. And you, apple, let us hear you sing.

APPLE   (*Singing recitative*).
Beware, you have lived long in error,
You who are deaf to repentance. This is the time
When heaven will punish all stubborn sinners
And reward the righteous.
(*Aria*)
Open the tomb
Where she's interred,
Dwelling on doom,
Forgotten, unheard.
Let her go free!
Let the bells ring!
Let us all sing:
Misery, flee!
And joy to the king!

EVERYBODY.   Brava! Bravissima! What a voice! Encore!

TARTAGLIA.   Wait a moment—don't get so excited. I'll interpret that song for you. "Beware, you have lived long in error, / You who are deaf to repentance . . ." Barbarina, you're the one living in error, because you don't want me for your husband, and you turn a deaf ear to my entreaties. Beware, then: that apple means you. So take my hand and let's have a little "joy to the king."

TARTAGLIONA.   Poet, it looks promising.

BRIGHELLA.   But if he doesn't marry her . . .

He'll get some wizards
To fry our loving gizzards.

TARTAGLIA.
The anger of heaven
May punish and pound us,
Its thunderbolts driven
To earth all around us.
Tartaglia, reign
Like a king once again!
(*To* BARBARINA)
The apple said it: take my hand.
That's also my express command.
The sky looks frightening—
Let's beat the lightning!

BARBARINA. We haven't listened to the green bird yet, Majesty. He's about to speak.

TARTAGLIA. I'm the king. I've heard enough of this. Let him shove his birdsong in some other woman's nest. Give me your hand, or I'll take it!

GREEN BIRD. Stop, listen, and be amazed! You cannot marry Barbarina. She is your daughter.

TARTAGLIA. My what? Daughter? What does this birdbrain think he's saying?

GREEN BIRD. I know all too well what I say. Tartaglia, we are approaching the moment of truth. Barbarina and Renzo are your twin children, thrown into the river by Pantalone. And your wife Ninetta, who was buried alive below the drains of the palace kitchen, has remained alive, thanks to me.

TARTAGLIONA. Brighella, Brighella, that's the end of me.

BRIGHELLA. And me. I can hear our gizzards sizzle.

FINAL SCENE

*Enter* NINETTA

NINETTA. Rescued! Who has saved me from that loathsome pit and brought me out to see the stars again?

TARTAGLIA. My lost wife! My own Ninetta—she lives! She does look older. A bit more worn. But I'll take her back as she is. I'm a loyal, royal husband. Did someone say children? You two? My children? So you're not puppies? I'm confused. I'm dizzy. It's like a play—time for the king to pass out . . . (*He staggers.*)

PANTALONE (*Holding him up*). I really wrapped those babies up. Venetian oilskin. There's nothing like it.

GREEN BIRD. Ladies and gentlemen, we haven't quite finished. Will you all kindly remain in your places. I have to work one or two transformations. Tartagliona, away!—join your playmates, the toads in a swamp. And you, poet, here's how we'll crown you—not with a laurel wreath but with ass's ears!

TARTAGLIONA. Poet, help! I'm turning turtle. (*She does.*)

BRIGHELLA. Oh, my angel, I'm turning head over ass. (*He sprouts an ass's head and other equipment.*)

TARTAGLIONA. My son, you have your revenge. Enjoy your Ninetta. As for me, I'll crawl into a lovely swamp or ditch and live a long, long time. (*She crawls off.*)

TARTAGLIA. Strictly speaking, she always was something of a turtle.

BRIGHELLA. Now I'll have to bray my divinely inspired verses to the music of a treadmill. (*Exit, kicking.*)

GREEN BIRD (*To the audience*). Attention, please, ladies and gentlemen. We will have one more miracle, the final one, for your entertainment. I am the king of Terradombra, as you heard earlier, compressed into this green shape by the ogre on the mountain. Our flight of fancy is finished, and so are my days of flying. You've guessed that Barbarina was bound to become my queen. We're all ready to start afresh. So . . . Mend your ways, everyone, and take your philosophy with a grain of salt. As for us up here, if our fairy tale can turn a profit, we'll conclude that such foolishness is the best philosophy of all.

(*He is transformed into the king of Terradombra and embraces* BARBARINA. TARTAGLIA *embraces* NINETTA. RENZO *embraces* POMPEA. TRUFFALDINO *embraces* SMERALDINA. TARTAGLIA *embraces his children, and so do* SMERALDINA *and* TRUFFALDINO *and*

PANTALONE. *They might even dance, swapping partners, to the music of the orchestral* WATERS.)

### Envoi

BARBARINA.

> I now propose
> That we repair
> Old Calmon's nose
> If you approve
> As soon as we move
> Away from here.

> Perhaps our show
> Went on too long
> Or seemed too slow
> Or weak or strong.
> But since we did it, well or flawed,
> Please applaud!

The end of

## *The Green Bird*

## Notes

1. Gozzi originally intended *The Green Bird* to be the last of his *Tales*, but later changed his mind: the play was followed by *Zeim, King of the Genies,* and by many "Spanish" comedies influenced by Golden Age theatre.

2. Far from being merely amusing, Gozzi asserts, *The Green Bird* has a serious purpose: to criticize the pernicious philosophy of the European Enlightenment. In the following paragraph, he suggests that all the characters of the play must be read in the light of that polemical project.

3. This is a reference to Louis-Sébastien Mercier's *Jenneval; ou, Le Barneveldt français,* an adaptation of George Lillo's *The London Merchant; or, The History of George Barnwell,* translated by Elisabetta Caminer Turra under the title *Jeneval dalle nobili passioni* and produced at the Sant'Angelo Theatre in the autumn season of 1771. Turra and other supporters of the French *drame bourgeois* are criticized in scathing terms in the *Ingenuous Disquisition and Sincere History of My Ten Tales for the Theatre,* where Gozzi claims that such comedies may corrupt the morals of Venetian audiences and are thus a danger to society.

4. In eighteenth-century Venice, upper-class weddings were often celebrated by the publication of a volume of poetry written for the occasion. Usually of poor quality, such collections were frequently satirized by literary purists. Gozzi is implying that Brighella is a bad poet, and that Pantalone shows poor taste in admiring him.

5. As Gozzi states in his preface, *The Green Bird* continues the plot of *The Love of Three Oranges,* and Pantalone is here referring to events that occurred in the earlier tale. In *The Love of Three Oranges,* Tartaglia, son of the king of hearts, has been ill for ten years with terminal melancholy, and no doctor has been able to cure him—if he does not laugh, he will die. Leandro and the princesss Clarice, aided by Morgan Le Fay, conspire against Tartaglia, but Truffaldino trips the witch and sends her sprawling, heels in the air, at which Tartaglia roars with laughter. Furious, she puts a spell on him, making him fall in love with the three oranges. Tartaglia and Truffaldino go on a quest for the oranges, overcoming a series of perils in order to steal them from the castle where they are hidden. Carrying the oranges, they flee through the desert. Thirsty, Truffaldino cuts open an orange to suck its juice. A princess emerges from the orange but, unable to find anything to drink, immediately dies. The scene is repeated with the second orange, but Tartaglia manages to save the third princess, Ninetta. Tartaglia falls in love with her but is tricked by Smeraldina, who turns Ninetta into a dove and takes her place. Noticing the switch, Tartaglia refuses to marry Smeraldina, but the king insists and gives orders to prepare the wedding feast. Ninetta, in the form of a magical dove, ruins the wedding feast by making the cook (Truffaldino) fall asleep and burn the roast. The court is in an uproar: everyone tries to catch the dove, who turns back into the princess. The king arrives and dispenses judgment, condemning Smeraldina and uniting Tartaglia and Ninetta in matrimony.

6. Tuscan Italian was the language of literary prestige, while purists of this time considered the Venetian dialect suited only to popular audiences and genres (such as the theatre). In fact, though, Brighella's poetic language oscillates between Venetian and Tuscan—another indication that by Gozzi's standards he is a bad poet.

7. For "flirtatious women" Gozzi uses the word *civetta,* with a punning double meaning, "flirt" and "owl." The ornithological theory is obviously false, since owls are predators which smaller birds ordinarily avoid. The hidden meaning is more logical. In Italian *uccello* (bird) is also a vulgar term for the male organ—thus its instinctual fluttering around *civette* (flirts).

8. These lines are a paraphrase from a parody of Petrarch by Francesco Berni (1497–1535). Berni, a satiric poet, was one of Gozzi's most admired models.

9. Tartaglia's memories have their source in *The Love of Three Oranges.*

10. Symptoms of advanced syphilis.

11. In the original, Gozzi names two famous Venetian prostitutes, whose reputation was well known to his audience.

12. This, and other poetic endearments of the scene, are distortions of the style of Petrarch inspired by Berni.

13. From Petrarch's *Canzoniere,* sonnet 124 ("Amor, Fortuna e la mia mente schiva"), lines 12–13.

14. According to Chasles, Cappello was a gondolier famous for storytelling. Again, Gozzi deliberately creates a clash between the "magical" atmosphere of his setting and the "realistic" reference to his own city. He does the same in scene 15 by introducing into the fairy's garden some of the most celebrated statues of Venice and nearby Treviso.

15. Truffaldino is referring to the exit aria usually sung by a tragic hero as he left the stage at the close of a scene in the operas of Pietro Metastasio.

16. The Venetian Campo dei Mori takes its name from the thirteenth-century statues of Levantine merchants still to be seen there. The three statues were popularly identified with a trio of Moorish brothers who lived nearby: Rioba, Alfani, and Sandi. Gozzi, in a sort of visual hyperbole, adds two more statues to the total.

17. The "puff-puff devil" is a character from *The Love of Three Oranges.* Following Tartaglia and Truffaldino with a bellows, he made it "magically" possible to travel vast distances in the compass of a single scene. The episode was intended to poke fun at Pietro Chiari's frequent violations of the Aristotelian unities of place and time.

# Afterword

ALBERT BERMEL

During this century a small portion of Carlo Gozzi's dramatic output has leaked into English, as well as other languages, but in the form of adaptations—some of them proficient, some not—rather than as translations. A collection of English translations as accurate as differences in language and time would permit seemed overdue, and the five included here are a beginning. They were provoked into being by Andrei Serban's determination to stage some of them at the American Repertory Theatre in Cambridge and by the impassioned backing of Robert Brustein, the A.R.T.'s artistic director. Who could have expected that the first out-on-a-limb venture, *The King Stag*, would draw favorable comments that verged at times on rapture from critics and spectators and would have warmed cantankerous old Gozzi's bosom? Not Serban, I surmise, although I have never asked him directly. He doesn't appear to give himself time to think about success, any more than Brustein does. He hurls his imagination into a work while he proceeds with a perfectionism worthy of Chaplin. As the production was taking shape, he confided that he would like nothing better than to devote himself to Gozzi's plays for the rest of his life.

He is far from being the first leading director in this century captivated by Gozzi. Vsevolod Meyerhold, Max Reinhardt, Giorgio Strehler, George Devine, and Benno Besson, among others, have measured their aptitudes against these rich and distinctive *fiabe*, which lend themselves to experimental staging because of their extravagance. They may not constitute a total theatre, since they do not incorporate music and dance, although these can be, and generally are, grafted on. But the miracles and transformations offer *metteurs en scène* chances to extend the resources of a stage (and an auditorium) to the limits. And beyond. Better yet, all the ostentation rests solidly on a powerful story line: Gozzi punches out one perilous episode after another to be endured by his principals and some of the secondary characters. Evil sometimes contends blatantly with good, the forces for good invoking Christian motives, an orthodox God-centered morality. From the commedia-derived figures there issues a flow of verbal and physical byplay that is partly or wholly improvised. Some of it intervenes during the peaks of heartrending suspense in a neo-Shakespearean fashion—the side-of-the-mouth comments from Pantalone, Tartaglia's stammering soliloquies, and the farcical antics and lines of Smeraldina, Truffaldino, and Brighella distantly recall Falstaff on the field of battle at Shrewsbury or Launcelot Gobbo with his father or the knocking on the gate of Macbeth's castle or the Fool in the storm with Lear, as they reveal the interior conflicts, the nagging, low, personal worries that attend high drama.

Moments of theatricalism, when the performance grows conscious of itself as theatre and the actors step outside their parts and allude to the audience's responses, amount to a pre-Brechtian alienation. Memories of Venice obtrude in a play laid in Cathay or Persia. Another "alienation effect," possibly indebted to Euripides, emerges from statements made early in the play that summarize the action to come, making it seem fated and the characters governed by mysteriously incontestable forces. Cigolotti's opening speech serves this function in *The King Stag;* so do the curse of Norando in *The Raven* (like Aphrodite's announcement at the beginning of *Hippolytus*), the poems of Brighella in *The Green Bird* (like the monologues of Polydorus or Poseidon that respectively launch *Hecuba* and *The Trojan Women*), and the colloquy in *The Serpent Woman* between Zemina and Farzana (like the argument between Apollo and Death in the prologue to *Alcestis*). Yet another outgrowth of the Greek drama is the Aristophanic parabasis, the author's statement, often dealing with contemporary circumstances, such as Calmon's preachings in *The Green Bird,* although we cannot tell whether to take these interjections as the author's precise views.

The thunderous, lightning-lit entrances and exits of the magicians; the exoticism of near- and far-eastern settings, costumes, and masks; the principle that on a stage anything can happen—people can swap identities and a palace can spring up or vanish in a trice; a plasticity that predates surrealism and Cocteau by 150 years; the rousing climax at the end of an act with its carryovers into the act to come; and the closing requests for applause . . . these splashes of spectacle provide further contributions to an unabashedly theatrical theatre.

Gozzi's plays, with many of their characters in what he calls "oriental" garb, sometimes reach outward to exotic overseas theatre, to the eastern end of the Mediterranean and the subcontinent formerly known as Asia Minor, or even all the way to the Far East, as when he introduces into *The Serpent Woman* Princess Canzade and her confidante, two fine specimens of the "fighting lady" role from ancestral Chinese drama and the Peking Opera—except that they perform no exploits on stage, only boast about them. Most of the plays also look back to a pretheatrical form, the epic quest, in which the hero finds his reward, his partner, and his courageous true self only by undergoing a stringent trial.

But this playwright's most compelling appeal to directors surely resides in the one component of his odd mix of antiquity and protomodernity that in a contemporary American play would be accounted its heaviest liability, namely, his characters. Seldom does he explain them (Turandot marking the exception that makes the rule more noticeable). For the most part they obediently move as he ordains, deterred only for an instant by their wonder at the unmerciful nature of their destiny, but then recovering their momentum as they take heart from their conviction that God must be on their side. Yes, they lack background or "roundness," but that is because all of them, commedia and noncommedia figures alike, are rooks, knights, and bishops in an epic chess game, *una divina commedia*. They resemble ideographs more than they do people. Far from being a handicap, their diagrammatic single-mindedness allows, even encourages, a production to interpret and organize them with almost absolute freedom.

How accurate can one be in haling a play across the barriers of language and culture and more than two centuries? Most translators I know—a meager sampling—would agree that anything like word-for-word transliteration does the original artist no service; it is the written equivalent of the work of simultaneous interpreters, helpful enough in transmitting ephemeral speeches at the United Nations or in diplomatic maneuverings, but sorely deficient in conveying whatever it is that keeps a play, novel, or poem alive in its own tongue. Conscientious translation needs to take transliteration as its starting point, but needs just as much to break further away from it with each succeeding draft.

Modern directors have inclined to make cuts in Gozzi (as they do with almost any script these days) before and during rehearsals, even Italian directors who present the work to homegrown audiences in Venice. The reasons are obvious, and may be defensible. Stretches of his originals, and especially the melodrama and the scenes of self-indulgent self-pity, go on at more length and with more passion and exclamatory phrasing than are required to get the drama across to our audiences—but with not enough vivacity to justify themselves as literature. To take full advantage of them we would need an older style of acting that made its brash "points" without shame. Exposition and explanations get repeated, almost surely on the strength of what Gozzi and his collaborators decided, after experience, was essential to keep the popular audience abreast of the action and reminded of what had led up to it. Still, if directors or others insist on cutting in these places, that is up to them; we have tried to provide plays that are as nearly intact as discretion, that elusive arbiter, would allow.

Adaptation imps tempted us to trim a few of the lines and stage directions having to do with weeping. We resisted, but it was a tough struggle, for sentiments that may have seemed harmlessly apt during the *siècle larmoyant* have grown bloated. Loyalty to the giant Gozzi won out over our desire to bring the plays into line with late twentieth-century tastes. In *The Raven*, for example, Jennaro weeps, Armilla weeps, Millo weeps, Pantalone weeps, Smeraldina weeps, Tartaglia weeps—the first three repeatedly and profusely. Perhaps some stanching should have been applied to these spills to allow the action to ford or even vault the salty aqueduct at moments of high flow. And yet Gozzi is not Gozzi unless he makes his full impression in print. Draining off some of his garrulity might modernize the tone more, but would be like letting his blood. That magnificent drama *Turandot* was virtually an opera before Puccini, Alfano, and their librettists got to it.

We have, though, slightly pared down the incidence of certain words and epithets that are Gozzi favorites (among them, *cruel* and *cruelty, pity* and *pitiless, traitor, barbarous*) but would surely raise unwanted guffaws in today's English. Occasionally we took out a direction to an actor that corresponds to the sense of the spoken line, but we kept most such directions ("BARACH [*Brokenly*]. I foresaw this disaster!") in order to hold onto as much of the Gozzi flavor as remains tolerable. Other than these sparing and tiny omissions, the plays are complete.

We followed no overriding technical principle in moving the plays into English, only the aesthetic demands of fidelity, energetic expressiveness, and sequences of consonants that ought not to choke the actors. These demands meant possibly reviewing each scene, line, word, once it was written, in the light of the surrounding material and, sometimes, the whole play. We have reproduced the obscenities, banal, anal, and erotic, many of which did not appear in earlier translations, while realizing that English cannot quite do some of them justice. The speeches in blank verse of the royalty and nobles became, when put into English-speaking mouths, reminiscent of the excesses of Stephen Phillips and other Victorians; it seemed desirable to manipulate them into prose. Some speeches, especially Pantalone's, are in Venetian dialect, but American regionalisms sound inappropriate and foreign to the plays; we hope that the generalized slanginess we settled for is less jarring than New Yorkese or hillbilly would have been. As for the passages of *canovaccio,* or prose scenario, which gave Antonio Sacchi and his colleagues opportunities—but restricted ones—to improvise on the Venetian stage, we have shifted them from suggestive prose instructions to explicit dialogue, in part as a weak protective measure against directors who may want to season the plays with items from yesterday's newspaper or this morning's talk show.

The translators are grateful for advice, always heeded, from Eric Bentley, the first editor in this country to publish Gozzi in English (in *The Classic Theatre*, vol. 1, recently reissued as *The Servant of Two Masters and Other Italian Classics* and in *The Genius of the Italian Theatre*); to our editors at the University of Chicago Press; to Ms. Joann M. Hoy, and Ms. Helen Merrill; Professor Franco Fido of Brown University, for his comments on the introduction; and to our wives for being exactly who they are. But please, let nobody fault our largehearted colleagues for the final versions, for which we insist on taking the credit and the rap. A personal word: this has been my first venture into translating in partnership, and I thank Ted Emery for sharing his scholarship, precision, good nature, and love of language.